Reporter vs. Publisher

By Janice Brownfield

Alpenstock Publishing, Santa Ana, California

ALPENSTOCK PUBLISHING
Post Office Box 1759
Santa Ana, CA   92702   U.S.A.

First edition, 1986

Library of Congress Cataloging-in-Publication Data
Brownfield, Janice
    REPORTER vs. PUBLISHER
    What Journalism Professors Don't Tell You

    Includes index.
1. Journalists--Legal status, laws, etc.--California.
2. Press law--California.
3. Brownfield, Janice
I. Title
KFC535.B76   1986   070'.9794   85-70671
ISBN 0-9614521-7-X Softcover

Contents

Chapter 1

Laguna Beach, long known as the art colony of Southern California, every year lures thousands of visitors who are attracted by its beautiful coastline. After the establishment of the art colony by the early artists, the cultural oasis bloomed with the arrival of others who had a creative bent. They included film-makers, actors, cartoonists and writers.

The first newspaper in Laguna Beach was published November 5, 1915. LAGUNA LIFE was followed by several other newspapers, including SOUTH COAST NEWS, which began publication on February 11, 1927. The NEWS was subsequently adjudicated a newspaper of general circulation on March 7, 1952, meaning it was then qualified to publish advertisements of local governmental agencies, including the City of Laguna Beach. It was also in 1952 that Vernon R. Spitaleri first visited Laguna Beach, known by then as the home of the "Festival of Arts," and was smitten by the picturesque village.

Born in Pelham, New York, Spitaleri had his first contact with the newspaper business through his father, who was a printer. While a teenager, Spitaleri worked as a "printer's devil" for a Long Island newspaper. In high school he was the editor of an underground newspaper which he printed himself and then circulated on campus. After receiving a bachelor of science degree in printing from Carnegie Tech, Spitaleri entered the U.S. Navy and saw active duty as a lieutenant commander with the amphibious forces during World War II. For his service in the invasions, including that of Normandy, France, Spitaleri was awarded three Purple Hearts and a Presidential Unit Citation. Following the end of the war in 1945 he returned to New York where he became one of the managers of the American Newspaper Publishers Association (ANPA). There he used his experience and education in printing to advise newspaper publishers of the most effective means of production.

One member of the publishers association was William W. Ottaway, who met Spitaleri at a conference in San Francisco. Ottaway requested Spitaleri to stop in Laguna Beach before returning to New York and suggest any possible improvements for the operation of SOUTH COAST NEWS. As Ottaway later wrote, "On the occasion of this brief visit to Laguna, Vern literally fell in love with the town and vowed that some day, God willing, he would make his home here." Spitaleri returned to his work with the ANPA in New York, where he was also enrolled in the Juilliard School of Music and the American Theater Wing. Trained to become a composer and concert baritone, Spitaleri chose instead to remain in the printing industry.

He left New York to join the Knight

2

newspaper group in Miami, Florida. Spitaleri worked to improve the production of the Miami HERALD as well as the other Knight newspapers--Chicago DAILY NEWS, Detroit FREE PRESS, Akron BEACON JOURNAL and Charlotte (North Carolina) OBSERVER. Then in 1957 Spitaleri and his wife Marjorie made their move west where he joined Sta-Hi Corp. of Whittier, California. He assumed the role of executive vice president of Sta-Hi, the largest newspaper equipment manufacturer west of the Rockies. Each day he drove for an hour to Whittier from the home he had purchased in Emerald Bay, an affluent private community northwest of and contiguous to the City of Laguna Beach. Unbeknownst to Ottaway, publisher of the SOUTH COAST NEWS, Spitaleri planned to purchase his newspaper.

There were two newspapers in Laguna Beach at that time competing for advertisements. While the NEWS was adjudicated to receive the City's legal advertisements (public notices, bids, etc.), the LAGUNA POST was not. Both were allowed to solicit paid advertisements from merchants, of course. Although the POST was not adjudicated to receive legal ads, it had become one of the liveliest papers in the country with Betsy Rose as editor. In early 1967 Spitaleri formulated a plan to buy both newspapers, thereby acquiring the NEWS, the one he was really after, and eliminating the POST, the local competition. In a contract entered into with Ottaway on February 9, 1967, Spitaleri purchased the NEWS for a total of $400,000. Of that amount, $200,000 was for hot type machinery and equipment; $100,000 was for the remaining assets, including the business as a going concern and for good will; $50,000 was for Ottaway's services as a consultant; and another $50,000 was for Ottaway's promise to not compete against Spitaleri with any other newspaper. The

3

LAGUNA POST was acquired with a much smaller financial investment. Merging the two newspapers, Spitaleri formed the NEWS-POST on March 30, 1967.

An exhibit to the contract with Ottaway stated that the SOUTH COAST NEWS had received $12,637 in legal advertising income in 1964 and $8,954 in 1965. To qualify for an adjudication to receive legal advertisements, Ottaway had filed a petition with the Orange County Superior Court in 1952. Pursuant to the California GOVERNMENT CODE, Section 6000, Ottaway presented evidence to show that the SOUTH COAST NEWS had been established, printed and published at regular intervals in the city for at least one year and that it had a bonafide subscription list. The newspaper was therefore adjudged to be a newspaper of general circulation qualified to print local government legal advertising, including that of the City of Laguna Beach. For any legal advertisement published in the newspaper, the NEWS needed to prepare an affidavit of publication and cite the court adjudication No. A21179.

After publishing the NEWS-POST in Laguna Beach for four months, Spitaleri filed a petition with the Superior Court to have the NEWS-POST adjudged a newspaper of general circulation in order to insure his continued receipt of the legal advertising from the City of Laguna Beach and other governmental entities, such as the County of Orange and school districts. In the petition he signed and which his attorney filed with the court on July 19, 1967, Spitaleri stated, "For more than one year next preceding the filing of this petition, said newspaper has been established under the name of the South Coast News, printed and published at regular intervals in said city. During the whole of such period, the mechanical work of producing the newspaper, that is, the

4

work of typesetting and impressing type on paper, has been performed in said city; the newspaper has been issued from the place where it is printed and sold in said city; it has been both printed and published in said city; and it has been published as a biweeky newspaper on Monday and Thursday in each calendar week. Wherefore, petitioner prays for judgment ascertaining and establishing said Laguna News-Post as a newspaper of general circulation, as defined in Section 6000 of the Government Code, for the City of Laguna Beach, for the County of Orange, and for the State of California."

The judgment and decree establishing the LAGUNA NEWS-POST as a newspaper of general circulation were entered and filed with the court on September 28, 1967, with the adjudication No. A57683. The court found the following proof offered by Spitaleri to be satisfactory: "For more than one year next preceding the filing of the petition herein, the petitioning newspaper has been established under the name of South Coast News and Laguna News Post, printed and published at regular intervals in said city" of Laguna Beach. Since there was no other newspaper in the city to contest Spitaleri's claims, the court accepted as fact the statement by Spitaleri that the NEWS-POST he had formed had been in existence for more than one year when it had actually been just six months earlier, on March 30, 1967, that the new newspaper had begun publishing.

Nevertheless, with his court adjudication in hand, Spitaleri continued to receive legal advertising from the City. Since in fact the NEWS-POST had not been in operation for the required one year, the GOVERNMENT CODE then in effect had a provision which dictated the methods by which governmental bodies were to select a newspaper to publish its advertisements when there was no adjudicated newspaper in its

5

jurisdiction. The code required notices to be sent to other newspapers which circulated their editions in the areas. They would then be qualified to print the legal advertisements. Although Spitaleri had secured a court adjudication, No. A57683, he continued to use No. A21179, the adjudication obtained 15 years earlier in 1952 by Ottaway when he was publisher of the SOUTH COAST NEWS, in the affidavits of publication for legal advertisements published in the NEWS-POST.

Spitaleri also continued his employment at Sta-Hi Corp., which had constructed a plant in Irvine, California, thus decreasing his travel time to approximately 30 minutes from his Emerald Bay home. As president of Sta-Hi, Spitaleri gave testimony in a trial involving that corporation and Tri-Q, which had been formed by three former employees. The lawsuit concerned the sale of newspaper manufacturing equipment. In 1965 the case was heard by the Supreme Court of California, which noted that both companies had attempted to defraud the state treasury and the Internal Revenue Service.

Regarding the NEWS-POST, Spitaleri had correctly anticipated that other newspapers would eventually seek to obtain legal advertising from the City of Laguna Beach. Besides the income, carrying the advertisements also improved that newspaper's status, thus helping to increase circulation, which is an added inducement for merchants and others to advertise. In 1972 Dennis Madison, publisher of the LAGUNA VILLAGE SUN newspaper, petitioned the Superior Court to be declared a newspaper of general circulation, qualified to publish legal advertisements. Because Madison was required by the GOVERNMENT CODE to publish his notice of intent, Spitaleri was informed and ready to take the offensive.

In objections filed with the court on September 22, 1972, Spitaleri's publishing corporation, Laguna

6

Publishing Company, contended that the LAGUNA VILLAGE SUN had "not been established, printed and published at regular intervals for at least one year preceding the 26th day of July 1972 in either the City of Laguna Beach or the County of Orange, within the requirements of Section 6000 of the Government Code." Spitaleri was therefore well-acquainted with the legal requirement that a newspaper be published at regular intervals for at least one year in the jurisdiction for which it was seeking the legal advertising. He did not, however, apply the law to himself when he sought his adjudication for the LAGUNA NEWS-POST in 1967, just four months after its formation.

By 1972 Spitaleri had been publishing the NEWS-POST for five years but had not yet shown a profit on his investment of $400,000. In an attempt to obtain advertising income from merchants in the surrounding areas in Orange County, Spitaleri had expanded the circulation area of the NEWS-POST. Still based in Laguna Beach, the NEWS-POST now had five editions: the Laguna NEWS-POST, the Laguna Hills NEWS-POST, the Mission Viejo NEWS-POST, the Laguna Niguel NEWS-POST and the South Shores NEWS-POST. The advertisements and most of the inside pages of the five editions were the same. Only the front pages used different stories; or leads to the same stories were changed to appeal to the readers in the five areas.

Another newspaper, known as the NEWS and published by Golden West Publishing Corp., had already established itself in the areas which Spitaleri was attempting to enter. Carlton Smith and Richard Birchall published three editions of the NEWS which covered the same areas: Saddleback Valley NEWS, Leisure World NEWS and Capistrano Valley-Beach Cities NEWS. In 1967, while employees of the LEISURE WORLD NEWS, a house organ published by Leisure World Foundation for all of the residents of its retirement community known as Leisure World in Laguna Hills, Smith and Birchall founded their own publication, the NEWS ADVERTISER. Smith was editor of the LEISURE WORLD NEWS, while Birchall was the advertising director. They assumed the same roles for their own publication, the NEWS ADVERTISER, which was circulated in the Saddleback Valley, just outside the guarded gates of Leisure World.

Unlike Spitaleri, who paid $400,000 for a newspaper which then failed to yield a profit after he purchased it in 1967, Smith and Birchall used the facilities and the advertising base of the LEISURE WORLD NEWS to operate their NEWS ADVERTISER, from which they made a profit. Smith and Birchall were able to offer low advertising rates in their publication because of the pick-up rate they gave to advertisers who were charged more for the same advertisements in the LEISURE WORLD NEWS. Recognizing that their two employees were profiting from the physical base provided by the LEISURE WORLD NEWS, two of the officers of Leisure World Foundation used their employer status to take over Smith and Birchall's Golden West Publishing Corp. in 1972. Smith and Birchall, however, resumed control of Golden West later the same year after Birchall filed a stockholder's derivative action lawsuit in Superior Court.

The following year Spitaleri filed a lawsuit against Golden West, Golden Rain Foundation, Leisure World Foundation (LWF), and Professional Community Management (PCM), which had been formed at the end of 1972 to take over the management functions of LWF. Spitaleri alleged that from 1967 to 1972 the cooperation exercised between the LEISURE WORLD NEWS and the NEWS ADVERTISER violated the State of

California's Cartwright and Unfair Practices Acts by creating an unreasonable restraint of competition for the area's advertising market. Smith and Birchall were also accused of conspiring with Golden Rain Foundation, which owns Leisure World, to keep the NEWS-POST out of the guarded, gated and private community. Spitaleri wanted to deliver the Laguna Hills NEWS-POST to all of the residents of Leisure World, including non-subscribers. Golden Rain Foundation would only allow him the same privileges that it allowed the LOS ANGELES TIMES, THE REGISTER and other newspapers--delivery only to subscribers.

To claim circulation to all of the Leisure World residents in representations to prospective NEWS-POST advertisers, Spitaleri began mailing his newspaper to all of the residents in 1969. Using the U.S. Postal Service employees as carriers was more expensive than the hiring of local residents as was done by Leisure World Foundation to deliver its LEISURE WORLD NEWS to all of the residents. It certainly seemed that Spitaleri should have been able to hire carriers, as other newspapers did, to deliver copies of his newspaper to only paid subscribers. His number of paid subscribers, however, would not be very appealing to potential advertisers.

Spitaleri did not limit his litigious attacks only to the two competing newspaper publishers. He also sued other community newspapers established in the area that he was trying to enter. Richard J. O'Neill, who had been chairman of the Democratic Party of Orange County and is a major landowner in Orange County, owned Capistrano Valley Publishing Corp., which published the GOOD NEWS newspaper. Like Spitaleri's NEWS-POST, the GOOD NEWS was struggling to exist. After a couple of years Larry Hill, the GOOD NEWS advertising director, purchased the GOOD NEWS, hoping to make it a financial success, according to his subsequent court testimony. Hill testified that by chance he met Spitaleri at a convention on the East Coast where Spitaleri offered him a job paying $35,000 a year, almost three times the amount paid to Michael Eggers, the NEWS-POST's managing editor at that time.

The day Hill returned to California he found that his GOOD NEWS offices had burned to the ground. Spitaleri subsequently entertained Hill at his Emerald Bay home, several times until 2:00 a.m., acting as if he were interested in buying the GOOD NEWS instead of hiring Hill. Spitaleri's attitude then suddenly changed. Hill found himself being sued for $2 million in alleged damages he had caused Spitaleri in the mere four months Hill had owned the GOOD NEWS. Spitaleri filed a similar suit against O'Neill and the Capistrano Valley Publishing Corp. One community newspaper in the area which Spitaleri did not sue was the RANCHO REPORTER. There was no need to sue a newspaper for unfair competition or any other reason when it went out of business on its own. Having to hire attorneys to defend himself against Spitaleri's lawsuit caused Hill to go out of business, and also thus ending Spitaleri's need to purchase the competing GOOD NEWS.

Spitaleri apparently was using the judicial system in an attempt to compensate for his lost profits while he was unable to sell the NEWS-POST. In 1973 he contacted Joe Snyder, a newspaper broker in Lindsay, California. Snyder told Spitaleri that if there were not so many competing newspapers in Orange County that the NEWS-POST would have been worth between $850,000 and $1.1 million. Instead, however, the NEWS-POST had been losing at least $20,000 and sometimes $75,000 a year during each of the six years Spitaleri had owned it. It appeared that

10

Spitaleri was trying to get almost $1 million from O'Neill through litigation because the NEWS-POST was unable to compete successfully in the free enterprise system. The following year, 1974, Spitaleri resigned from Sta-Hi Corp. in order to give his full attention to the NEWS-POST, according to an argument offered in court years later.

Seeing the need to have the NEWS-POST hand-delivered to all of the residents in Leisure World to keep down his costs and to attract advertisers in the Saddleback Valley adjacent to the retirement community, Spitaleri attacked the owners and management of Leisure World, claiming he had a First Amendment right to enter private property and deliver unsolicited copies of his newspaper. The NEWS-POST highly publicized on the front page of its Laguna Hills edition to Leisure World the various lawsuits filed concerning the management of the retirement community. A headline on the front page of the January 15, 1975, edition stated, "$189,000 Fraud Claim: Ed Olsen Hit with New Lawsuit." The story concerned Richard Birchall's stockholder's derivative action against Olsen, president of Leisure World's governing body, PCM, and Otto Musch, PCM's secretary-treasurer. Olsen and Musch were the employers of Birchall and Smith in their work at the LEISURE WORLD NEWS.

Because of his own financial interest in trying to acquire more advertising dollars for the NEWS-POST, Spitaleri used the news and editorial sections of the newspaper to attack the government of the private community of Leisure World. Yet the newspaper was essentially silent concerning its lawsuit against the Golden West Publishing Corp. and Leisure World entities alleging unfair competition and infringement on his First Amendment rights. The other four editions of the NEWS-POST did not receive as much attention from Spitaleri as the Laguna Hills edition

11

received.   Spitaleri did not have any lawsuits pending against the governing bodies in the areas served by the other four editions.

On February 5, 1975, the Laguna Hills NEWS-POST included one full page which featured in the center a drawing of a man screaming and carrying a sign over his head that read, "Why Didn't Someone Tell Us?"   Under his feet was the NEWS-POST's response, "Oh, But We Did!" Surrounding the caricature were reproductions of approximately seven NEWS-POST stories and editorials which had been printed in the past regarding conflicts at Leisure World.   One of the stories was headlined, "News-Post Banned from LW Meeting" and told of the reporter's efforts to attend a meeting of the Golden Rain Foundation at Clubhouse 3 of the private retirement community.   Part of a NEWS-POST editorial mentioned Golden Rain Foundation's "discriminatory practice" of preventing the NEWS-POST from being delivered through the guarded gates by carriers to non-subscribers.   The supposed purpose of the editorial was found in the lower right-hand corner in the form of a boxed editorial with a coupon at the bottom requesting Leisure World residents to check a smaller box saying, "Yes, I enjoy the Laguna Hills News-Post.   Please enter my subscription for one year at $6.00."   There was then a space for a resident to write his name and address, and instructions for mailing the coupon to the NEWS-POST.   The editorial above the coupon told the residents, "You Can Help Us to Help You."   The editorial then read as follows:

"For many months, the News-Post has attempted to obtain fair and equal treatment in regard to distribution of the News-Post in Leisure World.   So far we have been unsuccessful.

"The fact remains that the management of Leisure World does not want you to read any LOCAL newspaper but the Leisure World News which is a house organ controlled by the management. Only news favorable to the management is permitted to be published in this controlled paper.

"The Leisure World management knows we will report the news as we find it and let the residents of Leisure World make up their own minds about their affairs. For this reason the management has made it difficult and needlessly expensive for the News-Post to bring you the straight, unvarnished news.

"Despite these obstacles the News-Post has mailed its newspaper to you since 1969. This is expensive. We have absorbed many postal increases and we are facing another shortly.

"The Leisure World News is distributed to each resident by carrier. The News-Post should be allowed to do the same thing.

"The News-Post is a Wednesday newspaper yet you do not receive it by mail until Thursday, or Friday. If we had the same privileges as the house organ, you would receive your News-Post every Wednesday.

"The Leisure World management will allow us to use carriers to deliver your newspaper if you are a paid subscriber. However, the News-Post has many faithful readers on fixed incomes who do not feel they can afford to pay for the paper.

"The management tells us all of you are paying for the Leisure World News in your dues. That is the way they justify discriminating in favor of the Leisure World News.

"Did anyone ever tell you you were paying for the Leisure World News? All of the literature on Leisure World implies that you get it free.

"If you are paying for the Leisure World News, were you given a choice whether you wanted to buy it? If you chose not to buy it,

13

would your dues be reduced?

"The Leisure World management simply does not want the News-Post in Leisure World publishing all the news--both good and bad. A free press is guaranteed to all Americans by the Constitution. The tactics of the Leisure World management are hardly in keeping with the freedom of America.

"It is also most interesting to note that two officers of the corporation managing Leisure World are officers of the corporation which publishes the Leisure World News. It is not in their financial interest to allow any competition from the News-Post if they can help it. This is a clear case of putting self-interest above the public interest.

"We want to continue serving all of you Leisure Worlders with a truly free press. To help us do that we urge you to become a paid subscriber so we can deliver the News-Post by carrier on the day of publication. We urge you to help us help you!"

Spitaleri gave the impression that the NEWS-POST was a free press and that he was more interested in the First Amendment than in his advertising income. He was seeking the same permission which had been given to the LEISURE WORLD NEWS, unsolicited carrier distribution of the NEWS-POST to all Leisure World residents. Golden Rain Foundation then owned and still owns all the common areas, including the streets and sidewalks, within Leisure World. Not all of the residents of Leisure World were or are members of Golden Rain. Yet through a contract which Golden Rain had with the Leisure World Foundation, then publisher of the LEISURE WORLD NEWS, that newspaper was indiscriminately delivered by carrier to all residents whether or not they were members of the Golden Rain Foundation. The Leisure World Foundation

14

had an understanding with Golden Rain that no competing unsolicited, give-away newspaper could be distributed within Leisure World except by mail. The questionable arrangement, begun in 1964 when Leisure World was developed, continued after 1967 when Birchall, Smith & Weiner, Inc., the predecessor of Golden West Publishing Corporation, bought the LEISURE WORLD NEWS.

Newspapers such as the LOS ANGELES TIMES, THE REGISTER and others could only use carriers to deliver to paid subscribers unless they wanted the U.S. Postal Service to deliver copies to non-subscribers. Spitaleri usually excluded that fact from his editorials. Not dependent on Leisure World for their success, the daily newspapers were financially profitable and had no dire need to compensate for any possible losses in advertising revenue from that area. Being able to cite all of the thousands of residents in Leisure World as recipients of the weekly LEISURE WORLD NEWS, its publisher could make a better offer to potential advertisers. Spitaleri viewed the relationship between Golden Rain and the LEISURE WORLD NEWS publishers as financially damaging to his NEWS-POST, mailed once a week to Leisure World.

With no profits to show from the NEWS-POST, Spitaleri was having difficulty making the payments required in the $400,000 purchase of the SOUTH COAST NEWS. The heirs to William Ottaway's estate filed suit against Spitaleri and his wife Marjorie for their failure to pay the sums owed for Ottaway's consultantship. A one-day trial before a judge of the Superior Court on June 2, 1975, resulted in a verdict in favor of plaintiffs Barbara O. Duarte, William J. Ottaway, Steven R. Ottaway and Harriet R. Anderson. On June 23, 1975, the judge ordered the Spitaleris to pay $12,500 and one-half of the sums due on the $50,000 consideration to not compete.

15

Spitaleri did not yet have to contend with a competing newspaper located in Laguna Beach. As is true of many small town newspapers, the NEWS-POST was the recipient of the efforts of volunteers who enjoyed contributing stories and/or photographs of their clubs' activities. One such volunteer was Larry Campbell, a retired Marine officer, who was a member of numerous service and civic organizations in Laguna Beach. He also taught photography in the journalism department of Saddleback Community College in nearby Mission Viejo. Eggers, the NEWS-POST managing editor who received Campbell's contributions to the newspaper, had an advanced education which consisted solely of an A.A. degree in photojournalism from El Camino College, another two-year community college in Southern California. When Eggers found out about Campbell's teaching role he surreptitiously wrote a letter to Saddleback questioning Campbell's qualifications. Eggers' letter resulted in Campbell's dismissal although Campbell did hold a Community College Limited Service Credential in "Communication Services and Related Technologies, including Printing." That credential apparently was insufficient for teaching photography, in which Campbell was self-taught. Campbell seemingly did not know for several years that it was Eggers who initiated the steps toward his disengagement from Saddleback. Years later Eggers would be teaching photography to Leisure World residents through the Emeritus Institute of Saddleback.

Campbell's anger over the facts concerning his dismissal was directed at Spitaleri instead of at Eggers. In order to be more centrally located and to be closer to the majority of the prospective advertisers in South Orange County, Spitaleri planned to move his NEWS-POST offices from Laguna Beach to Laguna Hills, an unincorporated part of the County of Orange which is about nine

16

miles inland from the Pacific Ocean. Spitaleri had long since stopped using the hot type printing equipment and was sending the NEWS-POST out of the city to be printed offset. Despite a long and bitter feud with the Laguna Beach City Council in trying to have a new newspaper plant built on a parcel of land he owned on Laguna Canyon Road in Laguna Beach, Spitaleri was unsuccessful in obtaining a permit or zoning change. Spitaleri blamed Councilwoman Phyllis Sweeney for leading the rest of the council against his plans. Spitaleri then opted to lease office space at an industrial park in Laguna Hills near Leisure World, the private retirement community upon which he was trying, through litigation, to force receipt of his newspaper. In an editorial in the May 7, 1975, edition of the Laguna NEWS-POST, Spitaleri wrote, "Yes, we do plan to move to a new facility a few miles inland on the first of June...Our sole objective in making this physical move to a new facility is to improve our operations so we may better serve you." With no other newspaper now having an office in Laguna Beach, Campbell seized the opportunity and began publishing, in July of 1975, the TIDES AND TIMES, self-advertised as "Laguna's only hometown newspaper."

Chapter 2

Laguna Beach had first attracted me as a 16-year-old who enjoyed escaping the heat of Tustin, California, by traveling 25 miles to visit the seashore in the summertime. Born in Detroit, Michigan, I had moved with my family at the age of nine to California in 1963. I began writing letters to one of my aunts, who was favorably impressed with my ability to squeeze news of all the family happenings into single-page letters. She praised my tight writing and encouraged me to become a writer. With her continued encouragement and my desire to serve people in some manner, I studied a college journalism textbook at age 12 to determine if that was the career for me. During the next few years I had more exposure to the journalism profession. As a freshman in high school I prepared a report on Charles Dickens' attempts, through his books, to reform child labor laws and other ills.

It became evident to me that writing about social injustices and other evils, shedding light in dark corners, could improve the quality of life for many people. To do the most good as a writer, it seemed that newspapers would be the most effective medium through which to communicate to the most people.

In a parable by Booth Tarkington entitled "Freedom of Speech," used to accompany a Norman Rockwell painting with the same caption, a fictional encounter between Benito Mussolini and Adolf Hitler, both later to become dictators, is told regarding their political views. Meeting in a chalet in Austria in 1912, each recognizes himself as a future dictator. At that time one is a journalist and the other an artist. They agree that to become masters of their own countries they would first have to destroy freedom of speech. The parable reminded me of a quotation attributed to another dictator, Nikolai Lenin of Russia. In the same vein as Mussolini and Hitler, Lenin said, "Why should freedom of speech and freedom of the press be allowed? Why should a government which is doing what it believes to be right allow itself to be criticized? It would not allow opposition by lethal weapons. Ideas are much more fatal things than guns. Why should any man be allowed to buy a printing press and disseminate pernicious opinion calculated to embarrass the government?" I was yet to discover that local government officials could have the same view as notorious dictators toward the freedom of speech and of the press.

Neither my high school nor college education in journalism prepared me for what I would experience as a professional journalist. For that matter, neither did my independent study inform me that the First Amendment freedom of speech in this country would be abused not only by the government but also by the press establishment, journalism societies, a civil rights group, and the judicial system, including the United States Supreme Court. Ratified in 1791, the First Amendment is part of the Bill of Rights added to the United States Constitution to guarantee basic rights to all citizens, not just publishers or churches. "Congress shall make no law respecting an establishment of religion, or prohibiting the free exercise thereof; or abridging the freedom of speech, or of the press; or the right of the people peaceably to assemble, and to petition the Government for a redress of grievances." Therefore, the United States government guarantees that every citizen has the right to worship, to speak, to publish, to assemble and to petition. Just in 1976 Congress enacted the Civil Rights Attorneys' Fees Award Act so that citizens who successfully prosecute lawsuits will have their attorneys' fees paid for by the defendants because they should not have to pay to have enforced through litigation rights already guaranteed by the government.

According to several surveys, many Americans resent the claim of the press--newspapers, magazines, television and radio--that it has a First Amendment right to report the news. Many people apparently do not realize that the press is preserving the right for everyone, not just themselves. Thomas Jefferson, one of the writers of the Constitution and the Bill of Rights, said that if given the choice, he would rather have newspapers than government. The more that government actions are examined and exposed, the less likely the politicians will be able to become tyrannical and dishonest.

Before graduating from Tustin High School in 1972 I had made many visits to Laguna Beach, which seemed like an idyllic seaside community. I dreamed of living there and working for a local newspaper. The idea that either the Laguna Beach city government or the NEWS-POST, the local newspaper, could be corrupt never entered my mind at the tender age of 16. The beautiful scenery, quaint shops and charming homes gave a fairy-tale impression. I returned to my high school studies and served as co-editor-in-chief of the campus newspaper, looking forward to college at another seaside community, Malibu, California. I received a California State Scholarship which I used to attend the Christian-oriented Pepperdine University. In addition to overlooking the ocean and the movie star community known as "The Colony," Pepperdine was known for its award-winning publications and excellent journalism department. Because of a 3.91 grade point average I had been accepted with honors at entrance at UCLA. Attending a small college with a Christian emphasis in its educational program, however, was more important to me.

One of my basic education requirements was a class in English composition. Because I had to write a term paper, I chose to do it on a subject in journalism because that was my major field of study. In 1973 I turned in my term paper entitled "Administration and the Media." Using more than 12 news magazines as sources, I concluded that the "practices toward the media by the Nixon Administration, which includes the legislative and judicial branches, leave 'the freedom of the press,' guaranteed by the First Amendment to the Constitution, at stake." One of the examples cited, which I would soon see on a local level, was a TIME magazine article entitled "Nixon vs. the Vultures" in which reporters were pressured to "tell it like the Administration says it is." If the news media were to just be an extension of government, we could have a communist dictator instead of a democratic government and independently owned and operated

21

news media. The journalism profession has been called the Fourth Estate, numbered after the executive, legislative and judicial branches of government. Just as the three branches of government are designed to assure a check and balance system of power, the Fourth Estate is to give the people's point of view, which may or may not agree with the official version given by one of the governmental branches.

In my college journalism education my first class taught the basics of the "who, what, where, when, why" of newswriting. For additional credits toward my major, I began working on the campus newspaper, THE GRAPHIC. Within one year I rose from staff writer to features editor, to city editor, and then to news editor. I was subsequently enrolled in more advanced journalism classes, taught by James Fields, who had previously been a newspaper publisher. We did in-depth studies of communications law, including those applying to libel and to freedom of information. Above all, Fields stressed a journalist's role in being a "watchdog" on government agencies.

He encouraged his students to join the campus chapter of Sigma Delta Chi, the Society of Professional Journalists, which promotes the responsibility of journalists to the public. The society's motto is "He Serves Best Who Serves the Truth." Its watchword is "Talent, Truth, Energy." For my last trimester before graduation from Pepperdine I wanted to have an internship at a newspaper in exchange for class credits and perhaps an opportunity to be hired full-time. Because the only newspaper located in Laguna Beach at that time was the NEWS-POST, I arranged to have an interview with its publisher, Vernon R. Spitaleri, concerning an internship in which I would work without pay. Probably as a result of a life based on honesty and forthrightness, it never occurred to me to check the litigation history of the newspaper or the policies of the publisher. I assumed its editors and publisher would have the same journalism philosophy as my college instructors and textbooks. A perusal of their recent editions did not reveal any glaring irregularities. To assist me in obtaining either an internship or a full-time reporter position, Fields wrote me a letter of recommendation on May 14, 1975.

After noting my "A" grades, Fields wrote, "Janice was outstanding in her approach to a rigorous schedule of public affairs reporting assignments. All of her writing was impressive, but I was particularly impressed by her rigid meeting of the tight deadlines which were imposed on this work. She was the first in her class to complete the assignments. I have also been impressed by Miss Brownfield's stable personality which will surely be useful to her in contact with news sources and the public...During my years as an editor and publisher, I saw few young people with as much promise as her." Perhaps if Fields had mentioned that he sometimes referred to me as a "legal beagle" I would not have been given the internship and eventual full-time employment.

The NEWS-POST's oddities first struck me while I was applying for the internship. The lack of communication between Michael Eggers, the managing editor, and Spitaleri, the editor-publisher, was evidenced in my telephone call to arrange an interview. Eggers asked me to tell Spitaleri that he would not be present the following Saturday for the interview. When I finally met with Spitaleri, our conversation was interrupted by a woman telephoning to complain that she had received numerous calls from families seeking foreign exchange students for the summer because the NEWS-POST had printed the wrong number in the newspaper. Her call made me feel at ease since the apparently imperfect NEWS-POST would seemingly be less likely to expect perfection from me.

Luckily I was not wearing my best clothes for my first day as an intern. Since my interview at the NEWS-POST offices in Laguna Beach, its operations had been moved to Laguna Hills, nine miles inland in an unincorporated part of Orange County. Bound volumes of NEWS-POST predecessors dating back to 1915 had not yet been placed on the shelves at their new location. Spitaleri had me spend several hours sorting and lifting the volumes. After a few weeks I was told by some Laguna Beach citizens that there had been a fight between Spitaleri and the city council. Displeased with his newspaper, the city government would not allow him to build a newspaper plant in the wooded canyon portion of the city. The circumstances of the City's discontent with the NEWS-POST were unknown to me.

Although I was required to work only 16 hours a week for the internship, the NEWS-POST, a semi-weekly newspaper, had me working about 40 hours a week. Eggers had me running from one assignment to another without pay or gas money. Since I was hoping to be hired at the end of the internship, though, I accepted all of the assignments given to me.

Several days a week I worked in the production shop as a proofreader and paste-up artist. Both departments, production and editorial, were soon praising me for my work. I enjoyed feeling needed by them. During the middle of the internship Spitaleri said I could be hired full-time if I pasted-up pages more quickly. Shortly thereafter he told Eggers I was the best of the three paste-up artists.

Most of the workers in the production shop were married women who had children. I enjoyed

24

their company because they seemed more mature than the workers in the editorial department, where five of the seven employees were in their twenties. Most of the editorial workers were single and their main social life was with their fellow employees. Judi Bloom, whose desk was next to mine, was the nicest and she made the rough work bearable. When she accepted her job four months earlier, she had not been told that she would have to lay-out pages and paste them up herself. As an English major in college, Bloom had work experience just in writing, not in production. Her dislike for Eggers, for conning her into her job, was well-known in the editorial department. Rather than move closer to the NEWS-POST, she commuted about 70 miles each way to work for about six months until she found a writing job with another newspaper closer to her home.

Because I had minimal contact with Eggers at the beginning, my feelings about and impressions of him were not too clear-cut. I used my time to concentrate on my work assignments and nothing else. With Spitaleri I had even less contact. A quiet loner who usually walked with his head down, Spitaleri had Eggers relay his directives to the editorial workers. Aristocratic in appearance, Spitaleri had short, dark wavy hair, graying at the temples, and combed straight back. Typical of many of his heritage, he had a thin moustache, hardly noticeable. Mainly because of his trimmer physique, he would regularly tell Eggers that he was the better-looking of the two. Eggers did not appreciate the comparison. Nor did he enjoy hearing the Spitaleris compliment me, which caused him to refer to me as their "golden girl."

As the end of my internship approached, I asked Eggers to inform my supervisor at Pepperdine University that I had performed the required

25

duties and to suggest a grade for my efforts. In spite of any jealousies he may have had about me, Eggers wrote the following letter on July 24, 1975:

"Hopefully, this letter will serve as a critique of Janice Brownfield's internship at the News-Post Newspapers.

"Without hesitation I would classify Janice as an outstanding journalist who can, and will, do very well in the profession she has chosen for a career. Her photography work also shows promise.

"As is the case with any new experience, Janice spent the first few days of her internship becoming acquainted with her new surroundings. This doesn't imply that she sat back and watched what was happening around her. In the first issue after she joined our staff, she had a front page by-line story.

"As I told her before she joined our staff, the News-Post does not believe in weather-obit internships. Janice will attest to this. In addition to daily rewrites, she worked on several major feature and news stories. She also handled working on headlines, cutlines and dummying several pages. She was also trained in the production shop to handle editorial page pasteup techniques. Overall, she has done an excellent job.

"Perhaps one of her better qualities was that she was always willing to listen to instructions and carry them out in detail. This proved invaluable.

"Janice will attest to the fact that she worked very long and hard hours (double the 16 hour requirement), however, the experience gained was well worth the effort I feel. One measure of her value to our operation might include the fact that Jan will join our newspaper as a full-time employee on August 1.

"Although I could go on for pages, my sin-

26

cerest comment might be that Janice earned an 'A' grade for her work.

"I know she gained something from the job and I'm sure the entire News-Post editorial and production staffs benefited from her internship."

Spitaleri had offered me $500 a month to work full-time, 18 hours a week in the editorial department and 22 hours in the production department. At that time inexperienced receptionists could receive $800 at most businesses. JoAnn Carlson, a journalism instructor at Pepperdine, had encouraged students to enter the public relations field because it was more financially rewarding than newspaper work. On August 3, 1975, I was graduated cum laude with a bachelor of arts degree in journalism and a minor in family life. Because consumerism was a newsworthy field and since I had read that newspapers often prefer to hire specialists, I had taken several courses in family consumer problems in order to qualify for the minor. Ralph Nader, who wrote UNSAFE AT ANY SPEED about the dangers of the Corvair automobile, had become a consumer crusader whose work was very influential and which I admired.

With my hiring at the NEWS-POST I became the subject of a staff profile, which according to the editor's note at the end was a "continuing series." As I was to find out later, that could have been due to the NEWS-POST's "swinging front door."

Dorothy Korber, who had been a NEWS-POST staff writer for several years and covered the San Juan Capistrano beat, was assigned to interview me for the profile. As published in the newspaper the headline read, "Her Flashing Grin Hides Seriousness," and, of course, the article was accompanied by an appropriate photograph of me smiling. The profile began with, "News-Post staff writer Jan Brownfield is usually grinning, or

27

laughing, or smiling, or beaming.

"But when asked how she would describe herself, an unusual expression crossed her face. She looked serious.

"'I think of myself as--' Jan began, but was interrupted by eavesdropping reporter Bill Doherty.

"'She's a cute kid,' Doherty said.

"Jan flashed her familiar grin as she shook her head in perplexity.

"'I don't know why they always call me 'Kid' around the office,' she said. 'I'm 21 years old.'

"'You're the cutest and the kiddest,' Doherty retorted.

"Jan may well be the cutest and the youngest News-Post editorial staffer, but her constant smile belies the sincere, dedicated journalist behind it.

"She came to the newspaper as a summer intern from Pepperdine University, Malibu. Her ability was obvious almost instantly, resulting in the creation of a position for her on the staff.

"Working in the Laguna Beach area was natural for Jan. A resident of Tustin, she has long been intrigued by the ambience and beauty of the Art Colony.

"'I've always wanted to live and work in Laguna,' she commented, 'and Laguna is meeting my expectations.'

"In addition to a fairly regular beat covering Laguna Beach council meetings, Jan's feature-writing assignments have ranged across the south county area.

"She brings to her work a strong sense of the importance of journalism.

"'I became a journalist because I want to do something worthwhile, to perform a social service,' Jan said. 'I have high ideals, and I hope to work to get rid of society's abuses.'

"Jan laughed at her own seriousness, but her muckraking bent was clear.

"Part of Jan's enthusiasm and sincerity stems from her dedication to the Christian faith.

"'Every day, I try to act like a Christian,' she explained, serious again. 'It's hard.' She is active in the Calvary Chapel.

"Pepperdine's reputation as a Christian school and its fine journalism department prompted her to attend the Malibu university. She graduated this summer...cum laude.

"'I've wanted to be in the newspaper work for nine years,' Jan said. 'I decided in my first year of junior high. One of my aunts encouraged me and was a big influence.

"She was co-editor-in-chief of the Tustin High School newspaper, winning two regional awards in feature writing.

"Jan, the daughter of an insulator and a librarian, currently lives at home with her parents. She leads a physically active life, biking outrageous distances and swimming daily.

"But, regardless of the endeavor, she tackles everything with that smiling exuberance.

"Her philosophy?

"'I used to be a real worrier--I'd wake my mother up in the middle of the night to check a math problem,' Jan recalled. 'I've learned that I can work or study hard and still enjoy life.'"

Shortly after joining the NEWS-POST, I noticed that Michael Eggers, then the managing editor, received at least one telephone call a day from the Laguna Beach municipal services director requesting that pictures be taken of his municipal projects. After each call Eggers went into immediate action by requiring me to take the requested photographs, which then appeared in the NEWS-POST. Those pictures consisted of road patchings, sprinkler installations, road railings, tennis court installation, Cal Trans employees not working, group of tree plantings, city hall additions, viewpoint sign, new swing set, and city employees in Halloween costumes. At one point, when I asked Eggers if it was necessary to respond to every picture and story whim of Stanley Scholl, the municipal services director, Eggers answered that it was because Scholl sometimes provided the NEWS-POST with story leads. I never saw any stories resulting from his leads except for further publicity for himself and his projects.

If I had studied various back issues of the NEWS-POST before applying for an internship, I would have seen the tremendous amount of personal and business publicity given to Scholl and a slightly less amount given to the other city officials and to the Festival of Arts, from which both the City and the NEWS-POST profited financially. On May 7, 1985, a NEWS-POST photograph showed Scholl walking under telephone wires with a caption about an underground assessment district. On May 10, 1975, he was pictured with other city officials planting a tree at Bluebird Park.

Eggers continued to take and publish photographs of Scholl standing at the Ruby Street viewsite/park, looking at cliff erosion, inspecting water protection at the playhouse, examining a ditch under construction, standing between two city trams, posting a "Leaving Laguna Beach" sign, and looking at the ocean. Eggers also wrote stories about Scholl's vacations and placed them prominently on the front page of the NEWS-POST. Since Scholl usually went without his wife and instead was accompanied by other city officials, Eggers was able to ingratiate himself with more than one public servant at a time. Jon Brand, a councilman, and Douglas Schmitz, an aide to Scholl and son of the Festival of Arts president, were Scholl's frequent companions.

Besides keeping him in Scholl's good graces, the stories and photographs either prepared or ordered by Eggers were payment for the free meals, drinks and trips with which Scholl provided him. Eggers also used the NEWS-POST as a vehicle for giving himself publicity. A member of the Jaycees and the Exchange Club in order to obtain NEWS-POST advertisements from member merchants, Eggers would receive a percentage of the advertising income. Photographs of his son, daughter and wife would also appear on the front pages of the NEWS-POST when non-family members easily could have been selected to pose. If the photographs and stories were so newsworthy they might have been in other local newspapers, but they were not. They just "fell" into the NEWS-POST, as Eggers boasted that he "fell" into journalism.

Including Eggers and myself, there were seven individuals employed in the editorial department. Three, including myself, worked there only part-time. Dorothy Korber, who had written the profile about me when I was hired, was the editor of the South Shores edition and sat two desks away from me. She had worked there several years, joining at about the same time as Eggers in 1973. Korber often wondered out loud how much money Eggers had received from Rancho Palos Verdes Corp., owner of Sycamore Hills, for giving excessive press coverage to its lawsuits against the City of Laguna Beach concerning development plans for its 522 acres of scenic open space. She said she would not be surprised if Rancho Palos Verdes Corp. had given Eggers the down payment for his home in San Juan Capistrano which, according to the County Recorder's

31

Office, he bought on March 21, 1974. It was during that same time period, according to Korber, that Eggers gave preferential treatment to every story concerning Sycamore Hills. His salary was about $800 a month and he did not have any relatives from whom to inherit or receive a down payment on a home, she said.

Korber's suspicions were confirmed several years later on May 18, 1977, when Howard Miller, a consultant to Rancho Palos Verdes Corp., told me that he had "arranged" the financing of the house for Eggers because Eggers had credit problems. Miller was in close communication with Councilman Jack McDowell, who in the June 4, 1977, edition of the NEWS-POST was accused by then-Mayor Jon Brand of making "traitorous comments" and "working for the other side" over the issue of Sycamore Hills. The actions of Eggers and McDowell certainly seemed to indicate relationships with Rancho Palos Verdes Corp. that compromised their positions of public trust, that of a newspaper editor and that of an elected city officer.

Eggers, McDowell, the City of Laguna Beach and anyone else in a position to profit financially from Sycamore Hills were willing to ignore the Constitution of the State of California in order to ensure their economic gain. The constitutional violation was brought to the attention of the Laguna Beach City Council not by the city attorney or the landowner's attorney but by a Laguna Beach resident, Dallas Anderson, who had no formalized legal education. Another resident, Ronald Steinberg, had filed a lawsuit, criticized as being "silly" in a NEWS-POST editorial, because the city council had violated the state's Ralph M. Brown Act by discussing the land purchase in private meetings, closed to the public. Anderson had told the council that the sale also violated Article 16, Section 18, of the state Constitution which prohibits municipalities from making purchases greater than their annual tax revenue income. Superior Court Judge James Judge refused to acknowledge the violations and on July 14, 1978, allowed the City to proceed with purchasing the land for $6.75 million.

The constitutional violation was never mentioned in a single newspaper, including the LOS ANGELES TIMES, THE REGISTER and the DAILY PILOT, all of which had just reported the information handed out by the government. Only a year later, when Councilwoman Sally Bellerue, who had been a member of the council for three years, announced that the sale was unconstitutional did the press inform the public and the taxpayers. Under a June 28, 1979, NEWS-POST headline "Purchase Agreement Unconstitutional? Sycamore Hills Issue Flares," Bellerue was quoted as saying that the city council "had been advised that the City's 1978 agreement to purchase Sycamore Hills is apparently unconstitutional." Just scanning the local newspapers to check on their stories of government handouts, the LOS ANGELES TIMES reported similarly on July 1, 1979, with a story headlined, "Sycamore Hills Pact Invalid, Official Says." None of the newspapers quoted the article and section of the Constitution which forbade the acquisition.

The city government knew one year earlier when Anderson told the city council that the sale was unconstitutional. The city attorney, George Logan, was not competent to tell them because he did not even know how to legally assume the office for which he was receiving remuneration. Anderson constantly informed the city council of Logan's failure until finally, at one meeting, Logan took the oath of office. His associate, Stephen Chase, who had also been receiving payment for acting as the deputy city attorney, took his oath also. They did not offer to return the monies they had received before lawfully assuming their posts.

If the newspapers had been doing their jobs, they would have been acting independently of the city government instead of just an extension of it. They should have researched Steinberg's, Anderson's and other citizens' charges of actions not in conformance with the law and then written stories about them. But the press, especially Eggers, was not interested in serving the public. Eggers was more concerned about how to use the NEWS-POST for his own financial gain. In October, 1975, Eggers had the entire NEWS-POST editorial staff write stories promoting dog racing. It was the only subject, excluding the Festival of Arts which financially benefitted the NEWS-POST more than it did Eggers, for which the entire staff was ever assigned to do stories. The articles, photographs and columns were published in the October 22, 1975, edition of the NEWS-POST. Korber said she believed that Eggers was paid by a special interest group to provide the publicity, which was for the dog racing initiative to be on the November, 1976, ballot. About a week before the vote, the NEWS-POST printed a Copley News Service editorial on October 23, 1976, which recommended a "no" vote on the proposition. Two months earlier, on August 28, 1976, the NEWS-POST printed a column by Eggers encouraging a "yes" vote. As with all of his columns, Eggers' picture of himself was also included. It was apparent that promoters of the dog racing initiative had to compensate someone like Eggers to publish favorable columns and articles to give voters the impression that their local newspaper had given its endorsement.

My journalism education had not prepared

me for working under Spitaleri, the publisher and editor who had a degree in printing, and Eggers, the managing editor who had an associate of arts degree in photojournalism. Neither one of them took seriously the responsibility of being a watchdog on government. Each was more interested in using the NEWS-POST to his advantage. Spitaleri enjoyed being a watchdog on the private operations of Leisure World, a private community, because he wanted his First Amendment rights to be recognized in a way that he could increase his advertising income. Eggers wrote about city government officials' vacations, placing less emphasis upon their official actions which affected the taxpayers.

I had never heard Spitaleri or Eggers claim to be a member of Sigma Delta Chi, the Society of Professional Journalists, which I had joined while a student at Pepperdine University. They did not have to be members to know that it was unethical to use the NEWS-POST for their own advantage. The first standard of practice listed in the society's Code of Ethics is "Responsibility: The public's right to know of events of public importance and interest is the overriding mission of the mass media. The purpose of distributing news and enlightened opinion is to serve the general welfare. Journalists who use their professional status as representatives of the public for selfish or other unworthy motives violate a high trust."

The second standard listed is "Freedom of the Press: Freedom of the press is to be guarded as an inalienable right of people in a free society. It carries with it the freedom and the responsibility to discuss, question, and challenge actions and utterances of our government and of our public and private institutions. Journalists uphold the right to speak unpopular opinions and the privilege to agree with the

35

majority."

The third standard, "Ethics," which specifically delineated violations which Eggers and Spitaleri committed, states, "Journalists must be free of obligation to any interest other than the public's right to know the truth.

"1. Gifts, favors, free travel, special treatment or privileges can compromise the integrity of journalists and their employers. Nothing of value should be accepted.

"2. Secondary employment, political involvement, holding public office, and service in community organizations should be avoided if it compromises the integrity of journalists and their employers. Journalists and their employers should conduct their personal lives in a manner which protects them from conflict of interest, real or apparent. Their responsibilities to the public are paramount. That is the nature of their profession." The last paragraph of the Code of Ethics is a pledge, that "journalists should actively censure and try to prevent violations of these standards, and they should encourage their observance by all newspeople. Adherence to this code of ethics is intended to preserve the bond of mutual trust and respect between American journalists and the American people."

As indicated in its Code of Ethics, the society well recognizes that journalists are to serve the public's right to know. They are to obtain the information that the public would want to know. Because President Ronald Reagan did not allow the press to cover the invasion of Grenada in 1983, the public received information only from the governments of the United States and Cuba during the first two days. While the American government told its citizens that the United States had attacked Grenada with such precision that there were no civilian casualties, the Canadian press subsequently reported that at least 20 patients and orderlies at a mental hospital had been killed by the U.S. bombing. The American government then confirmed the press report.

The American government had also told its citizens that the day before the invasion, the Grenada military regime had closed the island's airport, making it impossible for Americans to leave if they so desired. The American press later learned that four commercial flights departed from Grenada the day before the invasion. Whether or not President Reagan was right to order the invasion, the American public had a right to know the truth before passing judgment. If all Americans do not support their First Amendment rights, they will lose them. They should let their government know that they will not tolerate restraint of their right to know. Later in 1983, the International Press Institute released its annual report, which covered 86 countries. In only 24 nations, mainly Western, is the press free, it reported. Journalists in other countries were killed, jailed or otherwise silenced for trying to report the truth to the public. The institute observed that "today only a small part of the globe can boast that free speech is respected and honored. The rest of the world is gagged...The role of the journalist has never been harder than it is today." The journalists in those repressive countries must have been aware of the penalties they could suffer at the hands of their governments for trying to protect the public's right to know. Americans should realize that members of its press do not necessarily dislike the United States when they report facts which may not reflect favorably on the government. The same is true of human relationships. Just because one likes someone should not prevent him from communicating honestly when they disagree.

As managing editor of the NEWS-POST, Eggers oversaw and sometimes assigned stories for the Laguna Beach beat which I covered. Like many people, Korber was enchanted by Laguna Beach and occasionally said she wanted my beat instead of the one she had--San Juan Capistrano and Laguna Niguel. Because Eggers was spending more time seeking a personal income in the advertising department, Korber often edited my stories before they were published. She usually did not make any changes except for a word or two.

From December 3, 1975, through February 25, 1976, Eggers did write seven stories, two with his byline, about candidates for the March 2, 1976, election for the Laguna Beach City Council. One article, published December 17, 1975, featured Jack McDowell's announcement of candidacy. Appearing across the top of the front page of the NEWS-POST, it was void of Eggers' byline. That was probably because Eggers was trying to keep it a secret from the other six candidates that he was being remunerated in more than one way to prepare McDowell's campaign brochures. In early February, 1976, he boasted to the NEWS-POST staff that he was going to the airport that morning with McDowell to fly to San Francisco where they would meet with McDowell's son-in-law concerning the preparation of the campaign brochures. On February 21, 1976, the NEWS-POST printed on its second page a political advertisement endorsing McDowell. The ad had the same writing and photograph as had appeared in the brochures.

Following my coverage of a meeting where one of the other candidates, Arnold Hano, told me that he knew of Eggers' participation in McDowell's campaign, I told Eggers what Hano said. Eggers' eyes shifted and he looked down as he quickly tried to determine how Hano had discovered his indiscretion. Eggers tried to act nonchalantly but later in the day asked me to try to find the source of Hano's information. I had no intention of doing so but kept my opinion to myself. After his election victory, McDowell complained privately to Dallas Anderson that he expected better news coverage from the NEWS-POST since he had paid Eggers more than $1,000 to work on his campaign.

Like Eggers, I did not feel financially secure with my salary from Laguna Publishing Company. For working 40 hours a week I received $550 a month gross. When I heard of an opening in the circulation department, I quickly applied. As the distributor to the racks and certain residences in Laguna Beach, I received another $150 to $175 a month as an independent contractor. Because the newspaper was published just two days a week, Wednesday and Saturday, the several hours for my extra job did not affect my full-time employment. The same day I assumed the additional duties in March, 1976, I also arranged to move out of my parents' home in Tustin to a place in Laguna Beach because I finally felt able to afford it.

Unknown to me at the time, on March 5, 1976, Spitaleri and his Laguna Publishing Company filed a dismissal of their lawsuit against Golden West Publishing Corp. which had alleged appropriation of trade secrets, including breach of employment contract, and interference with business relations. That suit was separate and apart from his other lawsuit against Golden West alleging unfair competition concerning the LEISURE WORLD NEWS. Spitaleri had charged that Golden West had sought Jon White, a NEWS-POST advertising salesman, to steal the names of the NEWS-POST advertisers and bring them with him to work for Golden West. White had been working for Laguna Publishing Company when I began my internship the year before. Spitaleri was forced to dismiss the lawsuit when the opposition proved that the names of his advertisers were public knowledge since they appeared in the NEWS-POST and that White chose to leave the NEWS-POST to work for the Golden West newspapers. It was absurd to consider the names of advertisers a "trade secret."

The week after moving to Laguna Beach I received a telephone call at work from a man who said he admired the stories I wrote about Laguna Beach City Council meetings and asked if I would be interested in hearing about wrongdoings by the mayor, who then was Phyllis Sweeney. After nine months at the NEWS-POST it seemed that at least one citizen appreciated my news stories concerning the city government. I agreed to meet with Dallas Anderson but kept in mind that he might have an axe to grind concerning Sweeney. After living near Sweeney for 10 years, he explained, he had grown to dislike her very much because she constantly trespassed on his property and allowed her dogs to run loose on his grass. I waited for more motives and Anderson supplied them. Seeing her in action as a councilwoman, he also came to dislike her treatment of the people's business. Her attitudes and actions were not conducive to good government, he said. Consequently, Anderson was motivated to investigate Mrs. Sweeney and her husband James through public records on file at the County Recorder's Office.

There Anderson discovered that James Sweeney was one of five partners in a business corporation which owned a building across the street from city hall. Mayor Sweeney had, according to Anderson, used her position as a government official to influence the state Coastal Commission to grant a remodeling permit for the building. That conflict of interest had been discovered when Anderson contacted Bob Joseph, the

40

City's planning director.   I interviewed Joseph, who had been the commission's area planner in 1974 when Mrs. Sweeney, then a councilwoman, telephoned him regarding Realex Investments' permit application for remodeling work scheduled for a public hearing on November 22, 1974.   Because of his work on other permits in Laguna Beach, Joseph knew that Sweeney was a councilwoman even though she only identified herself to him as an employee of Dorene Richmond, one of the partners in Realex Investments.   He was also sure that Mrs. Sweeney assumed he knew of her political position.

On the basis of Mrs. Sweeney's information that the City was actively working on a parking study and that Realtor Dorene Richmond and a tire dealer, the only occupants of the building, did not require much parking space, and that the critical part of the permit was getting the building facelifted in time for the 1975 summer art festivals, Joseph recommended the administrative permit, without a public hearing, which the commission approved on December 3, 1974.

After several people from Laguna Beach inquired about the Realex permit, Joseph said he pulled the file at the commission offices in the middle of May, 1976, two weeks after the City discharged him from his post as planning director. It was then that Joseph found out that Mrs. Sweeney's husband was a partner in Realex.   Her 1974 telephone call to him then became "questionable" in his mind.

My research for the story took two months because I did it on my own time.   I did not want Eggers to know I was working on the story and prevent my completion of it because of his unethical relationships with other city government officials.   Since Scholl did not like Joseph, neither did Eggers.   I finally turned my story in on May 25, 1976.   Instead of giving it to Korber,

41

whom I knew would automatically give it to Eggers because of its controversial nature, I chose to turn it in to Spitaleri. Still resentful of Sweeney's role in preventing him from building newspaper offices on his property in Laguna Canyon, Spitaleri was delighted with the story and ordered Eggers to print it. Mrs. Spitaleri had the same attitude toward Mrs. Sweeney and told me, "You should win an award for that story."

While working secretly on the Realex story I had been told by Eggers that he was going to recommend to Spitaleri that I be promoted to the position of Laguna Beach city editor. Although the four other regional editions of the NEWS-POST had a city editor for each, there was none listed in the masthead for Laguna Beach. Instead of trying to advance me because it was the right thing to do, Eggers was really trying to have himself promoted to the position of general manager, another title which did not appear in the masthead. Spitaleri vetoed the idea, claiming that it had been customary for the managing editor, Eggers, to assume Laguna Beach news responsibilities. Back issues of the NEWS-POST, however, revealed that other people had been listed as the Laguna Beach city editor while there had been a separate managing editor.

Spitaleri's reasoning was faulty in that I was writing all of the Laguna Beach news stories and Eggers spent so much time trying to obtain other income through the advertising department that he did not know what the major news stories in the city were. Although Spitaleri had previously said that I was the only one on the staff who was capable of covering Laguna Beach, he obviously wanted Eggers supervising the beat to protect the NEWS-POST's financial interest in receiving the City's legal advertisements and the Festival of Arts' publishing contract. While a government official's opinion concerning a reporter's ability would be the least reliable, according to all journalism textbooks, Eggers, never having read any apparently, told Spitaleri that Scholl said I had a "good grasp" of city news.

Destined to remain working part-time in the production department as well as in the editorial department, I received some sympathy from Korber, who said that my stories and photographs were too good to have my talent wasted by having to cut little pieces of paper to correct the typesetters' errors in the production shop.

It was with horror that I looked at the Realex story printed on the top of the front page on May 26, 1976. As part of the headline Eggers had written, "Joseph Labels Coast Panel Nod 'Questionable.'" The headline differed with the story, which stated that Joseph considered Mrs. Sweeney's telephone call to him "questionable." As the distributor to the Laguna Beach racks, I had been told by Spitaleri to put an increased amount of copies in the racks because he expected that issue to sell like hotcakes. Seeing extra copies with the incorrect headline was more upsetting. Back at the office after my route, I heard Spitaleri tell Eggers that someone had just called and told him, "Janice Brownfield is the best thing that ever happened to Laguna Beach." Spitaleri continued to receive many calls that were supportive of me and the story.

The city government, though, had a different reaction. When Scholl saw me walk into the City Clerk's Office that afternoon, he said to Councilman Jon Brand, one of his traveling companions, "Did you see the story in the NEWS-POST today?" After Brand replied that he had not, Scholl announced, for my benefit, that the "NEWS-POST has hit a new low." In the council chambers, however, Councilman Jack McDowell, an ardent foe of Mrs. Sweeney, told me, "You hit the nail right on the head." Frank Cankar, a resident who supported McDowell and had a father-son relationship with Eggers, told me, "Keep up the good work." The increased rack sales of the May 26th issue also encouraged me. During the two and one-half months that I delivered papers to street sale machines no other issue sold as well. The increased sales meant more income to me, which I cannot deny was enjoyable. When I told Spitaleri, in front of Eggers, what Scholl had said to me, he glared at Eggers and said, "Your friend Scholl." Eggers, who was seated, looked up at Spitaleri and replied, "I'm not the one who's paid by the City." Nothing else was said by either one of them.

Korber was obviously motivated by my Realex story because she wrote a column about Launa Beach government, which was not her beat, for the very next issue of the NEWS-POST, which was published May 29, 1976. Entitled "A Master of Manipulation" in her regular column known as "Curiouser and Curiouser," the featured subject was Stanley Scholl's constant manipulation of the NEWS-POST to print stories and photographs of his municipal services projects. Written in a humorous light and with no mention of Scholl's name or title, the column gave sufficient details so that only Scholl fit the description. "He expects us to document on film every city project, no matter how mundane or trivial. He rates a curb right up there with a new civic center." Korber got the idea for the conclusion when I told her about one photo session with Scholl and his projects. As it appeared in her published version, Korber wrote the following:

"Back at city hall, I wearily pulled myself out of his automobile.

"'Notice anything new about the car?' he queried innocently.

"Suspicious, I shook my head.

44

"'About the roof?' No, I told him. 'We had it repainted,' he said proudly, striking a smiling pose. 'Don't you think you should get a picture?'

"I gritted my teeth and snapped the shutter. I also left the lens cap on."

Even though Scholl was irked by Korber's column, it was not long before he began calling her at the NEWS-POST to have her write stories about the municipal services department's summer transportation program and a new city employee, Koko Grant. While she was intruding on my beat by accepting the publicity requests from Scholl, I continued to cover the Laguna Beach government beat. At an editorial staff meeting that summer, Spitaleri criticized a story I had written about Laguna Beach resident Barbara Smith questioning, at a city council meeting, the engineering capabilities of Scholl, who was city engineer as well as municipal services director. In addition to Smith, who was employed by an engineering firm at an earlier time, others at the same council meeting criticized Scholl's engineering ability and asked him for an answer, which was not forthcoming. Spitaleri said I should have found something more newsworthy about which to write. It was apparent that he was trying to protect Scholl or that Scholl had complained about the story.

No one dared to openly disagree with Spitaleri. Every employee quickly learned that Spitaleri only wanted employees who agreed with him. Consequently, I did not remind him that I had submitted another story at the same time as the one about Scholl's questioned engineering ability and that Korber had ordered it typeset and placed at the top of the front page. It was a follow-up story about Mayor Sweeney's husband selling his interest in the Realex Investments business. Since the NEWS-POST had published

45

stories about her questionable involvement in the business, it seemed appropriate to publish an article about them severing ties with the Realex business. Spitaleri had seen the typeset story in the production shop while I was working at a light table, which is used for pasting-up camera-ready copy. He took the story and said it was not going to be printed because it was not newsworthy enough. There was no point in my saying anything. The man clearly did not want to upset the city government. In the story's place he put a photograph of a scene from the Festival of Arts' Pageant of the Masters, from which, by being the official printer of its publications, Spitaleri benefitted financially, as did the City.

Because of the financial connections, he used the newspaper to promote the Festival. In one edition of the NEWS-POST Spitaleri was able to ingratiate himself with both the Festival and the city government in one editorial. Spitaleri wrote and published an editorial praising Douglas Schmitz, then 25 years old, for being named the City's new planning director. He is the son of James Schmitz, who at that time was president of the board of directors of the Festival of Arts. With no known experience in planning, Douglas Schmitz was chosen from more than 80 applicants who had legally applied for the position. Several months earlier, the City had stated that Schmitz, whose father also owns Beach Construction, would serve as temporary planning director, but that he definitely would not be named later as planning director.

Just as Spitaleri's financial arrangement with the Festival motivated him to give it un-limited publicity, he also censored anything that could possibly reflect negatively on the Festival. On July 10, 1976, the NEWS-POST had printed a short story I wrote about North Hollywood resi-

46

dent Bradley Steffens appearing before the city council to ask permission to sell, in front of the Festival, on City-owned land, copies of his own pamphlets about the Festival and Pageant. When the City denied his request, Steffens told the council that the interests of the Festival had been served at the expense of citizens' rights. Indeed, council member Sally Bellerue had said that the City would not think of doing anything that would upset the Festival. Being on City-owned land, the Festival gave the City more than $150,000 annually for the City's purchase of Main Beach Park. It did not seem to bother the Festival or the City that their exclusive relationship could infringe on other citizens' First Amendment rights. When I submitted a follow-up story about Steffens going to Orange County Superior Court to seek an injunction that would allow him to sell his pamphlets during that Festival season, Eggers said that Spitaleri did not want the story printed. Spitaleri received a profit for every copy of the official Festival pamphlet printed by the NEWS-POST. To increase his income from the pamphlets, he printed forms in the NEWS-POST for readers to order them directly from the NEWS-POST. Spitaleri had members of his family hawk the pamphlets on the Festival grounds to the summer visitors, a practice which of course kept the money in the family. Just one year later, in the summer of 1977, Spitaleri would testify in the LAGUNA PUBLISHING COMPANY vs. CAPISTRANO VALLEY PUBLISHING CORP. trial that the Festival pamphlets he printed were "very lucrative" for him.

The Festival and Pageant typically ran from approximately the middle of July to the end of August every year. All of the members of the NEWS-POST editorial department were required to attend the press preview night and then write reviews of the portion of the pageant that they were assigned. I subsequently turned my review in to staff writer Dorothy Korber, who approved it for typesetting. She did not know, however, that Marjorie Spitaleri would be one of the typesetters that day. Mrs. Spitaleri was editing the reviews as she typeset them. Since the idea of a review is that it contains opinions, the reviews contained comments that could be considered non-complimentary in some cases. Mrs. Spitaleri apparently deleted anything that she thought was not favorable to the Festival and her family's pocketbook. Korber became angry when she heard about the tampering and confronted Eggers with her complaint. Eggers did not even bother to try to discourage the editing by the wife of his boss. Although his formal journalism education was limited to photojournalism, I believe that Eggers knew such a practice by Mrs. Spitaleri was wrong. If either she or her husband had accomplished a formal or informal journalism education she would have known not to edit opinions. But the dollar signs may still have gotten in the way.

Later in the summer Dallas Anderson gave me a story lead which he said he had received from Councilman John McDowell. Anderson said McDowell had suggested that the bids for the city council chambers remodeling should be checked. I proceeded to go to the municipal services department at city hall one weekday morning to ask to look at the file for the bids. Rollene Billings, secretary to Municipal Services Director Stanley Scholl, informed me that Scholl was away from his office and that I would have to wait for his return because he first wanted to look at all files that anyone requested to view. When Scholl returned a few minutes later, he became enraged when he was told I wanted to look at the bids for the remodeling. He yelled and demanded to know "why" I wanted to look at

48

them.   When I asked him in turn what the problem was, he snapped back, "You don't write stories the right way!"   In response, I told him that if he felt that way about it he should talk to Spitaleri.   Scholl answered that he already had.

When I was finally allowed to look at the file, Scholl required me to stay in his sight, and not take the file to a desk in the hallway where it would have been more convenient.   After Scholl left, city employees Billings, Gary Frolenko and Sherry McGinnis told me that they were "shocked" at the way Scholl had treated me. They said they could not understand why he was so upset.   After arriving at the NEWS-POST I went to Spitaleri and told him about Scholl's outrage.   Spitaleri denied that Scholl had spoken to him about my stories and facetiously suggested that I ask Scholl what the "right" way was to write a story.   Spitaleri seemed to enjoy playing both sides--that of a publisher who believed in and practiced the First Amendment right to publish the news and views whether or not they were popular, and that of a businessman willing to change his product if it would mean continued financial backing from a valued customer.

McDowell had probably become suspicious of the bids for the remodeling of the city council chambers because on both the police station and human affairs department additions to the city hall, Scholl had incorrectly estimated both at $100,000, about $20,000 over on each.   For both projects, Noel Tomberlin Construction Company of Pomona had been awarded the contracts after Scholl had listed the inflated estimates.   It was conceivable that someone was receiving kickbacks by letting other bidders think the projects would cost more than they were actually worth.

One Wednesday morning that summer after completing my independent contractor delivery route for the NEWS-POST, I went with Dallas

Anderson for breakfast at the Coast Inn in Laguna Beach. It was about 9:30 a.m. and I did not have any other work responsibilities until later in the day when I would attend a city council meeting for approximately eight hours. When we walked into the restaurant we immediately noticed Scholl sitting at a table with Noel Tomberlin, the Pomona contractor. When Scholl saw us, he ducked his head and left after a few minutes. It was preposterous for him to think that we had not seen him and ridiculous for him to then think he could hide from our view. He apparently had reason for feeling guilty about meeting with a contractor away from his office at city hall. It was not until more than a year later when I was investigating the relationship between Scholl and Tomberlin that I discovered, through the state Department of Consumer Affairs, that Scholl was a licensed plumber in Pomona at the same time that Tomberlin was a licensed plumbing contractor in Pomona. Located in Los Angeles County, Pomona is more than a one hour drive from Laguna Beach. Scholl had left that area in 1973, three years earlier, when he moved to Laguna Beach. The notices for accepting bids for City of Laguna Beach projects were published in the NEWS-POST, which was not circulated in Pomona or within 50 miles of it. Even if I or anyone else could not find any proof about an illegal or just an unethical business relationship between Scholl and Tomberlin, they and God knew what they were doing.

Meanwhile, Scholl's supervisor, City Manager Alfred Theal, was going beyond the realm of his position. According to Councilman McDowell, Theal enjoyed bragging about his control over the local press. To demonstrate his influence in front of McDowell, Theal reportedly picked up the telephone in his city hall office to guide the DAILY PILOT in the printing of a story. Upon

50

McDowell's questioning about the NEWS-POST, Theal said that he did not even have to call the NEWS-POST on how a story should be written. Recalling that Eggers would change a direct quote by Theal in a story that I had written so that "Theal would look better," according to Eggers, I could readily believe McDowell's anecdote about Theal's control of the NEWS-POST.

Perhaps that control was made possible because the NEWS-POST was receiving income from the City for publishing its legal notices when the advertisements were supposed to be placed in the TIDES AND TIMES, the only newspaper published within the city limits. Six years later I discovered that on September 30, 1976, a hearing had been held in Superior Court regarding publisher Larry Campbell's petition to have the TIDES AND TIMES adjudicated to publish legal advertising. Spitaleri, on behalf of Laguna Publishing Company, had opposed the petition. He falsely informed the court that the NEWS-POST was published in the City of Laguna Beach and that it had been adjudicated for the County of Orange and for the City of Laguna Beach in 1922. The County Clerk's Office had no record of any such adjudication. The City was not even incorporated until 1927. Spitaleri apparently selected the year 1922 because of a case law which allowed newspapers established before 1923 to move their offices out of governmental entities' confines and still receive income from publishing their legal notices. In spite of Spitaleri's false claims, which were not countered by Campbell because apparently neither he nor his attorney had properly researched them, the court granted Campbell's petition to be established as a newspaper of general circulation.

On October 9, 1976, the NEWS-POST printed my story about McDowell publicly criticizing Scholl for an allegedly inaccurate report of an Aliso Water Management Agency meeting. Four days later I attended a luncheon at the Hotel Laguna which District Attorney Cecil Hicks addressed. James Yancey, president of the Laguna Beach Taxpayers Association, had invited me and provided me with a ticket to sit at his table. At the luncheon I saw Eggers and Spitaleri sitting together, not talking to anyone, just staring down at the floor. Both appeared to be sick. In his speech, Hicks condemned the dog racing initiative, which was to be on the November ballot. Just a year earlier, Eggers had the entire NEWS-POST editorial department write stories on the subject. And just six weeks earlier, the NEWS-POST had published a column by Eggers on August 28, 1976, very strongly endorsing the dog racing initiative. As previously agreed, Eggers took photographs at the luncheon and I wrote the story. After turning in my story to Korber, she immediately knew that it would need to be reviewed by Eggers because of his personal stance on the dog racing issue. Accordingly, he toned it down, questioning Hicks' charges about dog racing leading to organized crime activities.

Eggers and Spitaleri may have looked so uncomfortable at the luncheon because they were responding to pressure from the city government to terminate my employment in exchange for continuing to receive the legal advertising income, which was greater than my salary. Unbeknownst to me at the time, just two days earlier, on October 11, 1976, an advertisement for a reporter/photographer had been published in the CONFIDENTIAL BULLETIN of the California Newspaper Publishers Association. Applicants were advised to telephone Eggers at the NEWS-POST. On the evening of the Hicks luncheon, Eggers had a telephone conversation with Frank Cankar, his father-figure. Eggers said he thought he was going to have to get rid of me because the city government was pressuring him. I found out about the conversation the next evening when it was relayed to me by Dallas Anderson. Virginia Cankar, the wife of Frank Cankar, had told Trevor Cushman Jr., who in turn had told Dallas. The CONFIDENTIAL BULLETIN advertisement appeared again on October 18, 1976. While I did not find out about the ads until six weeks later, they documented the actions that Eggers was taking behind my back.

On the same day, October 14, 1976, as I learned six years later, City Clerk Verna Rollinger gave Larry Campbell a City legal notice for publication on October 22, 1976. Spitaleri apparently complained to then-City Attorney George Logan because the next day, October 15, 1976, Campbell wrote a letter to the City returning the ad at Logan's instruction. The ad was then sent to the NEWS-POST in Laguna Hills for publication.

On October 19, 1976, I turned in a story, which Eggers approved, about homebuilders' problems with the city government in obtaining building permits. The story was then typeset and in the production shop waiting to be pasted-up onto a page. While the story was in the shop, Adena Gay, a paste-up artist whose husband Ernest Gay was mentioned in the story because of his problems with the City, took the story and read it to him over the telephone. Adena Gay then went to Eggers and Mrs. Spitaleri and convinced them to omit the reference to her husband. Earlier the Gays had wanted the publicity and had asked me to write a story which had then been printed in full and unmolested, with references to them left intact. When I took the story to Vernon Spitaleri's office and asked him about Adena Gay's editing of it, he upheld her action, even though Eggers had ap-

53

proved the unedited version with the mention of Ernest Gay. That afternoon Adena Gay told me that their chances of having the City grant them a building permit for their home would be jeopardized if the story contained her husband's name.

On October 20, 1976, during the public communications portion of a Laguna Beach City Council meeting, Dallas Anderson told the council that City Attorney George Logan had failed to submit a resolution for attorney Stephen Chase to legally represent the City of Laguna Beach. Anderson also charged that city officials had been giving emoluments to members of the press, such as an executive editor, in an attempt to control the stories printed. That evening Councilman McDowell overheard Planning Director Douglas Schmitz tell others on the patio of the council chambers that it was Scholl who was trying to have me fired. Schmitz worked closely with Scholl on city business and had previously told me that they read the NEWS-POST on the tennis courts every Saturday morning before playing tennis. McDowell reported Schmitz's remark to Dallas, who then told me.

On October 21, 1976, I verified with City Clerk Verna Rollinger that Logan had failed to submit a resolution regarding Chase, a requirement set forth in the California GOVERNMENT CODE. The next day I turned in my story about Dallas' charges, and the responses by Rollinger, Theal, Logan and Mayor Sweeney. After reading the story, Korber again decided, as with the anti-dog racing speech by Hicks, to have Eggers review it for anticipated revisions. Eggers asked me what Anderson meant by referring to an executive editor receiving emoluments. Being the only executive editor of a newspaper in the area, other newspapers not using that title, Eggers apparently felt singled out by Anderson, which he was. Eggers knew better than I about all of the other emoluments he had received but had not bragged about in the editorial department. In addition to the political trip to San Francisco with McDowell, he had been on a Metropolitan Water District trip to Arizona with Scholl. He frequently telephoned Scholl and Theal to ask when they were taking him out to lunch. His house purchase had been arranged by a consultant to Rancho Palos Verdes Corp., one of the primary parties in a continuing series of stories concerning Sycamore Hills. Instead of reminding Eggers of those emoluments that even I knew about, I suggested that he contact Dallas if he thought such details were necessary for a more complete story. Eggers did so and then made several revisions to the story. One major and very ironic deletion that he made was the sentence that read, "The freedom of the press is being threatened by city employees conniving and engaging in conspiracy to influence the press with emoluments, Anderson charged." Later in the day Dallas told me that Eggers had telephoned him at his home that morning and asked for specific documentation concerning an executive editor receiving emoluments. Dallas had refused to provide him with any information, which Eggers pointed out in the story with my byline.

The October 23, 1976, edition of the NEWS-POST contained a Copley News Service editorial, titled "No on Prop. 13," which urged readers to vote against the dog racing initiative. I wondered if readers would recall that only 12 months earlier the NEWS-POST had devoted several pages to dog racing and that only two months earlier Eggers had written a column in favor of the initiative. Since the initiative was widely condemned by most government leaders, Spitaleri probably felt obligated to print the Copley editorial and adopt it as his own view as well. As a subscriber to the Copley News

Service, Spitaleri received its editorials every week and usually published at least one of them. As with the stories about homebuilders' problems, the Hicks speech and Anderson's comments, Eggers continued changing my stories and now started placing more of them toward the back of the newspaper.

On October 25, 1976, Dallas told me that McDowell had told him of a proposed meeting of Spitaleri, Theal and Scholl to discuss me at a place other than the NEWS-POST offices. On October 26, 1976, the appointed day, I observed Spitaleri leave the offices on schedule. While he was gone, I noticed that Eggers was very nervous. When Spitaleri returned to the NEWS-POST production shop where Eggers and I were, he told Eggers, "You've got it!" Both of them then smiled and laughed. Eggers became noticeably happy and relaxed.

In a separate but related incident in the production shop that day, Marjorie Spitaleri came in and started shouting at me for explaining her editing instructions to Kathy Jordan, a fellow paste-up artist. It concerned the pasting-up of an arts story written by Constance Morthland, a regular contributor to the NEWS-POST. Mrs. Spitaleri had told me earlier how she wanted that particular story edited when pasted up on a page. One of the reasons the Spitaleris had previously given me for my working in the production shop was to explain editing and to edit stories when the editors were away from the offices. Never before had Mrs. Spitaleri shouted at me. I knew that her reason for shouting was related to the city government's pressuring Eggers to terminate me. No one at the NEWS-POST was aware that I knew what was going on behind my back. Hoping that if I kept it to myself the pressure would end and I would continue working there, I did not mention it to any of my co-workers.

After hearing Mrs. Spitaleri's outburst, Mrs. Jordan said she was "shocked" by it and apologized to me for asking about the Morthland story. Adena Gay, another paste-up artist, then told me that Mrs. Spitaleri "really has the screws in for you."

On the evening of October 27, 1976, while Virginia Cankar and I were standing on the council chambers' patio during a city council meeting, she told me it was terrible that my stories were being buried toward the back of the newspaper. I had not even mentioned the subject, which she chose to raise on her own. Mrs. Cankar also remarked that my story about Richard Bofferding's lawsuit against the City of Laguna Beach, printed in that day's edition, was a good story and that it should not have been placed in the back of the newspaper.

On October 29, 1976, Korber notified me that Eggers said he would be the one attending and reporting on an emergency city council meeting scheduled for the following Monday for discussion of the City's participation in the Aliso Water Management Agency. Except during my vacation, I had covered all council meetings since joining the NEWS-POST 16 months earlier. I considered Eggers' intention to take over my duty as tangible proof that he was planning to get rid of me. Even though I would not be writing the story about the meeting, I decided to attend the council session on the morning of November 1, 1976. While walking toward the council chambers I encountered Dallas, who told me about another call he had received from Cushman about Eggers' intentions. The night before, Halloween, Virginia Cankar told Cushman about another conversation her husband Frank had with Eggers. When Eggers told Mr. Cankar that the reason he would give for firing me was that I was a "disruptive influence" on my fellow workers, Mr. Cankar told

57

him not to say that because it was not true. Ever since their previous conversation had been reported to me two weeks earlier I had been extra cautious at work because it appeared that the NEWS-POST would be trying to find an excuse to fire me. Eggers apparently did not feel qualified to write a story about the Aliso discussion because the NEWS-POST printed an unbylined story by Jim Van Rensslaer, a Laguna Beach resident, about the council meeting.

During the month of November of 1976 at least five more incidents occurred which further indicated that a conspiracy against me was in the making. It had been Spitaleri's custom to personally greet each editorial employee as he walked to his office in the morning. While he continued to greet the others, Spitaleri conspicuously began excluding me. At a city council meeting that month Scholl walked up to Dallas and asked him if he was going to talk about Scholl before the council that evening. Dallas just ignored Scholl, who must have recognized himself as one of the city officials conspiring and conniving to control the press with emoluments. Also in November, while Dallas was walking on a sidewalk near city hall, he encountered Scholl and Theal walking together in the opposite direction. Scholl asked Dallas if he was a "member of the bodyguard committee." We presumed that was in reference to the loyalty and support provided to me by Dallas Anderson, Trevor Cushman, James Yancey and others interested in a free press.

In the same month I began to notice that whenever I received a telephone call at work from Dallas that his name would be announced over the NEWS-POST public address system by the receptionist, Elizabeth Fleming. She did not announce the names of any of my other callers. I told Dallas of this new procedure when he told me of strange sounds he heard on the line plus

58

the delay in having his calls transferred to me. As is the practice at many other newspapers, the NEWS-POST had a telephone monitoring system to tape record the conversations of their classified advertising sales personnel. While Anderson called me at work only two or three times a week, Mrs. Spitaleri seemingly disapproved. At the same time, however, she heartily approved of employees who were also mothers talking on the telephones several times a day with their children. When I received one particular call from Dallas, Mrs. Spitaleri indicated that she wanted me to receive it at the telephone by the receptionist's desk. That desk was usually occupied by one of the classified advertising sales personnel. Consequently, it was very conceivable that she was directing the receptionist to tape record that call. I suspected that Scholl had told the NEWS-POST that Dallas was a subversive element in order to direct attention away from himself.

One day in November of 1976 while I was proofreading in the production department, Arthur Collins, the darkroom technician, came in after speaking with Eggers in the editorial department. Collins walked directly up to me and asked if I was going to work for the TIDES AND TIMES newspaper in Laguna Beach. He said it would really "burn" the NEWS-POST if I did. I told him that I did not even know Larry Campbell, the publisher. Marjorie Spitaleri, who heard Collins, then told me that Campbell had called her at her home in Emerald Bay several times in the middle of the night. He was drunk, she said, when he cursed her husband during those calls.

In an apparent attempt to further pressure the NEWS-POST to terminate me, Stanley Scholl gave a hand-out to the DAILY PILOT regarding so-called newsworthy projects of the municipal services department. Published on the second page of the November 16, 1976, edition of the PILOT, the story was headlined "Safety Tops City Work List." What would have been considered ordinary and expected improvements in almost any other city, Scholl had the audacity to describe as "high priority items" and the PILOT, exercising no news judgment of its own, gave Scholl the publicity he sought. Approximately seven inches of space were devoted to the story with the first paragraph reading as follows:

"Improvements in pedestrian safety, village esthetics, transit and parking, parks, sewage treatment and new development processing are being given the highest priority in Laguna Beach's department of municipal services."

Scholl was then quoted about such things as sidewalks, bus benches and trees. It would not surprise me if he kept a scrapbook of press clippings about his department. Spitaleri, envious of such a "major" story being in the PILOT but not in the NEWS-POST, expressed his anger the next day to those in the editorial department. He wanted to know why the NEWS-POST had not been the recipient of such a news tip. Spitaleri apparently did not recognize that Scholl was typical of officials at all levels of government who try to control the news. Members of the media who cater to officials of that caliber do not serve the public unless they discover and report the real news stories.

On November 23, 1976, I proofread a story by Korber about Laguna Beach resident Theresa Yale Eagles' involvement in civic affairs. That was the first time since Korber's May, 1976, column about Scholl and her July, 1976, stories about his bus proposal and his new assistant that Korber had reported on events in my beat. I never took the time from my beat to venture into hers. Before leaving work that day I found a note from Eggers in my message box. Because he wrote that he wanted to talk to me, I took the note into his office and asked him about it. He answered that he did not know that I was still on the premises and that he had not intended for me to receive the note until the next day. I waited the entire next working day for him to speak to me, but he did not. Observing Thanksgiving Day the next day with my family was a little unsettling, as I felt a cloud hanging over me.

Finally, when I returned to work on Friday, November 26, 1976, Eggers called me into the conference room in the afternoon and told me that an editorial department "reorganization" required my removal as of December 1, 1976, the following Wednesday. Looking down at a piece of paper while he spoke to me, Eggers said that he might hire someone in the future, but that for now I could continue working part-time in the production shop and keep my delivery route, or "You can just quit." Obviously preferring the latter, he gave it special emphasis. He offered to write a letter of recommendation for me, although, he added, he had already checked with the other newspapers in the area and found that there were no job openings. I told him that I would think about his offer rather than give him an answer then because he had had plenty of time before announcing the options to me. His "reorganization" plans indicated that Dallas' accounts of Frank Cankar's conversations with Eggers were accurate.

The next day, Saturday, November 27, 1976, Dallas and I went to the Orange County Law Library in Santa Ana to research my First Amendment rights. While there I telephoned James Fields, one of my journalism instructors at Pepperdine who was then working at California State University at Fullerton. He informed me of the October 11 and 18, 1976, advertisements

61

in the CONFIDENTIAL BULLETIN of the California Newspaper Publishers Association. Since the position advertised was that of a "reporter-photographer," Fields gave me the impression that he thought I had not been a competent photographer at the NEWS-POST. He had only taught me how to report the news and apparently was convinced that the NEWS-POST could not have complaints against my stories. Fields said, though, that he had seen some of my NEWS-POST stories in the racks when he was visiting Laguna Beach. The stories about alleged violations of the state's Brown Act (forbidding private meetings of public bodies on most subjects) probably irritated the city government, he said. When I asked him his opinion about me suing the government and the newspaper for violating my First Amendment rights by conspiring to terminate me, Fields discouraged my commencing litigation, claiming that it would "blackball" me in the journalism profession. I wondered to myself if he had ever had experiences similar to mine while he was an editor and publisher. I also wondered why he left the industry and chose instead to teach the theories.

On Monday, November 29, 1976, Dallas telephoned Spitaleri at the NEWS-POST and asked him who wrote the editorial printed in the Saturday edition. Lying, Spitaleri claimed that he wrote it. Actually, it was another Copley News Service editorial which I had proofread after it was typeset in the production shop several days earlier. Written in observance of the country's bicentennial, the editorial was about the principles on which the United States was founded. Before making the call, Dallas had told me that if Spitaleri wrote the editorial then he could not be behind Eggers' decision to get rid of me. As it was my custom on Mondays, I went to the city hall to pick up the agenda for the next council meeting. Because I was still being paid to work in the editorial department until Wednesday, I did not see any reason why I should shirk any of my responsibilities before then. Korber, however, had already assumed my duties by picking up the agenda. Living in San Juan Capistrano and working in Laguna Hills, Korber had to go out of her way to travel to the Laguna Beach City Hall. At that time I did not know that she had scheduled a move to Laguna Beach to coincide with her new job duties.

On November 30, 1976, Trevor Cushman attended a meeting of the Woman's Club in Laguna Beach because he had heard that Spitaleri was to be the speaker. More than 100 people, according to Cushman, heard Spitaleri announce that from then on the NEWS-POST was going to have a "stronger person" covering city hall. Later that day Cushman told me that after the meeting he had told Spitaleri that I was the "best reporter the NEWS-POST ever had" and that I "can't be bought by the city government." In private to Dallas, Cushman added that Spitaleri had told him that I was a "loner," that I was "temperamental" and that I cried. There was now no doubt that Spitaleri was definitely behind Eggers' decision to terminate my employment in the editorial department. Regarding his criticism of me, Spitaleri himself was the epitome of a loner, having no known friends and keeping to himself. Like many others of his ancestry, he had a short and hot temper, losing control of himself without knowing the facts about what was enraging him. As for crying, the only episode had occurred nine months earlier when Spitaleri broke his promise to me that I would not have to deliver the NEWS-POST to individual homes when I assumed the delivery route to the Laguna Beach street sale racks. I had felt deceived by him and his wife.

On December 1, 1976, Marilyn Angell, who

63

had attended California State University at Long Beach as had Korber and Richard Manly, another editorial department employee, began full-time work with the NEWS-POST as a reporter-photographer covering the San Juan Capistrano/South Shores area, Korber's former beat. Korber began attending the Laguna Beach City Council meetings that evening. I decided to continue attending the meetings because of my residency in Laguna Beach and status of a taxpayer. During a break in that first meeting attended by Korber, I saw her join Scholl and other city officials for drinks at the Ivy House restaurant across the street from city hall. After the meeting I submitted stories anonymously to the TIDES AND TIMES via Anderson. No one at the NEWS-POST had said that I could not write stories for other publications. That was a First Amendment right of mine. Working only about 20 hours a week in the NEWS-POST production department, I had plenty of free time. Even though I was not compensated for my contributions to the TIDES AND TIMES, neither were those who contributed regular features to the NEWS-POST.

A few days later I was fortunate to witness the expression of shock on Eggers' face when he received a telephone call from Scholl announcing that he would be leaving his position with the City of Laguna Beach on January 7, 1977, to accept a similar job with the City of Santa Monica. After Eggers had gone to the trouble of eliminating me and hiring another editorial department employee, Scholl said that he was leaving. It then became apparent to me that Scholl had been paranoid about the type of press coverage he received because he was being considered for a new job in a much larger city and did not want his chances to be hurt by truthful, but sometimes negative, reporting. If

Scholl had made the announcement just two weeks earlier, he would not have continued pressuring the NEWS-POST, I believe, for my termination. Scholl's fanaticism about press coverage was evidenced in another column written by Korber. Published in the December 18, 1976, edition of the NEWS-POST and entitled "All I Want for Christmas...," the column listed possible gifts for various public figures, including Scholl. For him she wrote, "To Stan Scholl, a full-time photographer assigned to him by the SANTA MONICA EVENING OUTLOOK."

Since assuming the Laguna Beach beat Korber was very friendly with Scholl, fraternizing with him and other city officials just as Eggers did. She apparently was the "stronger person" Spitaleri had promised. She had once commented facetiously that one night I sat by Scholl's wife at a Bible study and the next day sat on his lap. That remark indicated that Eggers had relayed the lie told to him over the telephone one day while I was at city hall. Standing in the hallway to Scholl's office, I heard him tell Eggers that I was there sitting on his lap.

On the evening of December 30, 1976, I went with Anderson to the Ivy House. While there, Larry Campbell of the TIDES AND TIMES and his wife Betty joined us in our booth. When it was about to close at 2:00 a.m., Campbell suggested that we go to the White House restaurant in Laguna Beach. Campbell told Anderson that the NEWS-POST kicked back 15 percent of the legal advertising income from the City. Campbell also said that John Wilson, the NEWS-POST business manager, had to be involved in the scheme.

One weekend in the middle of January of 1977 I contracted influenza while at my parents' home in Tustin. I was going to try to make it to work that Monday but could not do so. I called the NEWS-POST about an hour and a half before my starting time at about noon and told the receptionist that I was sick and would not be in that day. When I returned to work the following day, Adena Gay told me in the production shop that the Spitaleris and Eggers had a conference there the day before to discuss what to do with me. They complained that I should have given them more notice that I was sick, according to Gay. In 18 months at the NEWS-POST I had not missed a single day previously. When I was a full-time employee I could have missed up to three days a year and still have been paid. Now as a part-time employee I was paid hourly and; therefore, I lost about $19.50 by being sick. Emotionally stressed by my predicament at the NEWS-POST, I probably was very susceptible to catching a virus that made me sick.

Later in January, while proofreading in the production shop one day, I was shouted at by Mrs. Spitaleri for the second time. Her motive this time was most likely to try to get me to quit so that the NEWS-POST would not have to pay unemployment insurance if I was fired. Mrs. Spitaleri yelled that I had not replaced a lost or stolen placard from a NEWS-POST rack at the Safeway store. After apologizing for not noticing that it was missing, I then told her that I would replace it on my next delivery. She then started yelling that cleaning, maintaining and repairing the racks were part of my duties. In the 11 months as an independent contractor responsible for delivering the NEWS-POST to all of the racks in Laguna Beach, I had never been told of those responsibilities. I told Mrs. Spitaleri that her husband had promised me all summer, six months earlier, that their son Marc would clean the racks. Mrs. Spitaleri then left the production shop.

In the early evening of January 20, 1977,

while I was working in the production shop, the receptionist came in and told me that Mrs. Spitaleri wanted to see me in the conference room. When I went in, Mrs. Spitaleri said, "We're going to have to let you go. That includes your delivery route." No explanation was offered and I did not ask for one. She seemed very happy to give me the news. I had been aware that my presence at the NEWS-POST made the Spitaleris and Eggers feel guilty about removing me from the editorial department because of pressure from the city government. It was just a matter of time before they would dismiss me from the production department as well. The last seven weeks at the NEWS-POST, working only in the production department, had been a test of endurance. I had survived because I had not quit; I had been "let go."

Chapter 3

In order to receive unemployment insurance for my living expenses, I went the next day to the state Employment Development Department and applied for benefits. I found that I would be receiving $248 a month for six months and that I would be required to show what attempts I was making to find employment as a reporter, photographer, proofreader, and/or paste-up artist. It was fortunate that my monthly rent, including utilities, was only $145. Also, while receiving my $500 a month and later $550 a month gross salary from the NEWS-POST I had deposited approximately $150 a month in a savings account, which now provided some security.

I applied at all of the various newspapers in Orange County, including the DAILY PILOT, LOS ANGELES TIMES, THE REGISTER, SADDLEBACK VALLEY NEWS, NEWPORT ENSIGN, and TUSTIN NEWS. Some of them granted me interviews, none of which resulted in my being hired. The letter of recommendation that Eggers had volunteered to write for me did not recommend me for anything. Nor did it say that I had done anything well at the NEWS-POST, therefore contrasting sharply with the letter he had written to Pepperdine University regarding my performance as an intern. Dated December 7, 1976, the letter read as follows:

"Janice Brownfield has been a part-time employee of the News-Post editorial department for over a year. She also worked part-time in our production department serving as a paste-up artist and proofreader.

"Prior to joining our newspaper family, Janice served as a summer intern in connection with her Pepperdine University studies.

"During her tenure at the News-Post she covered the City Hall beat for our Laguna Beach edition. This included covering weekly city council meetings, some planning commission sessions and other meetings held inside the City Hall complex. In addition to reporting on these meetings, she was also responsible for shooting various photo assignments in connection with her assigned beat.

"The decision to take Miss Brownfield off the City Hall beat was a management decision dictated by a reorganization of the editorial department. Please feel free to contact me at the phone number listed below for any additional information."

Unlike the July, 1975, letter of recommendation for an "A" grade that Eggers signed as managing editor, the above letter was signed by him in his new capacity as executive editor, a title he had requested and was finally granted in October, 1976. At the same time, Korber had been given the title of city editor. A story about their promotions had been printed on the front page of the NEWS-POST at the same time that the CONFIDENTIAL BULLETIN of the California Newspaper Publishers Association was printing their advertisement for my replacement. There was no reorganization as Eggers had claimed in his letter.

It was not very comforting to read in a book I ordered that once an editor has been fired by a newspaper that he will not even be able to get a job as a deskman or as a reporter at another newspaper. Since I had been a reporter, and not an editor, I would be even less likely to be hired. The book, entitled HOW TO OWN YOUR OWN NEWSPAPER, stated that good journalists, when fired, are "tainted" in the eyes of other newspaper owners and publishers. The author told of a young editor who had experienced the greatest single editorial victory the author had observed in his 40 years in the newspaper business. The young editor worked for a morning-afternoon daily that was published in a city "controlled by a powerful self-seeking political ring which was draining the city white." The editor embarked on a two-year crusade which resulted in a new city charter, reduced government expenses, increased city services and new government officials. What did the editor get in return? He was fired from his job within one year because the powerful politicians had lost their jobs and the wholesalers now had to submit bids instead of charging what they wanted to the city. The editor had served the community by lowering their taxes and bringing honesty to government and in return he had to rent out his house and live in the garage so he could have money for groceries. I had nothing more to lose except my unemployment benefits which were not due to expire for three months. Even if I got a job on a newspaper, I probably would not be there for long because I believed in writing the

70

news and not only what the government officials wanted written.

Another book I had time to read was "1984" by George Orwell. After checking the book out from the Laguna Beach branch library, John Gabriels, a city hall watcher not held in high esteem by some people but a man whom I respected for voicing his opinions, saw me with the book. Because I had only read the first few paragraphs of the book at that point, I did not understand Gabriels when he compared Spitaleri to Big Brother. Gabriels then explained that Spitaleri was trying to take control of everything, just like Big Brother in the book. After reading further I found out that Big Brother, the head of the government in the book, had control of the newspapers. Copies of previous editions of the newspapers would be constantly updated in order to conform with the events of the day. When the government got rid of someone, old newspapers were edited so that there was no trace of that person ever having existed. If it was not in the newspapers it just was not so. The main character of the book, though, Winston Smith, knew the past could not be changed. No matter what Spitaleri printed or did not print did not change the fact that something did or did not happen. Some time later I discovered that the May 26, 1976, edition of the NEWS-POST, which contained the first controversial Realex Investments story, was missing from the bound volumes of the NEWS-POST. It would be just like Spitaleri to delete that edition as if he had never printed it.

In deciding what stories to write for the TIDES AND TIMES I based my selection on what the NEWS-POST and the DAILY PILOT would not be reporting about the Laguna Beach city government. I considered the TIDES AND TIMES as having the ability to be more like a news

71

magazine such as NEWSWEEK or TIME and to present stories that would not be reported in depth in the daily newspapers. The NEWS-POST had an advantage of being published twice a week, whereas the TIDES AND TIMES was printed only once a week. Therefore, it could not compete with the NEWS-POST, and the DAILY PILOT especially, for timely stories. When submitting stories to the TIDES AND TIMES I also included a suggested headline rather than risk having Larry Campbell write his own. There was some satisfaction in seeing news stories printed for the public to read. As a result of my stories in the TIDES AND TIMES, I received a call from Theresa Yale Eagles, editor of the FACTS (Freedom and Courage to Speak) newsletter in Laguna Beach. She wanted me to volunteer my time and replace her as editor, an offer I declined because I was busy seeking a paying job. The newsletter did little more than print stories that had already appeared in local newspapers. In past issues, many of the stories had been mine from the NEWS-POST. In fact, FACTS' policy was that if the story did not appear in another paper it would not be published in its newsletter. That policy did not demonstrate much freedom or courage.

The only newspaper in the area that I respected was the NEWPORT ENSIGN in Corona del Mar, which was six miles northwest of Laguna Beach. Arvo Haapa, the editor and publisher, regularly wrote editorials that served the public interest. His newspaper was truly a watchdog on the Newport Beach city government. When I heard that he was retiring and selling the newspaper to Herbert W. Sutton, publisher of the weekly PENNYSAVER advertising publication throughout the south county area, I decided to apply for a job, thinking that the ENSIGN might extend to the Laguna Beach area. My interview with George O'Day, Sutton's business manager, went very well. He had read the book and had seen the movie ALL THE PRESIDENT'S MEN and said that I seemed to be the type of person Sutton would want to hire. My subsequent interview with Sutton, however, was a big disappointment. Sutton's quotations in the ENSIGN had led me to believe that he wanted to continue Arvo Haapa's policy of being a watchdog on government. In person, though, Sutton told me that he wanted less emphasis on government news. He also said that once people are elected to office the populace should support, and not criticize, their actions. After reading the stories by me in my scrapbooks, he noted that I would have to be "controlled" in the choice of words I used, even though editors had reviewed my stories before they were published. Even if I had been offered a position with the ENSIGN I do not know if I would have accepted it because our philosophies about the responsibilities of a newspaper were so different that I would not have been happy there. Sutton had no formal journalism education and he had never published a newspaper before, deficiencies which in themselves did not disqualify him from producing a good newspaper. With Sutton's advanced printing equipment he did produce a much more attractive ENSIGN with graphics and art work. Unfortunately, though, the issue I saw not only looked like a Hollywood glamour magazine but read like one also. Sutton appeared to be catering to high society, of which he was a member. He was ignoring the press' responsibility of being a watchdog on government. Allowing government to operate in the dark was a great disservice to his readers.

My interview at THE REGISTER also failed to result in a job but for the stated reason that there were no openings at the time. The news director had read through my scrapbook and commented that I must have "rocked the boat" of the Laguna Beach city government. The interview had been arranged by Elizabeth Rogers, a 76-year-old former society editor of THE REGISTER who lived in Laguna Beach. Shortly after I had joined the NEWS-POST she told me that she had nothing but contempt for Spitaleri even though she had never met him. "He always wants to be the boss of everything," she said, adding, "I wouldn't trust him." Having worked for THE REGISTER for 20 years doing soft news, Mrs. Rogers was well-remembered and well-liked by the news director. George Grey, an investigative reporter for THE REGISTER who sometimes attended Laguna Beach City Council meetings, also had a low opinion of Spitaleri and assured me that he could get me a reporting job with THE REGISTER. "I'm impressed with you, kid," he said, and jokingly added, "Of course, you'll have to sleep with me." Some time later I saw him at a local gasoline station. He expressed his disappointment with THE REGISTER because it was unwilling to print any real news stories emanating from Laguna Beach. He showed me stories he had turned in about the government's activities. Only one of the approximately six that he submitted was printed. The least controversial, the story was about a memorial plaque being approved by the city council.

The TUSTIN NEWS was no better a prospect for employment. Having lived in the Tustin area and been graduated from Tustin High School, I was familiar with the newspaper, which not only had a poor appearance but also failed to print much more than stories about high school sports and social events. I had never wanted to work for the TUSTIN NEWS but because I needed employment I decided to apply. While working for the NEWS-POST I had learned that Spitaleri was acquainted with the publisher, William Moses.

74

But that was not surprising because their offices were only about 12 miles apart. When I telephoned the TUSTIN NEWS I found how similar they were. Moses was not interested in hiring someone whom Spitaleri did not want to keep. Their similarity was further revealed when I read a story in the DAILY PILOT on March 2, 1977, headlined, "2 Newspapers Endorse Dead Candidate." The story reported that Spitaleri's NEWS-POST had printed an editorial encouraging readers to vote for Dr. James Marshall, who died four weeks earlier, in that day's Saddleback Community College election. The TUSTIN NEWS had published the same editorial, written by Spitaleri. Robert Price, the only living candidate for the Laguna Hills trustee area, was an administrator in the Laguna Hills Leisure World retirement community. In the DAILY PILOT story it was Moses, not Spitaleri, who pointed out that the NEWS-POST was involved in litigation with the Rossmoor Corporation of Leisure World over circulation privileges in the private and gated retirement community. The PILOT also quoted Moses as saying that Price was a "front man for the (Rossmoor) outfit" and a corporation "stalking horse."

In addition to applying for jobs, reading books and contributing stories to the TIDES AND TIMES, I also went to the Orange County Law Library to research First Amendment cases similar to mine. Dallas Anderson did most of the research and found cases for me to read. On our way back to Laguna Beach on May 18, 1977, we stopped at the Ivy House restaurant and saw Howard Miller, who was on his dinner break from a city council meeting. He joined us for a little while and paid for our dinner, saying his clients, which included Rancho Palos Verdes Corporation, gave him practically limitless expense accounts. He got his money's worth from us, too. His eyes lit up as Dallas told him that City Attorney George Logan was a de facto officer because he had not been appointed in a resolution and had not taken an oath of office. I had to consciously prevent my eyes from widening when Miller told us that he had helped Eggers obtain financing for a home in San Juan Capistrano. I silently recalled the times that Dorothy Korber had told me she thought Rancho Palos Verdes Corporation, for which Miller was a consultant concerning Sycamore Hills in Laguna Beach, had given Eggers money to buy a house in exchange for favorable press coverage. Korber had said that at about the time Eggers had bought the home and for a long time afterwards, he gave excessive coverage to any news items concerning Sycamore Hills, the land for which Rancho Palos Verdes was trying to get a zoning change for City-approval of development plans. Rancho had filed a lawsuit against the City of Laguna Beach for preventing development of the 522 acres of open space. Miller had attended many city council meetings and said I had done an "excellent" job of reporting the news but that it had inevitably "ruffled the feathers" of some city officials. "I thought Spitaleri was a man of principle," he pondered. "The words he says and the editorials he writes are just that," I answered. I was disappointed to hear Miller tell us about Chicago politicians who had benefitted financially by graft, but that the public had also benefitted. In effect, he was saying that the end justifies the means. If some good is done for the public, he believed, what the city officials did was of no consequence.

Dallas and I were at the law library again on June 7, 1977, and during a lunch break at the cafeteria in the Orange County Courthouse we saw Spitaleri standing in line. After scurrying around to determine if Spitaleri was appearing in

76

court that day, we found that his lawsuit against Capistrano Valley Publishing Corporation was going to be tried in Department 14 of the Superior Court in which Judges James F. Judge presided. We were sitting on a bench in the hallway when Spitaleri approached, acting as if he were looking for his courtroom. When he got near us he just stood there staring, with his hands hanging at his side. He then limply lifted one hand and gave a weak wave to Dallas, who did not smile, speak or wave but nodded his head.

Inside the courtroom, we saw Richard J. O'Neill, head of the Democratic Party of Orange County and major stockholder of Capistrano Valley Publishing, sitting with the defense attorneys, headed by Glenn R. Watson of Los Angeles. The jury was still being selected for the trial, at which Spitaleri would charge that the GOOD NEWS, published by Capistrano Valley Publishing from 1971 to 1974, used unfair business practices by using lower ad rates than the NEWS-POST in an attempt to put it out of business. Before the day was over, we heard Spitaleri's attorney, W. Mike McCray of Tustin, present his opening statement to the jury.

McCray made so many misstatements of fact that I told Dallas I wanted to inform the defense about them. At my suggestion, we wrote a list of corrections and decided to put them in an envelope in a telephone booth at the courthouse the next day. After placement of the envelope, Dallas telephoned O'Neill's office and requested that an aide deliver the message to O'Neill that an envelope was awaiting him in the booth. Some of the misstatements that McCray made to the jury included the following:

--That the University of California at Irvine has a school of journalism;

--That 8,000 copies of the NEWS-POST were circulated in Laguna Beach;

--That the NEWS-POST was 60 years old; and

--That the NEWS-POST has won many awards.

In addition to correcting those statements, we included the fact that the NEWS-POST was printed at 8808 National Blvd., South Gate, Los Angeles County. We felt sure that the defense attorneys did not have the latter information or they would have petitioned the Superior Court long ago to have Spitaleri's adjudication suspended for having the NEWS-POST printed outside of Orange County.

Returning to court the next day, Dallas and I sat and watched an O'Neill aide walk into the courtroom with an envelope. He handed it to the bailiff, who in turn gave it to O'Neill. We had used a brown envelope for our message, but this one was white, apparently the message that there was another message elsewhere. During the first break Dallas and I got in an elevator to go down to the second floor to see if the envelope had been picked up yet. O'Neill's personal attorney, Crawford Cofer, had gotten in the elevator with us. Thinking quickly apparently, Cofer pushed the button for the third floor instead. When Dallas and I got off at the second floor, we waited near the elevators rather than going near the telephone booths. Dallas suspected that Cofer was on his way to pick up the envelope. Sure enough, Cofer walked down the line of booths without hesitating until he reached the second one from the end. He reached in, grabbed the envelope from a hidden slot underneath and headed back toward the escalator he had taken down from the third floor.

Both the plaintiff, Spitaleri, and the defendant, O'Neill, had been staring at us--Spitaleri knowing we were not on his side and O'Neill wondering which side we favored. In direct contrast to McCray, defense attorney Watson was extremely sharp. McCray's line of questioning was continually objected to by Watson and the judge usually sustained the objections. The first witness for Spitaleri turned on him. Larry Hill had bought the GOOD NEWS while he was the ad director because he thought he could make a financial success out of it. The Capistrano Valley Publishing Corporation had been feeding money into it for several years but it never came out of the red.

Spitaleri had met Hill at a convention on the East Coast. The day after Hill returned to California he found the GOOD NEWS burned to the ground. In his testimony, Hill revealed that Spitaleri then offered him the position of NEWS-POST advertising director with a salary of $35,000 a year--almost three times the amount Eggers received. Spitaleri entertained Hill at his home several times until 2:00 a.m., acting as if he were interested in buying the newspaper instead of hiring him. Spitaleri's attitude changed suddenly, Hill testified. Hill found himself being sued for $2 million for alleged damages he caused Spitaleri in the four months he owned the GOOD NEWS. Spitaleri then dropped the lawsuit in exchange for Hill testifying on his behalf. But Hill turned on him and quoted Spitaleri as saying he was going to "tear apart the corporate structure to get at Dick O'Neill." We learned that the Capistrano Valley Publishing Corporation had filed a cross-complaint against Spitaleri and his Laguna Publishing Company. With Hill's testimony, the defense had evidence of Spitaleri trying to put them out of business instead of the other way around.

Watson, trying to learn why Dallas and I were attending the trial, introduced himself to Dallas at the end of that day's session while we were waiting in front of the elevators. In turn,

Dallas gave his name, but slightly slurred it on purpose so that Watson might not understand it. Watson then asked, "Do you live in Leisure World?" When Dallas answered in the negative, Watson proclaimed, "Well, you are over 52." Dallas, who has white hair, answered, "Yes." Our elevator came and we departed while Watson conferred with his client. We did not want any of the defendants or their attorneys talking to us because it would be just like Spitaleri to then sue us all for conspiracy.

In the County Clerk's Office on the first floor of the courthouse I got to read the file of one of Spitaleri's lawsuits charging conspiracy. In the lawsuit, he alleged that Jon White, who was working as an advertising salesperson for the NEWS-POST during my internship there and for a short while after I became a full-time employee, had conspired with Golden West Publishing Corporation and had stolen "trade secrets" when he left the NEWS-POST to work for the SADDLEBACK VALLEY NEWS. Spitaleri claimed that White took a "secret" list of NEWS-POST advertisers to the SADDLEBACK VALLEY NEWS and that he gave Golden West inside information on a real estate tabloid the NEWS-POST was preparing. The court file indicated that at a hearing the Golden West attorneys produced a real estate tabloid that the SADDLEBACK VALLEY NEWS had published in April of 1975, four months before White left the NEWS-POST. Furthermore, a witness testified that White had vigorously tried to have the NEWS-POST publish such a tabloid while he worked there. Spitaleri had contended that White had given the SADDLEBACK VALLEY NEWS the idea and that it had not produced the tabloid until September of 1975. In response to Spitaleri's charge that White had stolen the names of the NEWS-POST advertisers, the defense attorneys pointed out that their names were public in-

80

formation because the advertisements were published in his newspaper. Spitaleri was accused of having a "vendetta" that was shrouded in "silence and mystery" and that he had failed to compete successfully in the free enterprise system. The court dismissed the case "with prejudice," meaning Spitaleri was precluded from filing another lawsuit against them for the same cause of action.

The next day Eggers and Elizabeth Fleming, the NEWS-POST receptionist who signed the affidavits of publication of legal notices, were waiting to be called as witnesses for Spitaleri. As soon as I sat down, Fleming rushed over to sit next to me and proceeded to talk incessantly. I did not want to be rude to her but neither did I want to be reprimanded by the judge or the bailiff for talking. So I just nodded or shook my head in answer to her questions. When she found out I was not employed, she suggested I apply at the NEWS-POST. "They need a proofreader desperately," she whispered. By this time Dallas was sitting behind me and whispered, "Get a drink of water." When I returned, I sat with him instead of Fleming, which is what he had expected me to do. Dallas hoped the defense would get the idea that we were not on the plaintiff's side. My switch in seating helped because the defendants then spent less time staring at us. Before leaving the courthouse that day we telephoned O'Neill's Santa Ana office to have another envelope picked up from the same place, a telephone booth on the second floor of the courthouse. The courthouse and the Employment Development Department were both located in Santa Ana, which made it convenient for me to pick up my unemployment insurance checks and report my job-seeking efforts. I was qualified to receive unemployment benefits for another six months because I had not been able to find employment in my job classification as a

81

newspaper worker.

Back in court the next week, we heard the testimony of Paul Ideker, who had served as editor of the GOOD NEWS when he was 23. Like Hill's, his testimony did not help Spitaleri. Contrary to McCray's statement that Ideker had been taken from the RANCHO REPORTER newspaper by O'Neill, his testimony showed that he contacted O'Neill after the RANCHO REPORTER owner said he could no longer afford him. After seven days of testimony by various witnesses, the judge said he had not yet seen any evidence of intent by the GOOD NEWS to damage the NEWS-POST. That statement indicated that if the plaintiff continued with his current line of evidence he would not win the case.

All along Watson had been tearing apart the credibility of the plaintiff's witnesses, including Karl Venstrom, the former publisher of the then-defunct RANCHO REPORTER. Venstrom was still a journalism professor at Santa Ana College as he had been while he was a publisher. He testified that the low ad rates charged by the GOOD NEWS had put him out of business. When Watson started questioning him, he produced a deposition transcript Venstrom had signed a few weeks earlier stating that the SADDLEBACK VALLEY NEWS was the one and only newspaper that had put him out of business. That transcript had been prepared during discovery proceedings of Spitaleri's lawsuit against Golden West, which published the SADDLEBACK VALLEY NEWS. Venstrom apparently had not known that the same attorney, who was also on the board of directors of Golden West, would be the lead defense attorney in this lawsuit.

Compared to Venstrom, his ex-wife, Janice Venstrom Harrison, was of even less help to the plaintiff. When Watson asked her why she resented Ideker, she said he had been disloyal to

the RANCHO REPORTER. Her husband had testified that Ideker had been a loyal employee.
Mrs. Harrison charged Ideker with conspiracy for
taking away all of the RANCHO REPORTER's
key employees to work for the GOOD NEWS.
She said she had expected Ideker to stay at the
RANCHO REPORTER and work for less pay although the exact amount had never been
discussed. To dispel any conspiracy on Ideker's
part, Watson asked her why Ideker mentioned,
several months before he left, his desire to publish his own newspaper.

Mrs. Harrison's anger was building up and
came to a peak when Watson asked her if her
former husband's drinking problem had anything to
do with the RANCHO REPORTER's demise. "Do
I have to answer that?" she demanded of the
judge. "Yes, you do," he replied. She said the
drinking had only affected their marriage and not
their newspaper. Watson's cross-examination had
been impressive. Coupled with the excellent performance as well as his failure to learn Dallas'
identity, O'Neill was moved to talk to Dallas as
we left the courtroom. "What did you think of
the trial today?" he asked politely. "Very
interesting," Dallas answered. O'Neill was smart
enough not to introduce himself to us.

A few days earlier, Carlton Smith, publisher
of the SADDLEBACK VALLEY NEWS, introduced
himself to Dallas in the elevator and asked him
what he did. "Where?" Dallas asked. "What
brings you to the trial?" Smith delved further.
"Interest," Dallas flatly stated. When the
elevator reached the first floor, Dallas announced
it as such. Smith was rather irritated by then,
but replied calmly, "It sure is."

We had already sent the defense a second
message. It was shorter than the first one, but
very important, we thought. The message told
where false sworn testimony of Spitaleri could be

found. We had finally found a use for the false information Spitaleri had given in Orange County Superior Court in November of 1976 when he tried to prevent the TIDES AND TIMES from being granted County adjudication to print legal advertisements. Spitaleri had stated that the NEWS-POST had been continuously published in Laguna Beach since 1915. In Watson's hands, that testimony could result in Spitaleri being charged with perjury.

For all the trouble Spitaleri had intentionally caused me, the least I could do was to make sure the truth was brought out and that justice was served. Dorothy Musfelt, a former Laguna Beach city clerk, had told Dallas that there was probably an effort to keep me from getting a job. She had said that I had done a good job of reporting the news and that I was a victim of terrible circumstances. A girlfriend from Pepperdine wrote to tell me that a former boyfriend of mine had also been such a victim. He had been at a newspaper for only six months before he lost his job because of politics. It was both consoling and discouraging at the same time to know that newspapers and governments elsewhere were violating the First Amendment and damaging not only the reporters, but the public, in the process. If a reporter was on the city's side, however, then his job was guaranteed along with the public's ignorance of what was happening in their government.

It was satisfying to see Spitaleri's witnesses torn apart by Watson. They had not helped to prove any malicious intent on the part of the GOOD NEWS. Because William Moses, publisher of the TUSTIN NEWS, did not show up that day to testify for the plaintiff, Spitaleri himself took the witness stand. When McCray asked him how old he was, Spitaleri looked down at his script, thought for a minute and then said, "This is

1977, so I must be...let's see...54. My birthday's in August." They proceeded to follow the script, with McCray asking the questions and Spitaleri reading his answers. They began with his high school days and how he won an academic scholarship and still had to work his way through college. "I washed dishes, waited on tables, played in the band, was a vocalist if necessary, and even was on the boxing team." It was incredible. He sat up there, with no modesty at all, bragging about himself.

Dallas and I sat expectantly, waiting for him to refer to the three Purple Hearts he received during World War II. Watson objected to the questions, saying they were irrelevant. McCray said they were necessary to disprove Watson's statement that Spitaleri was an industrialist. The judge, who also was obviously bored and surprised by the testimony, agreed with Watson but said any information regarding Spitaleri with the newspaper business could be revealed. The change in the script did not prevent Spitaleri from squeezing in that on his way to work for the American Newspaper Publishers Association after the war that he "happened to pick up three Purple Hearts."

It was unbelievable. Everyone in the courtroom, except Spitaleri and McCray, had a difficult time restraining their smiles. Yet the testimony continued. McCray asked him what important event took place in 1952. After replying that he came to Laguna Beach that year, Spitaleri was asked, "Weren't you married that year?" Spitaleri then put on a face of pondering and then recollection. "By jove, that's right," he replied. By this time Watson just let the questions continue, knowing the jury was not favorably impressed with them.

After an hour of similar questions, McCray finally reached questions relating to when Spitaleri bought the SOUTH COAST NEWS and the LAGUNA POST. Again Spitaleri lied and said the SOUTH COAST NEWS was founded in 1917 when in reality it was started in 1947. We prepared a third message for the defense. We referred them to the Diamond Jubilee edition of the NEWS-POST, which contradicted statements Spitaleri was making. The third message also included a reference to the lawsuit the relatives of the former SOUTH COAST NEWS owner had won against Spitaleri, who was ordered to pay $12,500 to them for breach of contract. The full satis-faction of judgment notice had been filed with the court on November 2, 1976.

After sitting through another day of useless testimony for the plaintiff, the judge said they could not assume that merchants would have ad-vertised in the NEWS-POST if the GOOD NEWS had not been in business. This remark came after Spitaleri showed charts he made indicating how much more the GOOD NEWS had charged for ads. He must have spent many hours calculating the percentages for each advertiser, and each city and town. Yet his work had been a waste of time because it had been based on assumption. Eight days had gone by and they still had not presented any admissible evidence. Watson ob-jected to having the jury exposed to Spitaleri's calculations, on the basis that it was prejudicial. The judge gave them until Monday to locate cases supporting their beliefs. Watson had al-ready cited federal cases but the judge wanted state cases.

Before going back to Laguna Beach, a 26-mile drive from Santa Ana, Dallas and I went to do some research at the main county law library, which, like the courthouse, was located in the civic center plaza. After we left the library and had gone halfway through the parking lot, I noticed Carlton Smith and Richard Birchall, his former associate, behind us. They got into their car, but Dallas and I had to walk several blocks to the free parking lot. When we got in my car I could see Smith in my rearview mirror. He stopped his car and it appeared that Birchall was copying down my license plate number. They followed us about 15 miles, all the way to the Sav-On drugstore parking lot in El Toro. From there we proceeded to the Laguna Hills Mall where I telephoned my father in Tustin. Even though they were no longer following us, I wanted to prepare my family for any telephone calls. I advised them to not give any information regarding me over the telephone.

Smith had become so frustrated over not knowing who we were that Dallas was afraid they would start talking to us even more. Dallas consequently decided to call Smith to assure him that we were on his side. He called the SADDLEBACK VALLEY NEWS and gave his name as Mark Johnson. Within minutes the operator reached Smith at his home. Dallas explained that he had given a fictitious name but still did not repeat his real name to Smith. "Don't be so concerned. We're on your side. Please don't talk to us in public, though. Tell the others also. Mr. Spitaleri knows us and he is a dangerous man." Smith immediately answered back, "I know he is." By now Smith was relaxed and did not act frustrated. He thanked Dallas for calling and agreed to tell the others.

Back at the courthouse the following Monday we left our fourth missive for the defense attorneys. In that, our final note, we included copies of ads that ran free of charge in the NEWS-POST. They advertised water lilies sold by one of Spitaleri's sons, Chris, although there was no name listed. Spitaleri's attorney had tried to make a big deal out of one of the GOOD NEWS' owners running a free ad for his mother's boutique. We also wrote that we heard that Spitaleri paid the City of Laguna Beach for its legal notices and that his newspaper was still failing to make a profit. When Dallas called O'Neill's office to leave a message about our fourth note, no one answered the telephone. So, Dallas gave a signal to Cofer in the courtroom. Dallas put his forefinger to the side of his nose and then pointed it down, indicating another message was waiting in a telephone booth on the second floor. In contrast to Dallas' discretion in signaling, Cofer, who was standing beside the defense table, looked at Dallas and pointed down to verify the signal. Right there in front of the judge and jury, Cofer practically invited attention. Nevertheless, the judge did not say anything and Cofer left the courtroom to collect the note from a telephone booth.

It was shortly afterward that I had to leave for the unemployment office to pick up my check. Later at lunch Dallas told me of how Cofer and O'Neill had laughed at the defense table while reading the first part of the note and then appeared very serious while reading the portion about the legal notices.

That afternoon a newspaper broker from Lindsay in Central California, Joe Snyder, testified that in 1973 Spitaleri contacted him because he wanted to sell the NEWS-POST. It was understandable that Spitaleri had tried to do so because the NEWS-POST had lost money every year he owned it. His losses ranged from $75,000 one year to about $20,000 another year, never making it into the black, according to the evidence introduced. Snyder told the court that the NEWS-POST should have been worth between $850,000 and $1.1 million but he was unable to sell it. He also testified that Orange County was one of the most competitive newspaper areas in the country. Spitaleri was more dramatic when telling the court the net worth of his newspaper. "It's valueless," he remorsed, "except for a few desks and typewriters worth $15,000 to $20,000." So Spitaleri was trying to get almost $1 million from O'Neill because the NEWS-POST could not successfully compete in the free enterprise system.

Every day in court Cofer and Watson constantly looked at us. I usually looked away, except once. When Spitaleri was on the witness stand I looked over at them to observe their reactions to his responses. At that moment Cofer turned his head, winked and smiled at me. I quickly turned my head away and looked straight ahead. If McCray, Spitaleri's attorney, could catch us motioning to each other, I feared he would call me to take the witness stand. He could not charge us with anything since Dallas and I were merely supplying the defense with facts to help ensure that justice would prevail.

When the court recessed for lunch, Dallas and I quickly left and waited in the hallway for an elevator. McCray was standing about 15 feet away talking with Spitaleri's oldest son, Marc. All of a sudden, Richard Birchall came from behind and patted Dallas on the back and thanked us for all the help we had provided. We were mortified. Neither Dallas nor I responded to Birchall's remarks. Acting as if nothing happened, we turned and took the stairway down instead of waiting for the elevator. It was obvious that Smith had not told the others to refrain from talking to us in public, especially in front of McCray. From then on we took the stairway to avoid any other confrontations.

After lunch, Spitaleri took the witness stand again to become a victim of one of Watson's best performances. While McCray had criticized the SADDLEBACK VALLEY NEWS during the trial for using advertising zone rates,

89

Watson informed the court that Spitaleri and the NEWS-POST did the same thing. McCray was startled. His own client, Spitaleri, had not even told him that he, too, offered the pick-up rates. The zone rate principle allowed an advertiser to place an ad in one of the newspaper's editions for a certain rate and then pay a much lower rate to have the ad also run in another zone the newspaper serviced. The SADDLEBACK VALLEY NEWS' pick-up rate was $1.19 and the NEWS-POST's was 50 cents. It was a typical case of the kettle calling the pot "black." Spitaleri kept trying to rationalize his pick-up rate as being a "penalty" for the advertisers. However, he could never explain how it was a penalty.

Watson scored another point when he asked Spitaleri about the financing of newspapers. Spitaleri had bragged himself up as an expert who had even served as a consultant to other newspapers to tell them how to succeed. Now when Watson asked him the question, Spitaleri responded, "You're asking me to make an assumption." Watson retorted with, "Well, we thought you were something of an expert." Everyone in the courtroom was smiling then and many were laughing outright. Watson continued to delve into Spitaleri's financial expertise, noting that the NEWS-POST was losing money even before the GOOD NEWS came into existence. Probably the best evidence the defense presented was a chart showing the NEWS-POST's losses actually decreasing while the GOOD NEWS was in business and then its losses increasing again after the GOOD NEWS went out of business.

Marc Spitaleri, then about 21 years old, apparently could not stand listening to the cross-examination of his father any longer. Earlier in the trial, he had guffawed at his father's "smart" answers. Now, he picked up his skateboard and left.

Watson ascertained from Spitaleri that he also worked full-time for Sta-Hi Corporation during the time he started the NEWS-POST and up until 1974. As vice president and chairman of the board of the company, which manufactured newspaper machinery, Spitaleri said he earned from $60,000 to $100,000 annually during those years. Watson tried to imply that if Spitaleri had devoted his time to the NEWS-POST instead, he would not have had the financial problems he was experiencing.

Watson proceeded to put Spitaleri in his proper place by producing the minutes of the Laguna Publishing Company meeting when the SOUTH COAST NEWS and the LAGUNA POST were merged to form the NEWS-POST. The minutes revealed that Spitaleri had made maneuverings in an effort to show that the SOUTH COAST NEWS and the LAGUNA POST were unprofitable. By this time Spitaleri was slouching on the witness stand. Then Watson asked Spitaleri where the NEWS-POST ledger cards were for advertisers during the years 1971 to 1974. Already knowing the answer, Watson heard Spitaleri tell the jury that they were thrown away after the Internal Revenue Service had conducted an audit and told him they did not have to be kept because he was "exonerated." Watson emphasized to the jury that Spitaleri had filed his lawsuit in 1974 and had known that the cards were necessary for evidence when he had them discarded. At first Spitaleri tried to place the blame on John Wilson, his business manager. After further interrogation he admitted to throwing them away himself.

The next day, June 22, 1977, Watson brought up the subject of other lawsuits in which Spitaleri had been a party. While he was with Sta-Hi three former Sta-Hi employees had formed their own company, Tri-Q. They then sued Sta-

91

Hi in an action to enjoin it from allegedly violating the state's Unfair Practices Act concerning the sale of newspaper manufacturing equipment. Another lawsuit, which we believed Watson had not known about until we sent one of our messages, was the one filed by Barbara Duarte, daughter of the late William Ottaway, former owner of the SOUTH COAST NEWS. Spitaleri had testified in court earlier that he had paid $400,000 for the newspaper. Now, Watson informed the jury that a lawsuit had to be filed before Spitaleri agreed to pay part of the sum. Watson also made Spitaleri say that the actual newspaper cost about $150,000, while he paid an additional $200,000 for printing equipment.

Larry Campbell, the TIDES AND TIMES publisher, told us later that Spitaleri had bought a large amount of lead from Ottaway to use with the printing press. He had no plans of using it all, though, because he switched to offset printing a few years later. Campbell said Spitaleri had paid one cent a pound for the lead and then waited for the price to increase when he sold it for 90 cents a pound. While Spitaleri had supposedly produced his financial books for the trial, there apparently was no mention of his making a profit from selling the lead. Spitaleri was just the type that kept two sets of books, Dallas said. One set would be for the Internal Revenue Service and trials; the other set was for himself.

As the trial was nearing its end, Cofer secretly met with Dallas in the men's room and thanked him for his help and opinions. Dallas had said he had noticed a change in the jury in the last few days. Whereas they had been thoroughly against Spitaleri earlier, he thought they were showing more sympathy toward him now. He told Cofer that Watson's instructions to the jury, therefore, would be crucial.

In the courtroom on June 27, 1977, we

heard Spitaleri being torn apart again by Watson. The defense attorney had informed the jury that Spitaleri had asked for $500,000 from the Capistrano Valley Publishing Corporation in this lawsuit and the same amount in his pending lawsuit against Golden West Publishing Corp., publisher of the SADDLEBACK VALLEY NEWS. Now Spitaleri was asking for almost $1 million from Capistrano Valley Publishing with O'Neill being the major stockholder. Watson also produced a copy of the NEWS-POST with an editorial by Spitaleri on the front page. It was written shortly after the GOOD NEWS went out of business. Spitaleri cited the reasons as being "inexperience and gross mismanagement coupled with insufficient capital." Spitaleri could fit into that category also, I thought. Watson also produced the last copy of the GOOD NEWS in which then-publisher Larry Hill placed the blame for the GOOD NEWS' demise on Spitaleri's filing of a $2 million lawsuit against him. Hill had his day in court, though, when he told the jury he had to hire attorneys who then made an "agreement" with Spitaleri's attorney. He gave the NEWS-POST all of the ledger cards for the GOOD NEWS advertisers, amounting to several hundred, in exchange for a dismissal of the lawsuit against him. That was really what Spitaleri wanted--the advertisers. He knew that it was O'Neill, who was left in the lawsuit to face the trial, who had the money.

In his instructions to the jury, Watson figuratively undressed Spitaleri to show the jury what he was like. He called Spitaleri "a conspirator, a discarder of records and a falsifier of records." And, in other words, he called him a liar. He portrayed Spitaleri as a man who, just because he has one or three Purple Hearts, thinks that the world owes him a living. In Spitaleri's eyes, Watson said, O'Neill was a terrible man with a fat pocketbook. Spitaleri had tried to show that having a lot of money was a crime.

Dallas and I had found O'Neill to be a nice man, friendly to all. Yet at the same time I realized that I could be wrong since we only saw him for two weeks and he was trying to make a good impression during the entire time. The jury's verdict was 12-0 in O'Neill's favor. The cross-complaint that he had filed against Spitaleri, however, was ruled in Spitaleri's favor. Neither party was awarded any damages. Standing in the hallway after the trial, I talked to two of the women who had been in attendance at the trial. Margaret Spencer was an attorney employed by Watson. Harriet Maas worked for Leisure .World Foundation, which was involved in the lawsuit filed by Spitaleri concerning delivery of the NEWS-POST to Leisure World. She had also worked for the Federal Bureau of Investigation for 22 years, during which time she said she never saw anyone like Spitaleri "on this side of the bars." She characterized Spitaleri as a rude, callous and insulting individual. He tried to make fun of the attorneys at his depositions, which she attended. Spitaleri's wife was just as unpersonable as was demonstrated when she threw a tantrum when the defense attorneys tried to take her deposition, she said. In further conversation with Maas, we were delighted to hear that Spitaleri was ordered to pay $500 in another court hearing the same day.

During the trial I had wondered how the defense attorneys had referred to us before they found out our names from Larry Campbell. I found out when I spoke with Spencer. It might have been just a coincidence, but "agents Alpha and Beta" had the same first letters as Anderson and Brownfield. Before we left the courthouse, O'Neill came over to ask us how we liked the

94

outcome. Dallas informed him that we had celebrated the night before and did not know how to erase it. "Well, what do you mean?" O'Neill asked nervously, thinking we might have wanted him to lose. "We wanted you to win more," Dallas replied. It was true. We had wanted Spitaleri to have to pay damages to O'Neill for taking up his time and causing him to pay defense attorneys.

When we got back to Laguna Beach, Dallas decided he wanted to be the first one to tell Campbell the good news that Spitaleri had lost. Campbell wondered aloud why Watson or Smith had not called him. He did not yet realize they had only called him to obtain more information to the lead we had provided. Out of the blue, Campbell told Dallas that he had talked with Eggers recently. Eggers reportedly told Campbell that he was receiving $900 a month at the NEWS-POST but that he could be "had" for $950. In court, McCray said the ad manager, the position Eggers also assumed, earned $18,000 a year. Maas had seen the financial statements and said the figure was closer to $13,000. Campbell was mystified with the information Dallas and I were throwing at him, especially the fact that the NEWS-POST had lost money every year of its existence.

The next day when Dallas and I were at the Ivy House restaurant, Campbell told us of taking Eggers with him in a plane to Fresno over the weekend. Dallas and I were sickened at the thought of it but kept our feelings from Campbell. Eggers had written a letter to Saddleback College to get Campbell dismissed from his teaching job there. Eggers also said many uncomplimentary things about Campbell while I was at the NEWS-POST. Yet Campbell provided him with transportation and liquor for the flight to an Exchange Club convention in Fresno. It

95

was disgusting. The only one at the NEWS-POST whom Campbell seemed to dislike was Spitaleri.

That evening my mother telephoned to tell me that Carlton Smith had called her in Tustin. He had obviously gone to some trouble to ascertain my name and my parents' telephone number. Smith wanted information, I presumed, to help him with his defense in the lawsuit Spitaleri had filed against the SADDLEBACK VALLEY NEWS. That trial was expected to be in court in a few weeks. I returned Smith's telephone call on July 5, 1977. He was anxious to meet with Dallas and me to discuss Spitaleri before the LAGUNA PUBLISHING COMPANY vs. GOLDEN WEST PUBLISHING CORPORATION trial that was scheduled to begin on July 11. We met for lunch a few days later at the Mission Viejo Inn with Smith and a friend of his, Jerry Clausen, who also formerly worked in the editorial department of THE REGISTER. Clausen was doing an investigational report for "Smitty's" defense in the trial. Smith and Clausen asked me many questions and I confirmed that my stories for the NEWS-POST had been censored or held back when they interfered with Spitaleri's financial interests. My examples included the Festival of Arts and Realex Investments. Regarding the latter, Spitaleri had told Theresa Eagles of FACTS that he had not printed my Realex follow-up for fear of being sued. One piece of information I knew they would like was the fact that Marcie Eden, a NEWS-POST typesetter, had told me that a woman named Marilyn, whom I had seen working as a circulation department secretary for about two months, had been hired in June of 1976 to spy on the SADDLEBACK VALLEY NEWS. Pat Ochoa, the circulation director at the NEWS-POST had told Marcie about Marilyn's job duties.

When Smith asked me about my employment status, I told him that I had been unable to get a job with any newspaper. Consequently, I was still receiving unemployment benefits. Only because Smith asked where I had applied for jobs did I tell him that I had been to the DAILY PILOT, THE REGISTER, and the SADDLEBACK VALLEY NEWS, to name a few. Smith appeared embarrassed after asking about my contact with his newspaper when I told him that Annette McCluskey had been very gracious and seemed impressed with my previously-published stories, but that she had not offered me a job. Smith did not do anything of which I was aware to change my job status.

It was July 7, 1977, and I was very anxious on our way back to Laguna Beach to see if the TIDES AND TIMES had printed a story I had submitted with the headline, "Local Citizens Charge Obstruction of Justice at County D.A.'s Office." During the six months that I had been unemployed I had reached the depths of depression several times because there seemed like no answer to my predicament. I was delighted to see that Campbell had published the story in full, approximately 25 inches of three columns on the top of the front page and an almost equal amount on two inside pages. I was at a county Board of Supervisors meeting when District Attorney Cecil Hicks submitted his budget request for the next fiscal year. Dallas was also present and ready to address the board regarding Hicks' failure to administer equal justice. My story began with the following paragraph:

"Two Laguna Beach citizens have charged Dep. Dist. Atty. William L. Evans with conspiracy, conflict of interest and incompetency amounting to obstruction of justice for failing to properly investigate and prosecute reported alleged crimes committed by the Laguna Beach city government." Other paragraphs included the statements that "if Evans prosecuted under the

97

law as the two (Dallas Anderson and Trevor Cushman Jr.) understood it, Laguna Beach City Atty. George G. Logan and Dep. City Atty. Stephen M. Chase would be removed from office and required to return the remuneration they had received from the City.

"The first complaint made concerning Logan alleged that he committed a crime by appointing one of the staff in his private law firm to appear on his behalf in City matters." The complaint was then expanded to include the allegations that the GOVERNMENT CODE, Sections 1192, 1303, 1367 and 36507, were violated by Logan and Chase by not taking the oaths of office, by Logan providing Chase's remuneration, by Chase accepting remuneration from Logan, by Logan not being named city attorney in a resolution and by Chase not being named deputy city attorney at the prescribed time.

The story reported that only after Dallas had been to the Santa Ana City Hall on May 13 and 16, 1977, regarding a 1972 loyalty oath Chase had taken to work for that City, a copy of which was sent to Dallas and Trevor by Evans in Chase's defense, that Logan finally took the oath as Laguna Beach city attorney on May 18, 1977. It was incredible that Evans would send a 1972 oath from one city and try to claim that it was sufficient for working for a different city in 1977. Other paragraphs from the story read as follows:

"Anderson and Cushman report that all of the oaths which they have seen for Logan and Chase are illegal for the following reasons:

"--Chase's oath with Santa Ana had not been acknowledged by the city clerk or dated, as required by state law.

"--A 1972 oath taken by Logan when he was a school district trustee for the Huntington Beach Unified School District was also submitted

98

by Evans in response to the charge that Logan had not taken the oath of office for Laguna Beach City Attorney.

"The trustee oath, however, had not even been filed with the County Clerk in accordance with state law."

That story and others I wrote for the TIDES AND TIMES increased the newspaper's circulation by about 400 percent. My only compensation besides bylines was the fact that important news, not published elsewhere, was available for the public to read. Kelly Boyd, owner of General Lee's store downtown and later a city councilman as well, said he had to be resupplied with the TIDES AND TIMES several times because so many people were getting copies to read my stories. Campbell finally had to admit that people told him my stories were great.

The trial against Golden West was delayed and so I continued to work on stories for the TIDES AND TIMES. One of the last stories of mine printed by Campbell appeared in the July 14, 1977, edition under the headline, which I also wrote, "Undergrounding Procedures Deviate from State Laws." The story referred to the state Special Assessment Investigation, Limitation and Majority Protest Act of 1931 which the City of Laguna Beach had not been following in trying to underground the utilities in the Temple Hills area. Even though a majority of the landowners, comprising 58 percent of the area, opposed the undergrounding, the City was trying to proceed, in contradiction of the state law.

The July 28, 1977, edition carried three stories by me but Campbell chose to give me a byline only for one of them because, he later told me, he did not think I should have more than one byline on a page. It infuriated me that he would take away my credit for the story since he had never paid me a cent for my work, even

99

though he was making a profit through increased circulation. The unbylined story was about an electrical outage at The Cellar restaurant when I was dining there one evening. The failure began at 7:00 p.m., but I quoted Bud Jackley of Southern California Edison as saying that Edison did not know about it until 9:00 p.m. I also reported that Jackley said Edison's emergency telephone number should have been called; though I told him there was no such number listed in the Laguna Beach directory. Just two days later I was at the TIDES AND TIMES offices when an Edison check was received in the mail for a one-year subscription to the newspaper. It was very satisfying to think that perhaps one story of mine resulted in at least one new subscription.

Chapter 4

In late August of 1977 Dallas telephoned Carlton Smith to find out when the LAGUNA PUBLISHING COMPANY vs. GOLDEN WEST PUBLISHING CORPORATION trial would commence. Smith indicated that it had been postponed until November and that in the meantime Watson, at Dallas' suggestion, had taken the deposition of Marjorie Spitaleri, Vernon's wife. Smith said that Watson had acquired a substantial amount of useful ammunition from her testimony. One day while on a trip to the law library, Dallas and I went to the County Clerk's Office in the same building to research a court order in another matter requiring Spitaleri to pay $500. The order had been entered the same day that the verdict had been returned in his lawsuit against Capistrano Valley Publishing Corporation. We finally located a file showing Spitaleri as the subject defendant. He had been sued by Golden

West Publishing Corp. for allegedly violating business ethics and lying to merchants in the Saddleback Valley. In the file was a January 31, 1977, letter written on NEWS-POST stationery and bearing Spitaleri's signature. Addressed to all individuals who had placed legal advertisements in the SADDLEBACK VALLEY NEWS, Spitaleri wrote that they should place their legal ads in the NEWS-POST because the SADDLEBACK VALLEY NEWS adjudication was being challenged in court. Spitaleri went as far as to say that notices in the SADDLEBACK newspaper were not valid legally.

Also included in the file was a letter written to Watson by an attorney, not McCray, retained by Spitaleri and stating that he was advising Spitaleri to tell people that the SADDLEBACK VALLEY NEWS was not a newspaper adjudicated for legal advertising. Spitaleri wrote that Elizabeth Fleming at the NEWS-POST would be happy to place their legal ads in his newspaper. We were startled to read that Spitaleri falsely told the addressees that the NEWS-POST had been serving the Saddleback Valley since 1928.

On November 15, 1977, Dallas and I went to the Orange County Courthouse because the mandatory settlement conference for Spitaleri's lawsuit against Golden West was to be held that day. The hearing lasted several days, at the end of which Dallas gave Smith a copy of an Affidavit of Publication of the NEWS-POST falsely claiming that it was published and printed in the city of Laguna Beach when it was actually published in Laguna Hills and printed in Los Angeles County. A few days later, careful not to let Spitaleri or his attorney McCray see him, Smith told Dallas that Watson was very appreciative of the affidavit. Harriet Maas, who was employed by the Leisure World Foundation and who had attended the previous trial, told Dallas that Spitaleri had an office in Suite 402 of a building next to the Jolly Roger restaurant in Newport Beach. McCray had just moved his law offices to the entire fourth floor. That information plus the report from Smith that the NEWS-POST was now being printed at a new location in Los Angeles County indicated to us that Spitaleri was under very close surveillance.

As the selection of a jury neared completion on November 22, 1977, Judge Walter Charamza stared at Dallas and me and said, "There are those who do not want an unbiased jury for this trial. I'm going to do everything I can to make sure this is a fair trial." Even though all of the seats in the courtroom were filled, Charamza only looked at Dallas and me when he spoke those words. It seemed that McCray had told the judge about our presence at the previous trial, Spitaleri's suit against the GOOD NEWS publisher, and he wanted something said to impede us from doing a civic duty.

While walking in the hallway to the courtroom the day after, attorney Watson came from the other direction and as he passed Dallas and me he said, "Hello, good citizens." It was like a signal from Watson concerning the judge's remarks the day before. Perhaps Watson had told the judge that Dallas and I were just good citizens attending the trial. Or perhaps that was the answer Watson thought we should give if we were questioned by the judge. At any rate, Watson had us pegged right. Being a city attorney for several cities, though, he might have said that to any citizens attending a council meeting.

About a week later, Marjorie Spitaleri and her two oldest sons, Marc and Eric, appeared in the courtroom to hear McCray give the opening statement of Laguna Publishing Company. Before the session began, Dallas went out into the

103

hallway to smoke his pipe. That left me sitting by myself in the front row and Mrs. Spitaleri sitting by herself in the third row. On the other side of the courtroom were Smith, Birchall and Maas. Mrs. Spitaleri took the opportunity to reach over the second row, tap my shoulder and ask, "How are you?" I just looked at the finger tapping my shoulder. Then I turned away and looked at the courtroom clock. I could hear Mrs. Spitaleri laugh. It was typical of her immaturity. How she could think that I would be as hypocritical as she and act like nothing had happened was beyond me. I enjoyed ignoring her. I remembered all of the cruel things she had done to me at the NEWS-POST just because I was reporting stories as I had been educated to do.

A few hours later, while Dallas and I were standing in the hallway, Mrs. Spitaleri was sent by her husband to make a call on the pay telephone, which was near us. She apparently dreaded taking each step in our direction. As she neared the telephone she began shaking her head at us. We were tempted to laugh. Her arrogant ancestry was evident in her assumption that she could go around shaking her head at anyone in an attempt to show that she was the boss. Mrs. Spitaleri had played the little Hitler type at the NEWS-POST for so long that she now apparently thought she could start bossing a laid-off employee.

Back in the courtroom, the judge announced that many documents to be used as evidence in the case had been found. Larry Peterson, a staff writer for THE REGISTER, was sitting in the courtroom only for the opening statements. He turned around and asked Spitaleri what the documents were. "Just some old documents," Spitaleri replied, obviously trying to minimize their importance. Later, Watson told the judge the documents numbered almost 500,000 and that he would need several days to peruse them. For some unknown reason Spitaleri had waited until the trial had begun to announce that the documents had been found. In the previous trial Watson had accused him in open court of being "a discarder of records." Before leaving the courthouse that day, Smith told us that Watson or Joseph Sullivan, his other attorney, was going to the Laguna Beach City Hall to find an Affidavit of Publication with Spitaleri's signature on it. The affidavits that we had supplied to them had Elizabeth Fleming's signature on them. We had also given Smith a copy of the California PENAL CODE section which states that it is a felony for one person to suborn perjury of another. It seemed that Spitaleri was having Fleming sign the false affidavits on command, thus making them both subject to the penalty of perjury.

Two days later Dallas and I returned to Santa Ana. In the courtroom, Judge Charamza announced that he, not the jury, would decide Spitaleri's First Amendment claim that he should be allowed to deliver the NEWS-POST to non-subscribers in Leisure World, a private community. That day in court we also learned that Smith and Birchall had filed lawsuits against their former employers, who had coerced them into giving up 51 percent of their corporation's stock. When Birchall was on the witness stand, I learned he had experienced trauma similar to mine. He had been demoted from advertising director, his pay was reduced and he said that he was forced into a very "traumatic" experience. Later, when Smith was on the witness stand, he gave credit to Birchall for standing up to fight against their former employers. It was Smith who had earlier demoted Birchall for his "attitude."

On December 6, 1977, Watson gave his opening statement for the defendants. Smith had told Dallas earlier that Watson was going to be

105

hard, but not too hard, in the statement. Watson called Spitaleri "an opportunist" and told of his "bag of dirty tricks." Spitaleri had, according to Watson, used his position with the California Newspaper Publishers Association (CNPA) to delay the acceptance of the SADDLEBACK VALLEY NEWS into the organization. Watson told the jury that Spitaleri had also used his position as president of the Emerald Bay homeowners association to prevent Smith's newspaper from being delivered, unsolicited, to every home in Emerald Bay, which like Leisure World, is a private community, in an unincorporated portion of Orange County. In regard to Spitaleri's alleged unfair trade practices, Watson said the NEWS-POST had given a carpet dealer free ads in exchange for 7,000 square feet of carpeting in Spitaleri's home. Watson also told the jury that Spitaleri had caused the SADDLEBACK VALLEY NEWS adjudication to be suspended for a year when its offices were relocated from Laguna Niguel to Mission Viejo. The requirements for newspaper adjudications would be presented later in the trial, Watson added.

We returned to the courtroom the following Monday to hear Birchall testify about attending a meeting in La Costa, in San Diego County, California. He said he had been invited there to meet with several millionaires who were interested in buying the SADDLEBACK VALLEY NEWS. Spitaleri was also at the meeting, according to Birchall, with hope of selling the NEWS-POST. None of the principal buyers showed up at the meeting, however. Dallas and I thought that perhaps Spitaleri had arranged it that way. It was very strange that they would be meeting in La Costa, approximately 80 miles away in San Diego County, which is south of where the two newspapers are located in Orange County. T h e December 14, 1977, edition of the NEWS-POST

106

contained a very biased story about Spitaleri's lawsuit against Golden West. The story also quoted Spitaleri's attorney, McCray, but not the attorney for the other side. Dallas and I were shocked to read that Spitaleri was seeking $7 million in damages. What he could not make in the free enterprise system he was trying to make by filing lawsuits. There was nothing presented in the trial so far by McCray to indicate that Spitaleri had been damaged by Golden West. Even if he was damaged, Spitaleri would have to prove that it was done with the purpose of trying to put the NEWS-POST out of business. McCray had told the jury that the SADDLEBACK VALLEY NEWS had given away coupons for free classified ads. He apparently did not know that the NEWS-POST did the same thing, which we demonstrated to Smith by giving him a copy of one that appeared in the NEWS-POST. We also gave him other information we thought might be helpful.

The next day the judge had a difficult time staying awake during McCray's boring questions. By the end of the day, the judge was really perturbed with McCray's fishing expeditions and told him, "Let's get some motion into this trial." McCray's style was worse than a layman's and Watson and Sullivan never failed to find the humor and make an appropriate remark during the trial. A few days later Watson walked up to Dallas and me in the hallway and said Spitaleri had complained that the trial was not serious enough, that too many jokes were made. Watson also commented that the trial seemed to be progressing the same way as the one against Capistrano Valley Publishing. The next day, before court was in session, Watson remarked, "Ready for another fast-moving session?" At the end of that day, December 20, the judge stopped McCray from referring to Birchall and Phil Weiner, the third member of their original publishing corporation, as Smith's "buddies" by saying, "That's a no-no." That remark also would have been appropriate if directed toward Spitaleri's oldest son, Marc, about 21 years old then, who carried his skateboard into the courtroom as he did at the previous trial.

Dallas soon found out from Smith that after we gave him a copy of a NEWS-POST Affidavit of Publication that the defense attorneys themselves or their employees went to the Laguna Beach City Hall for three days during the Christmas holiday while the court was in recess. They sifted through all of the affidavits that had been filed there from the time the NEWS-POST moved from Laguna Beach to Laguna Hills in June of 1975. They had hoped to find Spitaleri's signature on at least one of them but it was not to be found. If they had found one it would have been evidence that Spitaleri had committed perjury himself, rather than just suborning perjury by having Elizabeth Fleming sign the false affidavits.

When the trial continued on January 5, 1978, Milan Dostal, the mayor of Newport Beach, was called by McCray to testify concerning his role as attorney for Edward Olsen and Otto Musch of Professional Community Management (PCM), three entities Spitaleri had filed a lawsuit against in conjunction with his suit against Golden West. Olsen, Musch and PCM had cross-complained against Laguna Publishing Company for libel because of stories that had appeared in the Leisure World edition of the NEWS-POST.

Sullivan and Watson questioned McCray about the purpose of him asking Dostal about the government positions he had held. After Dostal said he was mayor, Watson remarked that it qualified him as a "politician." Just about everyone in the courtroom laughed at the joke. Then the judge added that Dostal had "disqualified" himself.   Since Charamza was a resident of Corona del Mar, a part of Newport Beach, he probably had read in the ENSIGN that just the week before Dostal announced he would not seek reelection as a Newport Beach city councilman.   Years later I learned that Charamza had been the city attorney for Newport Beach before becoming a judge.   I wondered if he had ever been acquainted with Dostal.

As in the questioning of others on the stand, McCray's questions of Dostal did not seem to help Spitaleri's case at all.   Dostal's chosen responses were "I don't recall" and "I don't remember."   It was another story when Watson started questioning "politician" Dostal.   Watson obviously had carefully planned his strategy.   He began asking questions at various levels until Dostal was cornered into answering that he remembered what he had done as attorney for Olsen, Musch and PCM.   The information concerned PCM's operation of Leisure World and how it related to Spitaleri's request to have the NEWS-POST delivered to every residence.

In court on January 11, 1978, Richard Birchall, outside of the presence of Spitaleri and McCray, thanked Dallas and me for our help. During the afternoon recess that day Dallas and I went to the courthouse cafeteria as usual so that he could have a cup of coffee.   After being seated we noticed Jerry Goldberg, editor of the CITY NEWS.   I had previously had an unsatisfactory interview with him at a restaurant after driving him there because he did not have a car. Subsequent to that interview, I noticed the December 16, 1977, edition of the CITY NEWS featuring on the front page a personality profile of Michael Capizzi, the assistant district attorney. Rather than being a watchdog on government, Goldberg wrote the profile in a manner that gave the impression that he rubbed shoulders with such

109

"important" people as Capizzi. After a few minutes, Goldberg got up from his table and sat down at our table, uninvited. Looking at me, he said he was looking for a courthouse reporter, but not one who would investigate the stories. I quickly replied, "Well, you don't want me then!" There was no doubt in my voice that I did not want to work for the CITY NEWS. Dallas viewed my answer as a cue to give Goldberg the negative treatment for the remainder of his stay at our table. I left to return to the courtroom, though, a few minutes ahead of Dallas. The way we handled it, we were pretty sure that Goldberg would never bother us again.

Otto Musch, who along with Edward Olsen had taken control of the Birchall, Smith and Weiner corporation through coercion, testified in court on January 12, 1978. McCray showed him two sets of minutes of a corporation meeting which appeared to be the same except for the dates. They were photocopies and Musch, as secretary of the corporation, identified his signature, also photocopied, on each set. McCray asked him to read over each set of minutes to see if there were any differences. Musch did not find any and apparently McCray did not either.

Once again, it was a different story when Watson cross-examined Musch. The dates on the minutes were about a month apart. Watson had Musch read a certain portion of one set of minutes and the portion on the other set that appeared to be the same. The difference was that on the earlier set, it appeared that Olsen and Musch had not been properly elected to the positions of chief executive officer and executive vice president/secretary, respectively, of the pub-lishing corporation. On the second set of minutes it was typed to appear that it had been done properly and lawfully. As Dostal had testified earlier, he was the one who had the minutes

110

typed by his secretary and prepared for Musch's signature. Dostal had changed the top page on the second set of minutes and made photocopies of the other pages, including the one with Musch's signature, which explained why Musch could not remember signing a similar set of minutes twice. Earlier in the testimony when Watson asked Musch if he wanted to speak to an attorney because Judge Charamza had affirmed the possibility of a criminal charge, Musch was given time by the court to make a telephone call to Dostal. Dostal, the mayor of Newport Beach, knew that he had committed a crime by changing the pages of the minutes and told Musch that he could not help him because he was not a criminal attorney. Birchall and Weiner would not have been through such depressing times if they had known before that Olsen and Musch had not legally taken over their corporation. Smith had been retained as president of the corporation, receiving a $52,000 annual salary and $10,000 in bonuses. Birchall and Weiner had been eliminated to make room for Olsen and Musch. Birchall later fought back by filing a stockholder's derivative action suit against the corporation to have his rights restored.

During recesses Watson started coming to Dallas on a regular basis to ask him his opinion of the trial's progress. He was usually careful, though, not to talk to us in the sight of McCray or Spitaleri. On one occasion Watson referred to Dallas as "my courtroom monitor."

After the trial had been plodding along for two months, the NEWS-POST printed a story in its January 18, 1978, edition which was all about Eggers and appeared to be written by him as well. Appearing along the bottom of the front page and accompanied by a photograph of Eggers, the story was about his "promotion" to the position of vice president of Laguna Publishing

Company. Eggers obviously did not know that the California CORPORATIONS CODE required that a corporation officer be elected, not promoted, by the corporation's board of directors. There was no mention of any action by the board of what happened to Marjorie Spitaleri, who according to records on file with the California Secretary of State was the vice president of the corporation known as Laguna Publishing Company. The story did point out that Eggers would be retaining his title of executive editor also.

In the same issue, on the back page, was another in a series of "People Behind the News," that is, the employees of the NEWS-POST. The accompanying photograph of reporter Ken Barnes, the featured subject, indicated that he was in his mid-30s. The story revealed that he had been a public information specialist in charge of West Coast aviation activities for the El Toro Marine Corps base until he left to join the NEWS-POST. The story reported that Barnes left the Marine Corps in September and was hired as a part-time proofreader by the NEWS-POST in October. Now, the story continued, he was the NEWS-POST reporter assigned to cover Leisure World. There was no mention of what happened to William Doherty, the reporter who had the beat for three years. The main thought in my mind, though, was that Watson had told the court in his opening statement that the Marine Corps had given the publishing contract of the FLIGHT JACKET to the NEWS-POST even though Spitaleri had submitted his bid 30 days after the deadline.

The following day in court provided more laughter than one would ever expect. While everyone in the courtroom had learned by that stage in the trial that McCray often twisted his words so that they left his mouth in an ususual fashion, most of us were amazed that day by some of the apparent thoughts on his mind. In questioning a witness, McCray said "Disneyland" when he was referring to Leisure World. Even Spitaleri, who had not been observed to smile or laugh in court or elsewhere, broke out laughing. McCray then added that he had not been there for 25 years, so he did not know why it was on his mind. Disneyland was on his mind because he had represented Disneyland in personal injury lawsuits filed against the local amusement park since it opened in 1955. While everyone in the courtroom was still laughing about the "Disneyland" slip, he then added, "I guess that's why people call me a Mickey Mouse lawyer." The volume of the laughter increased. After the proper decorum had returned to the courtroom, McCray proceeded to interrogate his witness. He was asking him about house organs, such as the LEISURE WORLD NEWS, and external publications, such as the NEWS-POST. McCray then asked a question about "internal and external organs" and after a moment's pause, felt he should clarify the question by adding "in reference to newspapers, of course." The reaction among everyone toward his earlier Disneyland and Mickey Mouse remarks was minor compared to the laughter that last line elicited. The judge was so broken up he could not contain himself. His body shook with laughter. Fortunately, or unfortunately, the end of the day was at hand and McCray did not have much more of an opportunity to be the court jester.

The following day in court Birchall told us that the out-of-court settlement between Laguna Publishing Company and Olsen, Musch and PCM was for approximately $60,000. According to a LEISURE WORLD NEWS story which I later saw, it seemed that Spitaleri was the one who paid. Birchall also told us that "Watson hates Spitaleri" and would feel especially bad if he did not obtain a favorable verdict in the lawsuit. Watson had found Spitaleri to be a "vicious man," according to Birchall. I had no reason to disagree with him.

We did not tell Birchall that we had gone to the El Toro Marine Base that morning on our way to the courthouse in Santa Ana. I had entered the base while Dallas walked around outside smoking his pipe. A few days earlier I had telephoned the press chief, a Staff Sergeant Morales, to arrange to look at back issues of the FLIGHT JACKET. Morales had asked me if I was a reporter. I told him that I was not and questioned him if that would have made any difference. He finally said I could see the issues. While there, several officers asked me if I was looking for something in particular as I paged through the 1976 and 1977 issues. I found a story with the byline of SSGT. (Staff Sergeant) Ken Barnes in a 1977 issue. With all of the observers around I dared not write it down but instead committed the dates and the page numbers to memory.

Later in the day we gave Smith copies of the NEWS-POST stories about Eggers and Barnes. I also included in the package a report that Barnes had his byline on at least two stories in the FLIGHT JACKET. My report also stated that Staff Sergeant Morales was the press chief at the base and since Barnes had been staff sergeant and public information specialist, that he may also have been the press chief at the time of the FLIGHT JACKET contract negotiations.

That day we witnessed Karl Venstrom, a journalism professor at Santa Ana College, again get caught by Watson in his testimony. Venstrom had testified in Spitaleri's suit against Capistrano Valley Publishing Corporation. At that time he had claimed that the GOOD NEWS ad rates had put him out of business, while his deposition transcript in this case showed that he declared

114

the SADDLEBACK VALLEY NEWS ad rates were the only ones that put his newspaper, the RANCHO REPORTER, out of business. This time testimony extricated from Venstrom indicated that with the full schedule he had as a junior college professor he had not been able to spend much time working on the RANCHO REPORTER, indicating that was one reason for its demise.

The following day Venstrom's former wife, Janice Venstrom Harrison, was called as a witness by McCray. She came across as vindictive and hostile as she was during the previous trial. Watson was allowed to read into the record a portion of the Venstroms' divorce suit. The former Mrs. Venstrom had accused her ex-husband of excessive drinking, which affected his work performance at the RANCHO REPORTER. Watson also produced for the court a note that Mrs. Harrison had mailed to Birchall shortly after she had read an October, 1973, newspaper account of Laguna Publishing Company filing a lawsuit against Golden West. "It couldn't happen to a better bunch," she wrote.

The highlight of the testimony that day came when Watson cross-examined Frank Good, an advertising salesman who had worked for Golden West for about six months, several years earlier. Good had apparently refused to testify for the defense because Birchall and Smith refused to pay him for it. In a telephone conversation Good reportedly told Birchall that Birchall would have to "grease my palms" with $10,000 to testify in court. When Watson asked Good if he told Birchall that "money talks," Good replied, "And bologna walks." Good's testimony made me wonder about what incentive Spitaleri may have offered him in exchange for testifying since Good had allegedly said he would not testify in court for anyone. At the end of the day, Watson came to where Dallas and I were standing in the hallway and asked, "Can you believe the quality of witnesses McCray has been calling?" It was true that none of the witnesses called so far in the two months of the trial appeared to be helping Spitaleri.

On February 6, 1978, Dallas told Smith, at my request, that the witness then on the stand, Art Krause, had run a "Squawk Box" column in the NEWS-POST for a few months in 1976. By the time Smith got the information to his attorneys they could not ask Krause about it. The next witness, though, was able to testify to that effect. Robert Merritt was the news director for Leisure World's cable television station, which McCray tried to imply dropped Krause's "Squawk Box" segment because the Golden Rain Foundation management thought it was too critical of them. Golden Rain was a co-defendant in Spitaleri's case against Golden West. When Sullivan asked Merritt if Krause then took his "Squawk Box" in written form to the NEWS-POST, Merritt answered affirmatively. I remembered that it did not last long there either. Its short duration in either communications medium most likely meant that it was not very popular with the public. Krause was sitting in front of us next to Spitaleri at the time. When Krause heard Sullivan referring to the "Squawk Box" in the NEWS-POST he looked surprised.

Some of the witnesses called by McCray were on the stand for only a few minutes because the judge sustained defense objections that the materials had already been covered with other witnesses. Others brought out some new information. One witness, as a representative for an automobile dealer, had placed ads in the SADDLEBACK VALLEY NEWS and the NEWS-POST. He told of a salesperson from the SADDLEBACK VALLEY NEWS telling him that Spitaleri "is a nut and nuisance" and that there would be no NEWS-POST after Spitaleri lost the lawsuit. Sullivan then asked the witness if he had known that Spitaleri had sued another newspaper and had lost that lawsuit. The witness, who answered that he had not known that, then sank back in his seat and his face turned red. Asked if he continued to place ads in the NEWS-POST even after he had been told it would soon be out of business, the witness responded, "Yes."

That afternoon, February 8, Major Ruth Pulaski of the El Toro Marine Base took the stand. She was accompanied in the courtroom by what appeared to be a female attorney dressed in a similar Marine uniform. Watson produced evidence of about five publishing firms submitting bids to Pulaski for the FLIGHT JACKET publication contract. All of the bids shown, including the one made by Golden West, had been submitted prior to the February 28, 1977, deadline. Watson then showed Pulaski the bid made by Laguna Publishing Company dated March 30, 1977, and asked her why she awarded the two-year contract to Spitaleri. She then proceeded to tell about an alleged error of not notifying all of the publishing firms in the area. Page 153 of the 1977 AYER DIRECTORY OF PUBLICATIONS at the marine base was missing, she said she later learned, and that it had contained the name and address of Laguna Publishing Company. Spitaleri had somehow learned about the bids being sent out, she said, and called her several days before the February 28 deadline to say he was interested in making a bid.

During the noon recess Dallas and I went to the Santa Ana Public Library, just a short walk from the courthouse, to check the 1977 AYER DIRECTORY OF PUBLICATIONS. Just as we had thought, there were many publishing firms on page 153 and on the other side, page 154,

117

that were also in the area. We wondered if
Pulaski had notified them that bids were being
taken when Spitaleri supposedly called her a few
days before the February 28 deadline. I made
photocopies of pages 153 and 154 and we gave
them to Birchall upon our return to the
courthouse. I pointed out that Laguna Publishing
just listed its address as P.O. Box 637, Laguna
Beach, instead of its actual address in Laguna
Hills. Birchall noticed that Spitaleri had told the
compilers of the directory that the NEWS-POST
had a circulation of 48,000. That was a "gross
lie," Birchall told us, adding that advertisers look
at such directories to decide which newspaper will
give them the most coverage. Birchall then
showed the copies to Watson, who did not want
to use them because he did not want to an-
tagonize Major Pulaski.

Dallas and I could not understand that
reasoning. Watson would not ask Pulaski if the
other allegedly omitted firms had been given a
chance, like Spitaleri, to make bids. Watson did
elicit from her, however, that she had put no
time limit on Spitaleri submitting his bid. Watson implied to the jury, of course, that several
days was more than a sufficient amount of time
and that Spitaleri then could have met the
February 28 deadline. Watson then had Pulaski
read aloud a letter she had prepared for her
superior's signature. The letter was written in
response to a letter Smith had sent to Con-
gressman Robert Badham concerning the awarding
of the FLIGHT JACKET contract to Laguna Publishing Company, which submitted its bid 30 days
after the deadline. Badham had presented the
complaint to the House Armed Services Committee in Washington, D.C. The only investigation that resulted from the complaint was that
Pulaski conducted an investigation of her own
actions, prepared a letter on the subject, and had

her superior sign it. The judge looked astonished after hearing how the U.S. Marine Corps handled complaints of alleged violations of the law. Six months after the awarding of the contract, Ken Barnes began working for the NEWS-POST.

On February 9, 1978, Watson produced in court copies of Publisher's Sworn Statements signed by Spitaleri for the year 1974. They had been used by NEWS-POST advertising salesmen to show potential advertisers what the circulation figures were for the NEWS-POST. The statements to which Spitaleri swore stated that the NEWS-POST had a circulation of 40,255. The judge would not allow the statements into evidence, however, until the signature was identified as Spitaleri's. He had yet to take the witness stand in his trial and he refused to identify the signature as his during a court recess.

The inevitable was delayed for only a short period of time. A former advertising director of the NEWS-POST called by the plaintiff identified the signature as Spitaleri's when he was cross-examined by Watson. Records from the Bonita Publishing Company in Los Angeles County were also produced by Watson, who told the court that the records were also for the year 1974, during the time that the NEWS-POST was printed by Bonita. The press run records showed that less than 30,000 copies of the NEWS-POST were printed at the time Spitaleri swore to statements that the NEWS-POST had a circulation of 40,255. During a court break that day, Carlton Smith told Dallas and me that Spitaleri was a "God-damned crook." Smith's attorney, Watson, told us that the trial was a "fiasco" in that the information elicited from the plaintiff's witnesses helped the defense more than it did Spitaleri.

Sherill Warren, a U.S. Postal Service employee based at the Laguna Hills branch, was a good example of a witness called by the plaintiff

119

who helped the defense far more. Mrs. Warren was in charge of weighing newspapers, such as the NEWS-POST, when they were brought to the post office to be mailed. McCray was trying to imply that Smith had done something wrong by reporting an irregularity in one of the NEWS-POST issues that was to be sent through the United States mail to residents in Leisure World and elsewhere. In his cross-examination, though, Watson ascertained from Warren that she would have noticed the irregularity herself when she weighed a copy of the NEWS-POST. To Watson's next question, she answered affirmatively that the post office welcomed reports from the public concerning possible cases of mail fraud. Mrs. Warren described the irregularity in that specific issue of the NEWS-POST as an "illegal pagination" because a tabloid-sized insert in the newspaper did not have the proper page numbers on it. Spitaleri stirred in his seat over the mention of "mail fraud" and "illegal pagination."

The next day, February 15, 1978, Watson presented records which showed the NEWS-POST was paid for delivering 21,000 copies of K-Mart store advertisements with the newspaper, when in reality, only 18,000 copies had been printed for distribution. The NEWS-POST had been paid about $50 for each 1,000 copies of K-Mart advertising inserts that it claimed to have distributed. A representative of Sav-On, another discount store, testified that stores usually advertise with the newspaper which gave the most circulation coverage.

The following day Watson produced for the court information concerning the California Newspaper Publishers Association (CNPA). In questioning Tom Watson, a former general manager of the NEWS-POST, attorney Watson noted that during the time Spitaleri was on the board of directors of the CNPA that Golden West was "black-balled" from joining the association. That information came after Tom Watson bragged to the jury about the NEWS-POST winning a CNPA general excellence award while he was with the newspaper. Then attorney Watson revealed that the NEWS-POST was no longer a member of the CNPA. Tom Watson, in continuing his testimony that day, said Spitaleri did not receive any checks from the NEWS-POST while he was there because Spitaleri had a full-time job as chairman of the board of Sta-Hi Corporation, a manufacturer of newspaper equipment. Attorney Watson then produced copies of cancelled checks made out to Spitaleri during that time period. In one year, they totalled more than $20,000. Tom Watson, hearing the truth come out, then explained that it was done for income tax purposes. That way Spitaleri could report to the Internal Revenue Service that his company was losing money.

Before going to court on the morning of February 20, I went to the South Coast Community Hospital in South Laguna to apply for a typesetter position advertised in THE REGISTER classified section. After determining that I did not want to work in a basement on a complicated machine I had never seen before, I returned to the hospital lobby and saw a November 24, 1977, edition of the LEISURE WORLD NEWS. It contained a story about the settlement made between Spitaleri and PCM. Spitaleri dropped PCM, Olsen and Musch from the lawsuit and paid them a "substantial sum of money," the story reported. In return, Olsen and Musch had dropped their libel lawsuit against the NEWS-POST. I did not recall seeing a NEWS-POST story about the settlement. But then again the NEWS-POST did not even have a story about the trial in progress until December 14, 1977, a full month after the trial began. By that time all the major dailies in the county had already printed stories on the subject.

The trial had been in progress for three months and still no evidence had been presented by McCray that Golden West had used unfair trade practices or that it had done so with the intent of putting the NEWS-POST out of business. One of McCray's witnesses, William Wineska, did not help Spitaleri at all. He had been advertising director for the RANCHO REPORTER and was now employed by a newspaper in El Cajon. He testified that a pool supply company in Mission Viejo had advertised in the RANCHO REPORTER until a salesman from the SADDLEBACK VALLEY NEWS had supposedly offered the company a much lower rate. Wineska said the company representative had shown him a SADDLEBACK VALLEY NEWS rate card with a rate of $1 an inch.

McCray asked Wineska about a telephone call he had received from Richard Birchall a few weeks earlier. Wineska said Birchall told him that his side was winning the lawsuit so far and that the trial was like a circus. By 4:30 p.m., the time court was adjourned each day, Wineska was still on the witness stand. He would have to return the following morning because the court had not excused him.

The following morning in court there was no Wineska on the witness stand. He had failed to return to continue his testimony. Talk about a circus, I thought. My guess that Spitaleri would then call Eggers in as a last-minute witness turned out to be correct. Eggers began by responding to McCray's questions concerning his education and background. Eggers testified under oath that he had "degrees in journalism and photography." He also said he had 55 awards from civic groups and journalism contests. Eggers even tried to include the general excellence

122

award the NEWS-POST received from the CNPA one year as one of his own personal awards. Of course, Spitaleri was on the board of directors of the CNPA that year.

I remembered looking at the plaques on the walls in Eggers' office one day while I was employed there and counting the ones that were actually journalism contest awards. There were less than a handful. All of the rest were for merely placing stories and/or photographs of various community groups in the newspaper. The groups then gave him plaques for being such a good publicist. During the afternoon recess, I wrote a short note for Watson about Eggers testifying that he was vice president of the NEWS-POST. I questioned how he could be vice president of a newspaper and not of a corporation. Only four weeks earlier there had been a story on the front page of the NEWS-POST about Eggers being "promoted" to the position of vice president of Laguna Publishing Company, not of the NEWS-POST.

When court resumed that afternoon Watson asked Eggers how he could be vice president of a newspaper. Eggers said that he had been "promoted." After further questioning, Watson showed the jury that Eggers did not know that there has to be an election to become vice president of a corporation; and Laguna Publishing Company was a corporation. When asked what his new duties as "vice president" were, Eggers said he did not yet know. He also could not say who the "president" of the newspaper was.

McCray then questioned Eggers about his attempts to have the NEWS-POST delivered by carrier to non-subscribers in Leisure World, the private retirement community in Laguna Hills. Eggers added that he had tried to have NEWS-POST reporters attend meetings of the private community and corporation held on the private

123

property. Eggers had taken photographs of other newspapers being delivered by carriers to Leisure World residences but the judge ruled that they could not be submitted into evidence.

Almost as soon as I got home I prepared six pages of typed information that Watson could use in cross-examining Eggers. I wrote that he went only to El Camino College, a junior, two-year college, so he therefore could not have "degrees in journalism and photography." I also wrote about Eggers being paid by John McDowell to work on his campaign for election to the Laguna Beach City Council in March of 1976. In addition, I noted that if Eggers were vice president of Laguna Publishing Company, what happened to the previous vice president, Marjorie Spitaleri?

The next day, February 23, the errant witness, William Wineska, returned as a very subdued man. He looked as if he had been dressed down by the judge and McCray in the court chambers. Before court reconvened, Watson indicated to Dallas that my note regarding Eggers' vice presidency certainly did help in his cross-examination the day before. Watson also assured Dallas that he "had it on Eggers" for that afternoon. With Wineska, Watson gave him all the time he wanted but he was not able to find the alleged pool supply ad that he had claimed appeared in the SADDLEBACK VALLEY NEWS after the company stopped advertising with the RANCHO REPORTER.

Watson then asked Wineska about the publishing contracts Coastline Publishers had with Birchall and Smith, and the Leisure World Foundation in 1968. In that year Wineska was employed by Coastline Publishers. He had testified earlier that the contract for the NEWS ADVERTISER (Smith and Birchall's first publication), and for the LEISURE WORLD NEWS (then owned by the

Leisure World Foundation) was combined for both publications. When questioned by Watson, Wineska said the publisher of Coastline had signed the contract. Watson then produced the contract, which was just for Smith and Birchall's NEWS ADVERTISER and was signed by the assistant publisher of Coastline, Wineska, and not by the publisher of Coastline. Wineska's credibility as a witness was now 100 percent nil.

That afternoon my heart pounded when Eggers was back on the witness stand and Watson asked him what college he had attended. Eggers said, "El Camino College," as he stirred in his seat. "Is that a junior, two-year college?" Watson asked. I could tell he was enjoying the privilege of exposing the real Eggers. Again, Eggers answered in accordance with the information I had supplied them. Further questioning by Watson caused Eggers to retract somewhat from his testimony of the day before. He now had only an associate of arts degree in photojournalism and not "degrees in journalism and photography." Juror No. 8, like several other jurors, smiled and laughed to himself. I had never seen such a reaction in him before. I remembered that when he was being questioned during jury selection that he had both a bachelor's degree and a master's degree. He undoubtedly knew the difference between those and an associate of arts degree.

My own prejudice aside, it appeared that the jury had more disdain for Eggers than any other witness that had been on the stand. They looked at him with expressions of disgust. When Watson asked Eggers if the NEWS-POST had a policy which precluded employees from working on political campaigns of candidates in the NEWS-POST circulation area, Eggers replied that he was not aware of one. Additional related questioning by Watson caused Eggers to say that the decision to allow an employee to work on a campaign would be a "management decision." And, of course, Eggers was managing editor at the time he worked on McDowell's campaign. To my knowledge, he was the only NEWS-POST employee who had ever been paid by a candidate to work on an election campaign. Watson asked the proper question for Eggers to admit he received personal remuneration to work on such a campaign. McCray then asked re-direct questions by laughing and asking Eggers on whose campaign he had worked in 1976. Eggers smiled and laughed and then said, "Jack McDowell's." Regarding the amount he was paid, Eggers answered, "Just a small amount--$200 or $300."

If that information elicited from Eggers was not impressive enough, Watson then presented the information he had alluded to earlier when he spoke with Dallas. Watson had a copy of a memo written by Laury Jaros, who had been the NEWS-POST advertising director for just a few months while I was employed there. It had been given to Eggers for him to give to Spitaleri. In the memo Jaros told of merchants not wanting to advertise in the NEWS-POST because they could not get results from that newspaper. She also told of the hostility that the management of Laguna Hills Mall showed toward the NEWS-POST. Watson's questioning showed that neither Eggers nor Spitaleri did much to correct the merchants' attitudes. It was also revealed that Eggers did not know much about advertising, even though he had earlier stated he had served several times as co-advertising director with Spitaleri and that he was in charge of all departments at the NEWS-POST.

Watson had presented to the court another memorandum only the day before. It was written by Eggers soon after he was hired by Spitaleri in 1972. Eggers wrote that he wanted to correct the "swinging door" at the NEWS-POST in regards

to the lengths of time employees remained there.
When he wrote the memo he was the only one of
about seven editorial department employees who
had been at the NEWS-POST for more than a
year. While Watson tried to show that if the
NEWS-POST had paid them more they might have
stayed longer, Eggers said there was no way to
keep reporters who wanted to join large daily
newspapers. Watson also pointed out that Eggers
had been promised $1,000 a month when Spitaleri
hired him, but that instead he had received just
$800 a month to start. It was obvious that Eg-
gers did not like Watson's line of questioning.
He even smirked and snickered when Watson was
not looking at him. The jury, though, did not
miss it. When Watson asked Eggers what the
term for the nameplate on the front page was,
Eggers responded, "Masthead." Watson was looking right at me, so I shook my head to indicate
that Eggers' answer was wrong. The nameplate
was always referred to as the "flag" in my journalism textbooks. Eggers then called the real
masthead the "staff box." It seemed that Watson
was not sufficiently self-assured about the subject
to pursue it because he then switched to another
matter.

In an attempt to counter the NEWS-POST's
image of a "swinging door" employer, McCray had
Eggers prepare a list of editorial department
employees and the number of months they had
been employed by the NEWS-POST. When Eggers
started reading the names my heart began pounding again and I tried to relax by breathing
deeply. I did not want the jury or the judge to
guess who I was by my flushed face. Of all the
names announced, mine was the only one for
which McCray prompted Eggers. McCray said,
"Jan..." Eggers then said, "Jan Brownfield, part-
time, 17 months, laid off." I was startled to
hear that I had been laid off and not terminated

127

from employment. I feared that McCray would next ask Eggers, "Is she in the courtroom now?" My fear was not realized, thank goodness.

Eggers then named William Doherty as "Bill Doherty, editorial consultant, 36 months, terminated." McCray mentioned that Ken Barnes, a former Marine, had taken Doherty's place. Before the day was over, Watson was able to ask Eggers if he had learned since the day before whether he was vice president of the newspaper or of the corporation. Eggers said that he had discussed it with someone overnight but he was still unable to say. He did testify that his new title had resulted in his taking Spitaleri's place on the board of directors of the Laguna Beach Chamber of Commerce. Watson next asked him about Marjorie Spitaleri, who was the vice president of the corporation. Eggers' answer indicated that she still had that title. It was amazing. There was no president of the newspaper, but Eggers tried to tell the court that he was the vice president of the newspaper.

Dallas and I had smiled often during Watson's examination of Eggers. Watson had noticed that because when the court was recessed that day, he came over and said that "white-haired juror No. 16," meaning Dallas, had laughed many times in court that day. He did not know that Dallas had been the foreman each of the several times he had served on juries. Both Dallas and I were a little disappointed that Watson had not kept Eggers on the stand until the end of the day so that he would have to return on Monday morning. Watson had ended his questioning at about 4:25 p.m., just five minutes before the 4:30 p.m. adjournment. After Watson joined Dallas on his right-hand side, Sullivan then joined us and stood at Dallas' left-hand side. I had to step back into the apparent circle that was forming as Carol Watson, his daughter; and Richard

128

and Alithea Birchall joined us. We all faced Dallas as if he were a muse. He assured them that we had enjoyed listening to Eggers being cross-examined. After awhile, as everybody left, Watson turned to us and grinned when he said, "Vice president of what?"

By Monday morning I had prepared a seven-page packet of information which refuted practically everything Eggers had said on the witness stand on Thursday. The trial was not in session on Fridays in order to allow other court business to be conducted. I hoped that the defense attorneys would either be able to use the information in questioning Spitaleri or Eggers when they presented their own case, as cross-complainant, near the end of the trial. I quoted from the glossaries of four college journalism textbooks, giving the definitions of "flag" and "masthead" and pointing out how they differed sharply with Eggers' definitions.

Concerning Eggers' paid involvement in McDowell's campaign, I noted that he had received $1,000 to $1,200 remuneration, according to what McDowell had told Dallas. Also, I wrote that Eggers had come to the NEWS-POST on a weekday morning before going to San Francisco with McDowell. In his testimony Eggers had implied that a reporter other than himself had written the NEWS-POST stories about McDowell when Eggers himself was the one who actually wrote them. Sullivan's objection to Eggers' statement in court that all of the candidates had received fair and equal coverage in the NEWS-POST was sustained by the judge. My information to Watson and Sullivan also stated that McDowell's campaign story, written by Eggers, was one of the few that appeared across the top of the front page.

The rest of the seven pages noted that a story in the January 18, 1978, edition of the

129

NEWS-POST reported Eggers' "promotion" to the position of vice president of Laguna Publishing Company. It seemed as if Spitaleri had wanted to protect his wife and son Marc from possibly being called to the witness stand to testify as officers of the corporation. There was no other apparent reason for a story about the alleged "promotion" being printed during the trial.

Regarding Eggers' testimony about Doherty, I pointed out that he was "terminated" by the NEWS-POST at the time the libel lawsuit against it was settled. It appeared that the NEWS-POST wanted to dissociate itself from Doherty and any liability for stories written by him by claiming that he had just been a consultant instead of an employee. All of Doherty's bylines had stated that he was a "staff writer" just like the rest of us other employees. He was also listed in the masthead as the Laguna Hills news editor. On the witness stand Eggers falsely testified that neither Doherty nor any other NEWS-POST reporter had ever had their names listed in the masthead, or as Eggers described it, a staff box. If Doherty was an "editorial consultant," then the NEWS-POST's executive editor, Eggers, should have said his services were discontinued, rather than saying he was terminated. I also questioned why Eggers stated that I was "laid off" but that Doherty was "terminated." If I was just laid off I should have been called back to work at the NEWS-POST when a position was available, according to Webster's dictionary, and law books such as WORDS AND PHRASES.

On February 28, 1978, I wrote a description of Lynne Inglis' and Sheila Crane's work performances at the NEWS-POST because Dallas had seen them with Spitaleri in the courthouse cafeteria practicing holding their right hands up as in the manner of swearing to tell the truth. Since we presumed they would be the next witnesses, we gave the information to Sullivan. Both Inglis and Crane gave practically the same answers to questions asked by McCray. When Sullivan cross-examined her, Inglis admitted that she and Crane had been supplied with a script by Spitaleri so that they could read their answers to the questions posed by McCray.

Ken Barnes made his second appearance at the trial that day. As on his first visit, he was escorting a witness from Leisure World and was wearing hiking clothes and boots. Two ads that I had noticed in the personal section of the NEWS-POST classified ads seemed to meet his description. They read: "BACHELOR--in mid-30s wants to meet female under 40 in South Orange County to go hiking and camping. P.O. Box 2670, Laguna Hills 92653...MALE DESIRES--to meet female in So. Orange County for dancing, theatre, etc. P.O. Box 2670, Laguna Hills 92653." The address listed was that of the NEWS-POST.

Birchall was becoming very impressed with the material we supplied to him, Smith and their attorneys. He mentioned to me several times the agriculture magazine he had started six months earlier. He also showed me the book he was studying in preparation for buying a typesetting machine. Dallas informed me that Birchall asked him if I knew anything about agriculture. He also complimented Dallas on his keen perception, which would be very helpful in a salesman posi-tion for a publication, Birchall added. He was giving us all of the signs that he was interested in hiring us. But agriculture was not a main in-terest of Dallas or myself. It was comforting to know, though, that I could probably get a job with Birchall if I so desired. I would have to relocate, however, to North San Diego County where the Birchalls lived and worked. Birchall was one of the few publishers who knew what

Spitaleri was really like and therefore was more likely to hire me than was someone who believed what Spitaleri might say about me.

March 6 ushered in a very prominent person in the newspaper field to testify on Spitaleri's behalf. Edward Estlow, president of the Scripps-Howard newspaper chain headquartered in Ohio, came to California to tell the court what happens to one newspaper when another one has the bigger share of the advertising market. His answer was that the newspaper with the fewer ads is more likely to go out of business. That made sense. However, it did not necessarily mean that the more successful newspaper had violated fair trade practices to receive the lion's share of the ads. It could mean that the successful newspaper had followed wise business practices in order to survive in the free enterprise system. Because Golden West had started out on a shoestring budget, it could not afford to invest huge sums into ideas. It had to follow tried-and-true business principles. Laguna Publishing, on the other hand, had started out with hundreds of thousands of dollars and did not have to adhere as closely to wise business methods. After a while, though, Laguna Publishing had no more money to throw away on faulty ideas.

Dallas was confident that Estlow did not fly to California just to testify, as he had stated. Sure enough, as Watson interrogated him, Estlow told of how he had been studying the area with the idea of purchasing a newspaper to add to the Scripps-Howard chain. Estlow's knowledge about newspapers seemed to be very deficient. He could not give an adequate explanation concerning the difference between a shopper and a newspaper. He was also very stubborn. Estlow insisted on telling Watson that "in fact" Golden West published two newspapers and Laguna published four newspapers. In reality, Golden West was publishing three newspapers and Laguna was publishing three editions of one newspaper. After further questioning by Watson, Estlow revealed that about one year earlier a Sta-Hi salesman travelled to Ohio and gave him a copy of the Laguna-South Coast edition of the NEWS-POST. Spitaleri had resigned from his position with Sta-Hi at the end of 1974. It appeared that in 1976 or 1977 Spitaleri asked a Sta-Hi salesman to give Estlow the copy, hoping that he might be able to attract a buyer. After Estlow had completed his testimony, Spitaleri's son Marc, a senior in college, arrived with his skateboard in hand to take Estlow to the airport.

As Dallas and I left the courthouse that evening we were somewhat surprised to see juror No. 3 talking freely with Sullivan, Watson, Birchall and Smith in front of the courthouse near the street. The juror seemed upset and was talking continuously as we passed them. Dallas and I decided that the juror had been excused from serving on the jury because he had been away from his employment for almost four months. About a week earlier Dallas had told Watson that the juror was about to come "unglued" because of the way McCray was dragging the trial. The next day the judge announced that juror No. 3 had been excused for unexplained reasons. The trial had started with four alternates and there was more than a month left of the trial. Watson told Dallas that day that he was absolutely right about the jury's view of the trial. After the juror was excused he had told Watson and company that the case "should have been thrown out weeks ago."

On March 7, 1978, we were treated with listening to Spitaleri testify about the purpose of a newspaper. He said the primary purpose was to be a "watchdog on government." While he continued his dissertation, he kept his head down, but the tone in his voice was as if he were pontificating. "Let the truth be out and the people be informed...Shed light in dark corners...Report the news honestly and objectively..." Yes, he certainly did know the supposed purpose and he knew the right words to say, but Spitaleri also knew that he did none of those things. Not once during his monologue did he look straight ahead, where Dallas and I were.

During the day Dallas gave Watson a note from me suggesting that he look at the three volumes of the SOUTH COAST NEWS that Marc Spitaleri had carried into the courtroom. By looking at the volume number on the front page of one of the newspaper copies, Watson would be able to ascertain if the publisher of the SOUTH COAST NEWS, William Ottaway, had considered 1915 its starting year as the NEWS-POST did. In the note, I also pointed out that Spitaleri testified that he was a member of Sigma Delta Chi, the Society of Professional Journalists. Watson could then ask him if he knew about the society's Code of Ethics, which prohibits journalists from working on political campaigns, as in the case of Eggers and McDowell. While the age of the NEWS-POST and Spitaleri's knowledge of the Code of Ethics did not constitute any evidence about unfair business practices, the purpose of the trial, information such as that could be used to test Spitaleri's veracity in front of the jury, which would then consider his credibility on other matters.

The same day Birchall told Dallas that Spitaleri did not have an engineering degree as he had testified earlier in the trial as having. Spitaleri's wife did not even know it, Birchall said, without explaining that statement. Watson had subpoenaed Spitaleri's college transcript from Carnegie Tech in Pennsylvania. I wished that

134

they had also subpoenaed his high school records since he had also testified that he was the editor of his high school newspaper. Spitaleri had once told the NEWS-POST staff, however, that he had to pay to have the newspaper published and printed.

We wasted a trip to Santa Ana on March 8. Spitaleri had "collapsed" during the night, according to McCray. He supposedly had not called a doctor, though, until morning. Mrs. Spitaleri reportedly had told McCray that her husband also had low blood pressure. Watson remarked that he hoped Spitaleri would get well soon so that he could "work him over." The judge telephoned Spitaleri's doctor, who reported that his patient had influenza and a temperature. Smith retorted that he had to testify in the case even when he also had influenza. Perhaps the day was not totally wasted because after I returned to my Laguna Beach home that afternoon, I received a phone call from Metro News, to which I had sent my resume after seeing its ad in the SADDLEBACK VALLEY NEWS seeking a courthouse reporter. An interview was scheduled for the following Tuesday.

In court on Monday we heard Spitaleri claim a circulation statement with his signature on it was a "fraud." He and McCray seemingly tried to show the jury that the defense had made a photocopy of his signature and placed it on a phoney circulation statement. That was the statement that Watson had introduced into evidence. Spitaleri's signature on it was identified by Tom Watson, former general manager of the NEWS-POST. It was a sworn circulation statement indicating the NEWS-POST circulation was 40,255 for each edition in 1974. In reality, according to press records introduced by Watson, the NEWS-POST was having only 29,525 copies printed. At the end of the day, Spitaleri was

135

noticeably irritated when Sullivan received the judge's permission to take the notes Spitaleri had with him at the stand. Sullivan then had them marked for identification, a preliminary step to having documents introduced as evidence. Spitaleri had said they were just there to refresh his memory but the jury noticed that he shuffled some of them away before Sullivan reached the witness stand.

The following day, at Watson and Sullivan's apparent request, the judge lectured Spitaleri for about five minutes concerning his outbursts on the stand and his use of the word "fraud" in front of the jury. Many times Spitaleri's answers to questions had to be stricken from the record because they were "nonresponsive." He editorialized every answer yet claimed he did not know how to answer the questions any other way. After court was adjourned I went to the Metro News office on the second floor of the courthouse.

It seemed that I was the only one who had applied for the courthouse reporter position, which was an independent contractor job. I would be paid 75 cents an inch for published stories and an additional 10 cents an inch for stories I had edited, including my own. David Concannon and Richard Chavez, two of the business partners, were ready to hire me as an editor. They gave me two contracts to study overnight, and also told me that I would be paid an additional $50 a month as editor. The big selling point was that I could write stories during breaks of the trial I was attending. The next day I returned copies of the signed contracts.

On March 15, 1978, I wrote a note for Dallas to deliver to Watson. It concerned Spitaleri's testimony earlier in the week in which he claimed that he had contacted the public information officer at the El Toro Marine base when he "suddenly realized" that two years had elapsed and he should have received a bidding notice for the publishing contract of the FLIGHT JACKET. I also wrote that Ken Barnes, a NEWS-POST staff writer, was public information officer at the time the bidding notices supposedly were mailed. I also noted that Major Pulaski had testified that Spitaleri contacted her when he found out from several other publishers that they had received bidding notices. In addition, I wrote that in the LAGUNA PUBLISHING COMPANY vs. CAPISTRANO VALLEY PUBLISHING CORPORA-TION trial in June, Spitaleri had said his zone advertising rates were meant to be a "penalty" to advertisers. In this trial, he made it sound like an advantage, which it really was. Also, Spitaleri had said the proceeds from the sales of the Fes-tival of Arts pamphlets Laguna Publishing prepared went to philanthropic organizations in Laguna Beach. He also said members of those organizations sold the pamphlets. I informed Watson that Spitaleri's own children sold the pamphlets at the Festival grounds and that they could be bought at the NEWS-POST in person or through the mail by using an order form printed in the NEWS-POST. Concerning Spitaleri's alleged First Amendment right to deliver the NEWS-POST to those in a private community who had not subscribed to it, I wrote about Bradley Steffens. He had filed a lawsuit against the City of Laguna Beach for depriving him of his First Amendment right to sell pamphlets he had made about the Festival of Arts. Spitaleri had refused to print the story about the lawsuit, I wrote, ob-viously not wanting Steffens' pamphlets to inter-fere with Spitaleri's profits from the pamphlets Laguna Publishing made and sold. In denying Steffens' petition for an injunction, the Superior Court judge pointed out that the First Amend-ment issue had not been addressed in the decision. Another alternate juror was excused at the

137

end of the day. Just as Dallas had told Watson and Sullivan, alternate juror No. 1 said the jury could reach a verdict in a short amount of time. "Give them 15 minutes and they'll have it decided," he said in reference to the remaining jurors. It seemed that the way McCray was making the trial drag he was hoping to have a mistrial so that Spitaleri would not have to pay court costs or damages.

On Thursday, March 16, 1978, Marjorie Spitaleri made her first appearance in the courthouse since the beginning of the trial in November. On that prior occasion, she had listened only to McCray give the opening statement for Laguna Publishing. She did not stay and hear Watson tell about her husband. Now it appeared that she came to take notes for her husband while he was on the witness stand. I heard Vernon Spitaleri tell his son Marc the week before that his mother would be in some of the time the following week to relieve him of taking notes. Marc apparently needed to return to college in Claremont to work on a term paper. William Price, the attorney for Golden Rain Foundation, told us about the day that Mrs. Spitaleri's deposition was taken. Watson's questions apparently became too probing for her and she burst into tears. Spitaleri then yelled at her, "God damn it! Shut up!"

Their son Marc, who Harriet Maas said wanted to become an attorney, apparently had told her how the trial was progressing. This time she did not laugh and shake her head at Dallas and me. Though she was subdued, that did not stop her from trampling my heels as I walked into the courtroom. Before the day was over, she heard and should have learned extensively about her husband. Vernon Spitaleri testified that whenever he hired an attorney, he let the attorney do the work. When Watson replied,

"Yes, I know," juror No. 10 started laughing and bowed her head. Near the end of the day Watson proved that Spitaleri had removed the 1965 financial statement of the SOUTH COAST NEWS sales papers and replaced it with the 1966 statement. Spitaleri's action showed that he was trying to correct his error of basing his 1967 purchase price of the SOUTH COAST NEWS on out-of-date statistics. Dallas accurately predicted to me that Marjorie Spitaleri would not be back on Monday after listening to her husband on the witness stand. Watson remarked to us that Spitaleri was just "digging a deeper hole" for himself.

On March 20, 1978, Dallas and I were privileged to hear Watson read aloud the testimony Spitaleri had given concerning his education. Watson and Sullivan paid for an additional court reporter so that they could receive a transcription of the testimony sooner. Spitaleri had told the court that he had received a bachelor of science degree in engineering from Carnegie Tech. Watson introduced Spitaleri's college transcript, which showed that the college of engineering had awarded him a degree in printing. Watson asked Spitaleri to read all of the courses listed on his transcript and pointed out the lack of calculus, algebra or other similar subjects to indicate that he never studied engineering. While Watson did not ask Spitaleri to read aloud his grades, Birchall had told us earlier that he had received very few, if any, "A" grades. Spitaleri never admitted that he did not have a degree in engineering. He explained that he had tried to give the "equivalent" of the degree he had actually earned. If he really thought that was the case, why did not he explain that when he said he had a degree in engineering? Spitaleri also refused to acknowledge that he did not have a bachelor's degree in management and technical

139

engineering as he had also claimed earlier before Watson introduced his transcript.

Later in the day Watson asked him about the CNPA general excellence award that Spitaleri had been bragging about earlier. Watson then presented evidence, including letters written by Spitaleri to the CNPA, showing that Spitaleri had to ask the CNPA to give the award under what appeared to be false pretenses. The NEWS-POST, in about 1971, had entered the annual CNPA contest, but in the wrong category. The NEWS-POST had included as its newspaper circulation a shopper which it also distributed. The CNPA then notified the NEWS-POST that the circulation category it had entered was higher than its actual newspaper circulation. Spitaleri wrote to the CNPA suggesting it give the NEWS-POST a general excellence award, but not announce it at the award presentation ceremonies. He apparently just wanted to hang the plaque on the wall for the public to see, and publish a story and a photograph in the NEWS-POST announcing that it had earned the award.

Before the day was over, Watson produced photographs of the shed on Spitaleri's property in Laguna Canyon, several miles from his Emerald Bay home and on the way to the NEWS-POST offices in Laguna Hills. Spitaleri had used the wooden shed to store newspapers and advertising inserts that had not been distributed. On one of the bundles inside the shed there was a sign that read, "To P.S." Watson used a magnifying glass to read it, but Spitaleri refused to acknowledge that he could read the same thing. The front door of the shed also read, "P.S." Watson asked if those initials meant "paper shed." Spitaleri claimed that hippies in Laguna Canyon must have put the letters "P.S." on the door. He then rambled on about Dr. Timothy O'Leary and the drug users in the canyon that had been arrested many years earlier, before the photographs were taken. Watson asked, "Isn't it strange that hippies would paint ' P.S.' on a door?" Spitaleri did not find it strange at all.

The next day Watson continued to expose Spitaleri for what he was. Watson had him tell the jury that Ken Barnes was the public information officer at the Marine base before being employed as a staff writer at the NEWS-POST. Watson also asked Spitaleri about his lawsuit against Jon White, a former NEWS-POST ad salesman who left to work for the SADDLEBACK VALLEY NEWS. Watson did not have to mention the word "vendetta." The jury got the message when Spitaleri blurted out, "There was no vendetta."

It was also my fourth day working for Metro News as a stringer and editor. In checking the criminal calendar for people being arraigned in Superior Court that day, I noticed the name of Kevin Mocalis, the son of the city manager of San Juan Capistrano. He was being arraigned on drug charges. Also listed on the calendar as his attorneys were James Okazaki and Patrick Duffy. Okazaki, I recalled, was the city attorney of San Juan Capistrano. Richard Chavez, my immediate supervisor, called the DAILY SUN-POST to inform it about Okazaki's name being listed and to ask if the newspaper was interested in receiving the story by telephone in order to meet its press deadline. The newspaper was surprised and eager to receive my story, which I read over the telephone at 11:25 a.m., five minutes before its deadline. I wrote that Duffy claimed that Okazaki was not the principal attorney in the case and that Duffy was being remunerated in the normal manner as with any other client. It was exciting to have just met a daily newspaper's deadline. The time element was not much of a concern at the NEWS-

POST, then a semi-weekly newspaper.

In the Laguna Publishing trial the defense had rested and McCray was now presenting the rebuttal for the plaintiff, Spitaleri. He put Richard Manly, David Cunningham and Mike Stockstill on the witness stand one after the other. The first two had worked as staff writers and editors while I was employed at the NEWS-POST. Stockstill had preceded us. All three testified that they had written letters to the NEWS-POST thanking the management for the experience they had received there. It was inconceivable that any of them would have volunteered to write such letters. Noticeably absent were Dorothy Korber, William Doherty, Peggye Swenson and all of the others who had passed through the NEWS-POST's "swinging door." Some had probably left before Spitaleri even launched his lawsuit career and thought of soliciting such letters for use at trial. The letters did not contribute, however, to any evidence of unfair business practices allegedly committed by the SADDLEBACK VALLEY NEWS. All had left, they testified, to receive more remuneration at other jobs. Sullivan questioned Stockstill, who told the court he was hired fresh out of college, with no full-time experience, to become an editor at the NEWS-POST. Stockstill also testified that as an editor he just had responsibility for writing stories for one to three pages each week because the newspaper was the same in each regional edition except for about three pages. That testimony, elicited by Sullivan in cross-examination, helped establish that the NEWS-POST was one newspaper with several editions rather than being several different newspapers.

In the last few weeks of the trial Dallas had noticed that McCray was trying to be friendly toward him. They had even discussed a murder trial in progress in another courtroom on that floor. Unlike the Laguna Publishing trial, the murder trial was receiving nationwide publicity in the media because it was one of the first times that a physician, Dr. William Waddill, was accused of murder for performing a saline abortion on a fetus that was more than several months old. On March 28, Spitaleri himself began making friendly overtures. During a recess, he was at McCray's table orchestrating the next session as usual. As he walked back to his seat in the audience portion of the courtroom, he lamented, "It's a long haul, Dallas." McCray and Spitaleri had only talked to Dallas, though, while I was somewhere else. We could not figure out exactly what they were seeking. When Dallas told Watson about it, he could not understand the overtures either.

The same day in court we heard testimony by the president of VAC (Verified Audit Circulation). He had the results of audits conducted on the circulations of the Laguna Publishing and Golden West newspapers. In his testimony, he told the jury that the Golden West newspapers had about a 95 percent "penetration" rate in their circulation. He described that as an "excellent" rate because it meant that the Golden West newspapers were actually being distributed to the number of homes and businesses which it claimed in its circulation figures. Laguna Publishing, on the other hand, had only a 56 percent penetration rate. Each publisher who chose to have his publication's circulation audited was allowed to select the names of the competing publications to have those contacted in the survey to specify which publication they subscribed to and the reasons for their selection. Spitaleri selected the LOS ANGELES TIMES, the DAILY PILOT, THE REGISTER and one or two other publications. He did not list, however, any of the Golden West newspapers, which were his main competitors or he would not have been suing Golden West.

The following day Watson presented a chart showing the percentage of advertising THE PENNYSAVER, a shopper, had received in the past 10 years compared to the percentages Golden West and Laguna Publishing had received. THE PENNYSAVER had received a much greater percentage than the other two, according to the chart. By 1977 THE PENNYSAVER sold about $3 million worth of advertising, while Golden West and Laguna Publishing sold about $2 million and $500,000, respectively.

While earlier in the trial Spitaleri tried to imply that the defense had photocopied his signature onto a false circulation statement, the defense presented a witness who testified that a copy of the statement was in her files when she began a job in 1975. On March 30, the advertising representative of the Laguna Hills Mall told the court that the statement was in the files of her predecessor when she was hired. Another witness that day, the certified reporter who had recorded the out-of-court discussions of William Wineska and Frank Good with the defense attorneys, verified that Wineska and Good actually made the statements Watson had presented in court. By mid-afternoon, unbeknownst to Dallas and me, Watson ran out of witnesses so he rested for the defense. Later in the day, he was somewhat apologetic in telling Dallas that reason for his "inauspicious" ending.

While in the courthouse cafeteria during a court recess on April 3, Dallas was spotted by Norm Blandell, a sergeant with the Laguna Beach Police Department. He told Dallas about a story that had appeared in the TIDES AND TIMES about Chief Jon Sparks. Blandell was disgusted with Campbell for printing a story that made it sound as if it were not for Sparks the whole city

144

would fall apart. That was the way Campbell, a retired Marine officer, viewed people in uniforms. He often wrote in news stories, especially those appearing on the front page of his newspaper, "A tip of the T 'N T hat to our men in blue." The police were paid to perform public services and were paid handsomely for the much sought-after jobs on the force. That same day Ken Barnes, also a former Marine, testified in court. McCray called him to the stand and asked him when his "last arrival date" was at the El Toro Marine base. Barnes answered that it was in July of 1977. His answer was obviously meant to indicate that he had nothing to do with the awarding of the FLIGHT JACKET contract to Spitaleri. The wording of the "last arrival date," though, was very suspicious and did not eliminate the possibility that Barnes was there between February 28 and April 4, 1977, for the awarding of the contract. Watson and Sullivan were not prepared, however, to cross-examine Barnes.

All of a sudden, on April 4, Harriet Maas and Richard Birchall asked Dallas and me on separate occasions when I was planning to file a lawsuit against Spitaleri, an intention that I had revealed to them near the start of the trial in November of 1977. They were very concerned about the date I had in mind. My answer was that I would sue him soon after the trial in progress ended. Dallas and I just waited for more information to come our way and it did the very next day. While I headed toward the Metro News office during a break in the trial, Birchall invited Dallas and me to coffee in the cafeteria. The two of them got off the elevator at the third floor for the cafeteria but I had to get off at the second floor, where the Metro News office was located. During the break Birchall told Dallas he hoped that I would sue Spitaleri soon after the trial ended so that Spitaleri would not be

145

able to sell the NEWS-POST. Any potential buyer, namely Herbert Sutton of THE PEN-NYSAVER and the NEWPORT HARBOR ENSIGN, would be deterred from buying the NEWS-POST if it was involved in litigation immediately after the current lawsuit was completed.

On April 26 the jury voted 9-3 in rejecting Spitaleri's claim and 10-2 in favoring Golden West's cross-complaint. The following morning Dallas and I returned to the courthouse to hear the arguments regarding the First Amendment issue upon which the judge still needed to rule. Sitting on the hall bench that the jurors walked by into the deliberation room I saw a NEWS-POST issue from 1973 which announced it being awarded a CNPA general excellence award. Spitaleri and his second son, Eric, had been removing boxes and papers from the courtroom that morning to take back to his office. The words "General Excellence" appeared in type about two inches high and caught my attention immediately. Two men, involved in another court proceeding, were sitting on the bench next to the NEWS-POST. When I brought Dallas to the bench the two men were reading various sections of the newspaper. When they left I returned the NEWS-POST to the original position in which I had first seen it on the bench.

When Watson was informed by Dallas of the finding he started acting like he had authority over the hallway and told people not to touch the newspaper. Watson then directed Sullivan to take photographs of the newspaper with the door of the jury deliberation room in the background. Watson asked me questions about how I found the newspaper yet he did not pay attention to what I said. He finally understood the sequence of events after Dallas went back to him to explain that Spitaleri could not accuse me of planting the newspaper there because the two

146

men were sitting on the bench with the newspaper when I arrived that morning. One of the men, Thomas Lingo, a Laguna Beach Realtor, had even told me that he recognized Spitaleri as he was taking boxes and papers away that morning.

The last couple days of the trial Watson had been very uptight. In asking Smith questions on the witness stand, Watson seemingly did not have the questions or information in mind that he wanted to present to the jury. Apparently because the jury had been listening to the case for almost five months, Watson wanted to rush the last few days. The jury awarded Golden West $5,000 in actual damages and $50,000 in punitive damages for Spitaleri's unfair business practices. The $55,000 did not begin to cover Golden West's attorney's fees. Perhaps Watson would receive stock in Golden West Publishing Corporation as part of his payment.

I had prepared a story on the trial before the jury returned the verdict, just leaving blanks for the jury's verdict and the amount of damages to be awarded. When the verdict was returned I filled in the blanks and sent copies of the story to Golden West, and to the DAILY SUN-POST in San Clemente. Golden West understandably chose to write its own version for the SADDLEBACK VALLEY NEWS, the LEISURE WORLD NEWS and the CAPISTRANO VALLEY NEWS. Its version did not include any of the evidence presented against it by Laguna Publishing. Watson and Price had told Dallas that they were surprised McCray did not emphasize to the jury the conspiracy evidenced in the letters between Smith and Olsen by which Smith received a $52,000-a-year salary in exchange for Leisure World Foundation taking control of the newspapers. I was thrilled when I saw that the DAILY SUN-POST had printed the first 21 inches of the 42-inch-long story and even

147

gave me a byline. The DAILY SUN-POST had much of the same circulation area as Golden West and Laguna Publishing so it obviously did not mind printing a story of a trial between two of its competitors.

At my request, Dallas had asked Spitaleri after the verdicts were announced, "Are you going to appeal?" Spitaleri just glared at him and McCray answered, "We don't know yet." Besides having to finish my story and mail it, another reason I did not stay in the courtroom after the verdict announcement was because Watson still did not know my name. He had to ask Dallas when the episode of the 1973 "General Excellence" tale was being told to him. It was unfathomable to think that he did not know my name after five months of sitting in the courtroom and providing him with much beneficial information, albeit in the form of unsigned memos, which he had used in the trial. Even his clients were on a first-name basis with me.

Watson had learned, though, that Dallas and I were right about many things which perhaps affected the trial's outcome. Early in the trial Dallas told Watson that juror No. 11 did not like Watson at all. It was evident in her facial reactions while he questioned witnesses. But he had not noticed. It seemed that she was the one who had prevented the jury from reaching a verdict earlier. After the fifth day of deliberations she did not return to the courthouse, reporting that her baby was sick. The last remaining alternate then took her place and within a few hours the verdicts were reached. Golden West had gotten by on the skin of its teeth. A vote of 9-3 was the greatest differential allowed in a civil trial in state court. The DAILY PILOT quoted Smith as saying "we never doubted" that Golden West would win. He had been very worried not only about the trial's outcome, but

148

also by his wife's filing a petition for a legal separation shortly before the verdict was reached.

It was not surprising that the NEWS-POST did not have a story about the jury's verdicts. It had already been reported in other newspapers, including the LOS ANGELES TIMES and THE REGISTER. On April 29, 1978, THE REGISTER printed a partial retraction of the story it had printed two days before. In its first story it said Spitaleri had been found to have misrepresented his newspaper's circulation and sold advertising below cost. The second story said that it had erred in making that report, and that the jury had actually found Spitaleri to have used unfair business practices by sending out leaflets misquoting the circulation figures of Golden West. It seemed that Spitaleri had convinced Clarence Hoiles, publisher of THE REGISTER and called as a witness by Spitaleri during the trial, to change the story.

After most of the other newspapers had already printed a story about the verdicts, the NEWS-POST finally printed not a story but an editorial about the outcome on the front page of its May 3 edition. Just as at the beginning of the trial in November when other newspapers had stories about the trial commencing, the NEWS-POST did not have a story until about a month later and then gave the impression that the trial had just started. Spitaleri's editorial began, "As a matter of principle we believe that legal differences should not be tried in the press." He certainly did not follow that principle in the Leisure World edition of the NEWS-POST a few years earlier when he devoted a full page to his legal quest to deliver unsolicited copies of the NEWS-POST to non-subscribers residing in the private retirement community. His editorial continued with, "In view of the considerable amount of misinformation and distortion of facts published

149

in the area press this past week we feel compelled to at least set the record straight." Spitaleri's editorial, not other newspapers' stories, was distorted and false. He mentioned only the 9-3 vote, which showed three of 12 jurors in his favor, and not the 10-2 vote in the cross-complaint against him.

It was sickening, but not surprising, to read his editorial, which ended with, "In addition to the constitutional issues yet to be tried by the court we plan to continue this legal battle until a final decision is reached based on the facts, the evidence, and the law and not on any trumped up, irrelevant emotional issues used as a smoke screen to cloud the real issues. We feel confident that true justice will ultimately prevail." It was Spitaleri who tried to cloud the issues of fact and law with such an emotional and irrelevant issue as his receiving three Purple Hearts in World War II on his way to the American Newspaper Publishers Association.

McCray had been quoted in another newspaper as saying the reason he lost the trial was because Judge Charamza refused to let him argue the free press constitutional issue to the jury. "In order to prove conspiracy we had to show the overt acts and we couldn't do that without mentioning the constitutional issues," he said. But Charamza was the judge who would rule on the First Amendment issue at a separate hearing on May 8. After two and one-half days of argument, Charamza ruled on May 10 that Laguna Publishing had no constitutional right to enter Leisure World and distribute free, unsolicited, copies of the NEWS-POST. "I'm not to rule on the rights of the Leisure World residents. That's not the case before me," Charamza stated. He concurred with Golden Rain and Golden West that owners of private property may exclude from their property people asserting

First Amendment rights.

At the first day of the hearing Smith had thanked me for the "very nice story" I had written about the trial for Metro News and which had appeared in the DAILY SUN-POST. As usual, the NEWS-POST did not print anything about its injunction application being denied by Charamza. The other newspapers printed the judge's ruling, not minding one bit to print a story about a competitor losing in court. The DAILY SUN-POST printed my follow-up story and again gave me a byline.

The TIDES AND TIMES, Laguna Beach's self-proclaimed "hometown newspaper," had not printed anything about the NEWS-POST's legal battles. On April 14, 1978, shortly before the trial ended, Campbell gave Dallas a story I had written in September for him about allegedly illegal towing activities in the city. I had asked for the story back in November because Campbell had not printed it and he had not paid for it. All of a sudden he found the "lost" story, which he had typeset before deciding not to publish it. A week later, in the April 20 edition of the TIDES AND TIMES, the byline of "Mayor Jack McDowell" appeared with the top story on the front page. He reported that the City had agreed to purchase Sycamore Hills for $6.74 million through a soon-to-be-formed non-profit corporation, thereby ending the Rancho Palos Verdes Corporation lawsuits seeking $37 million from the City. The plan had been reported days earlier in other newspapers but the TIDES AND TIMES was the only one that let McDowell write his own story. Campbell was not what one would call a watchdog on government. And it seemed very clear that Councilman Jon Brand was right when he called McDowell a "traitorous liar" working for the other side, meaning Rancho Palos Verdes, as reported in several other newspapers.

Now that Laguna Publishing's courtroom battles appeared to be over for a while, Dallas and I could spend time concerning my own legal concerns. Dallas telephoned Smith, asking if he could recommend an attorney who could take my civil rights case. Smith responded by saying Watson was busy with other clients that had been somewhat neglected during the five-month trial. Watson, who was 60 years old and was city attorney for several cities in Los Angeles County, had excellent ratings for his legal ability, according to the MARTINDALE-HUBBELL directory of attorneys in the United States. Dallas suggested that we were also interested in challenging the NEWS-POST's legal adjudication. Smith, though, said that Golden West planned on doing that and that Mitchell Abbott, a 26-year-old attorney in Watson's law firm who had been a special assistant to U.S. Senator John V. Tunney, was researching the matter. If Watson was such a good attorney, we wondered if Smith did not question why they had not considered challenging the NEWS-POST's legal adjudication until now. Before the trial had begun we gave Smith a copy of one of the NEWS-POST's Affidavits of Publication of legal notices, claiming it was published and printed in the City of Laguna Beach when it was actually published in Laguna Hills and printed in Los Angeles County. Before then, Watson had told Smith and Dallas that the NEWS-POST received the legal notices because of a grandfather clause in the law. But Watson had not even bothered to check the NEWS-POST's affidavits on file with the Laguna Beach city clerk until we gave them a sample copy. McCray's portrayal of Smith as "Napoleonic" was correct, according to Birchall. Smith had gotten what he wanted and now we were of no more value to him.

Dallas also contacted William Price, the attorney who defended Golden Rain Foundation in the trial. Like Watson, he was given excellent ratings in the MARTINDALE-HUBBELL directory. Fifty-three years old, he had several years of experience in the federal courts, as evidenced by his role as an assistant U.S. attorney for the District of Columbia in the 1950s. Price said he did not have enough time to do my case justice and recommended another attorney, William Dougherty of Tustin. His ratings were not as excellent as Watson's and Price's, but he had received much publicity for representing Christopher Boyce, THE FALCON, convicted for selling defense secrets to the Soviet Union. Dougherty had worked for the U.S. Attorney's Office in Los Angeles and was a certified criminal law specialist. My telephone call and letter to his office were never answered.

Believing that other journalists would be interested in hearing about the legal battle I had witnessed between two newspaper publishing corporations, I submitted a story about the trial to THE QUILL, the magazine published by Sigma Delta Chi, the Society of Professional Journalists. My story was returned, however, by Halina Czerniejewski, associate editor. She wrote that she had consulted with Editor Charles Long and they had agreed the story was more about business practices than about the First Amendment. That was the reason they gave for not printing a story about a publisher, Spitaleri, who had held top positions with the American Newspaper Publishers Association, Knight-Ridder newspapers and Sta-Hi, the newspaper equipment firm. THE QUILL was filled with stories that had nothing to do with the First Amendment. The EDITOR & PUBLISHER magazine did not mind printing a story about the trial that just seemed to contain information from Spitaleri. Printed in the July 10, 1978, edition of the magazine, the short story on the last page reported that Spitaleri's attorneys would be seeking a new trial or appeal the decision. Golden West seemingly had not been contacted before the story was printed because it contained such false statements as the allegation that the LEISURE WORLD NEWS, published by Golden West, was "the only newspaper allowed inside the retirement village" of Leisure World. In reality, any newspaper was allowed to be delivered by carrier there if it was being sent to a subscriber.

Chapter 5

During one of my trips to the Orange County Law Library to research the law and cases related to my civil rights claim, I found two appropriate books published by the American Civil Liberties Union (ACLU). They were entitled AN ACLU HANDBOOK: THE RIGHTS OF REPORTERS and THE ENGINEERING OF RESTRAINT. I was assured by the first book that "if legal assistance becomes necessary the ACLU and its local offices throughout the country are ready to represent or support any reporter whose First Amendment rights are being infringed." The second book documented the Nixon Administration's attempt to control the press. Fred Powledge, the author, wrote, "Attacks on the press by officers of government have become so widespread that they constitute a massive federal level attempt to subvert the letter and the spirit of the First Amendment."

From experience I knew that such pervasiveness was also present at the local level of government. Encouraged by the ACLU's view of the government and the rights of reporters, I contacted the Orange County chapter of the ACLU. My request for legal representation was sent to the lawyers committee, which was composed of a few attorneys and law students who met at the law library once a month to discuss civil rights litigation.

Lewis Sandler, a 28-year-old law student at Western State University in Fullerton, was the only one in the group, he later told me, who was interested in helping me. As it turned out, a relative of his had told him that reporters should be supported in their attempts to be watchdogs on government. After meeting with Sandler in the summer of 1977 and discussing the conspiracy against me by the Laguna Beach city government and Laguna Publishing Company, he told me that he could authorize ACLU funding of the costs of such a case to vindicate my First Amendment rights. The ACLU, however, would not be able to provide an attorney or attorney's fees. So much for the ACLU standing ready throughout the country willing to "represent or support any reporter whose First Amendment rights are being infringed." I did not consider Sandler's offer to be official or authoritative since he was only a law student and he did not supply me any written guarantee of funding. Concerned about the statute of limitations, the time within which I could file a lawsuit, I was told by Sandler that I had more than one year from the date of my dismissal to file the lawsuit. He did not know what the time limit was, however.

It was now May of 1978, more than a year since I was removed from the editorial department of the NEWS-POST and then dismissed from the production department, not to mention relieved of my independent contractor duties distributing the newspaper to racks. I had been working for Metro News at the courthouse for about two months when Richard Chavez, my immediate supervisor, told me about a former REGISTER staff writer who had become a civil rights attorney. I telephoned the attorney, George Comroe, at his Anaheim office and told him about my case. He invited me to come to his office later that day for a free consultation. Before going there I checked the MARTINDALE-HUBBELL directory of attorneys which listed their birthdates, schools attended and the years they were admitted to the state bars to practice law. I found out that Comroe was 61 years old and had been an attorney for two years, since shortly after graduating from the Western State University in Fullerton in 1976. When I met with him in his office he told me that the one-year statute of limitations had already expired and that I should have taken my complaint to the Equal Employment Opportunities Commission within the first 180 days that I knew my civil rights were being violated. Comroe also said the ACLU was negligent in telling me I had more than one year to file my lawsuit. He had attended some of the ACLU lawyers committee meetings and had surmised that the members just played with people's cases and did not help them.

My heart sunk when Comroe told me that I had no choice but to do nothing. For 18 months I had lived to file a lawsuit against the Spitaleris, Eggers and Scholl for violating my rights and blackballing me in the newspaper field. Every day, day and night, that was my prayer and dream. Before the long drive, about 35 miles, from Comroe's office to Laguna Beach was over, I had shed a few tears. When I told Dallas Anderson what Comroe had said, he stated that he had not trusted the ACLU and that I should not have taken my case there in the first place. But I had been concerned about a one-year statute of limitations I had read about and only went to the ACLU after 11 months had expired since I was removed from the NEWS-POST editorial department in November of 1976. Within 24 hours Dallas had again researched my case at the law library and told me that Comroe was wrong and that I had at least a three-year statute of limitations for filing a lawsuit for conspiracy to violate my civil rights.

With the knowledge that I had three years to file a lawsuit, I could wait until the end of November of 1979 to do so. In the meantime, I continued to try to find more gainful employment in the journalism profession. At Metro News I was only receiving approximately $300 a month. I also had time to read other books besides ones at the law library. I found a 1977 book entitled THINKING BIG, which is about the LOS ANGELES TIMES and was written by two outsiders, Robert Gottlieb and Irene Wolt. The book showed how the publishers of the TIMES, the Chandler family members, were responsible for much of the development of Los Angeles. The book also cited the lack of sufficient newspaper competition for its ability to wield much power in controlling the area politics.

There was too much competition in Orange County for local news as Metro News found out after just a year. In September of 1978, after I had been with the news service for just six months, Chavez told me it was going out of business because they were not able to get enough subscribers. Metro News owed me several hundred dollars from previous months because Chavez had been paying his long distance telephone bills with the income from newspapers that printed my stories.

Laguna Publishing Company was also suffering financially. At the end of September, 1978, Judge Charamza denied Laguna Publishing's motion for a new trial. On October 7, 1978, I noticed one of Eggers' "Sidelines to the News" columns published in the NEWS-POST under the headline, "Unbelievable Week: Is It Over?" Eggers began the column with the following:

"I knew last Friday that this was going to be a tough week. There I was, Friday night, pondering the realization that once again I would be pounding the streets of the Laguna Beach beat for the News-Post.

"Now the thought of covering the Art Colony doesn't frighten me. I've been through the high-rise fight, numerous city council and school board elections and the ever popular fight over dogs on the beach.

"Granted this sleepy little resort town, excuse me, village, has a reputation of eating green reporters, but I knew I could handle it. After all, I had seen it all in the last six years."

The column continued in the same tone for another 18 paragraphs. The part that interested me was that the City of Laguna Beach had a "reputation of eating green reporters." It reminded me of the "swinging door" testimony at the LAGUNA PUBLISHING COMPANY vs. GOLDEN WEST PUBLISHING CORPORATION trial. I also thought of the "stronger person" Spitaleri had announced was going to be covering the Laguna Beach city government. That reporter, Dorothy Korber, stayed on the Laguna Beach beat for two months, until February 15, 1977, before leaving the newspaper completely. After graduating that same year from San Francisco State University with a degree in English literature, Marshall Krantz began covering the Laguna Beach beat later in February. He stayed 16 months, the same amount of time I had been a full-time employee there, before he left the NEWS-POST.

159

The next so-called "green reporter" was Ken Barnes, who had been a subject of testimony at the Laguna Publishing trial. Covering the Laguna Beach beat for just four months, he left in October of 1978. For an unknown reason Eggers was returned to a reporting position even though he retained his title of executive editor. He had joined the NEWS-POST in 1973 and had been the Laguna Beach writer for approximately 24 months before I began my internship in July of 1975 and started assuming his reporting duties.

I was not able to find employment as a reporter. While Eggers had testified in court that I had been "laid off," the NEWS-POST never contacted me about the openings in the editorial department. The NEWS-POST would not have to just hope that a new reporter would cover the Laguna Beach beat the "right" way. Because he did not have a formal journalism education, Eggers did not have to be told to skip the textbook approach when covering the Laguna Beach city government. Seeking any suitable employment in October of 1978, I went to the state Employment Development Department and examined the job descriptions posted on the bulletin board. The only job that interested me was that of a paralegal for a law firm which dealt with medical issues. Haight, Dickson, Brown and Bonesteel was conveniently located at Newport Center, just six miles northwest of Laguna Beach. Impressed with my writing experience, the law firm hired me to write summaries of plaintiffs' medical records. I felt somewhat secure in taking the job because I had spent so much time observing two trials and because I had reviewed many court files in writing stories for Metro News. Since I had not yet been paid the money owed by Metro News, I filed a small claims court action in Santa Ana on October 23, 1978, the day before I began working for the law firm. On November 13, 1978, just

160

two weeks on my new job, it was necessary that I go to the courthouse in Santa Ana for the hearing. When the judge asked me the nature of the stories I had written for Metro News, everyone in the courtroom laughed when I said, "About lawsuits and trials such as this." The judgment was entered in my favor and the judge gave the defendants until the end of the month to pay me.

My starting pay as a paralegal was $800 a month, which was $300 a month more than my starting salary at the NEWS-POST as a newspaper reporter with a bachelor's degree in journalism. While working in the legal profession I hoped that I would be able to learn more about lawsuits and be in a better position to select a capable attorney to represent me in my civil rights lawsuit.

One of the few journalists in Southern California whom I thought was best serving the public interest lambasted the media itself in a commentary delivered on Channel 2, a subsidiary of the CBS television network. Bill Stout, who worked at the Los Angeles station, criticized the local media, including his own station and the LOS ANGELES TIMES for failing to report on corruption in government. On a previous Sunday evening "60 Minutes," the national investigative television news program on CBS, had aired a segment exposing corruption among the officials of GLACAA (Greater Los Angeles Community Action Agency). Stout was very disturbed by the fact that it took a team of reporters whose beat is the world to expose a scandal based in Los Angeles. Stout chastised the TIMES and the local station for ignoring complaints brought to them earlier by GLACAA employees making charges against GLACAA officials using federal funds for their own personal use instead of for the poverty-stricken residents for whom they were intended. Stout continued to attack the TIMES for then printing only a small story about the fraud several days after the "60 Minutes" broadcast. The criticism was justified and I am glad that there is at least one person in the journalism profession who shares my belief that the news media is not serving the public.

The news establishments in Orange County fare even poorer than those in Los Angeles, in my opinion. Like the NEWS-POST, most of the newspapers seem to cater to their advertisers and do not really want to serve the public if it means the loss of any income. The press avoids controversial stories unless they are politically expedient in their direction. The record at the Orange County Courthouse revealed that Spitaleri had filed an appeal to the jury's verdict in his lawsuit against Golden West Publishing Corp. The transcript of the five-month trial would cost $23,000, according to the court reporter. I did not see any story about the appeal in the NEWS-POST or any other newspaper serving the area.

I continued to seek an attorney to represent me in a lawsuit against Spitaleri and the others. The Reporters Committee for Freedom of the Press gave me the name of Stephen Rohde, an attorney in Beverly Hills. Rohde wanted a retainer of $5,000 to $7,500 before he would work on the case. His estimate was based on the number of depositions, approximately 10, which he believed would need to be taken during the discovery process after a complaint was filed in court. Rohde had previously represented a film maker in a case completely different from mine; and that seemed to be Rohde's experience in working with the press. He did claim that he was well acquainted with Fred Okrand, legal director of the ACLU Foundation of Southern California, headquartered in Los Angeles. Rohde offered to contact Okrand for funding of the anticipated costs of my suit, which were separate

162

from attorney's fees, because I did not have any confirmation from the Orange County chapter of the ACLU that it would financially assist me. Rohde suggested that we contact the Reporters Committee for Freedom of the Press and the Society of Professional Journalists for financing his estimated attorney's fees of $5,000 to $7,500. Since Rohde knew Jack Landau, director of the reporters committee, he decided to write him a letter requesting funds. I agreed to write to the society for funds as well. A 1970 graduate of the Columbia University law school in New York, Rohde seemed confident that he could successfully litigate my case.

That evening, November 15, 1978, I was watching the Channel 11 television news at 10:30 when I saw Stanley Scholl being interviewed. When I found out the subject of the news story, I could see that his idea of news had not changed since leaving Laguna Beach. He was telling the reporter that certain types of garbage bins were dangerous and that the City of Santa Monica, his current employer, was trying to correct the hazard. I could not help but wonder if it was Scholl who contacted the television station with such a big story or if it had been the other way around as it had been with the NEWS-POST.

In my correspondence to the Society of Professional Journalists seeking funds to sue Scholl and the others, I told Russell Hurst, the executive director, that I well recognized that a commercial establishment has, in most instances, the right to terminate employment for cause. When, however, that commercial establishment is a newspaper and terminates an employee without cause but because of governmental interference and conspiracy, the First Amendment of the Constitution is violated and the civil liberties of the terminated employee have been infringed. In my own perusal of THE QUILL, the society's monthly

163

magazine mailed to members such as myself, I knew that the Legal Defense Fund had little more than $6,500, and that the Reporters Committee for Freedom of the Press had just received an unrestricted grant of $150,000 from the Knight Foundation. Consequently, it seemed that the reporters committee was more financially able to provide assistance.

Because the legal fund was "quite small," Hurst wrote to tell me on March 8, 1979, that the society would not be able to provide me with any financial assistance. He added that "contributions in the past few years have been limited, for the most part, to the more clear-cut freedom of information-type cases involving open meetings and open records laws. Our officers do not feel that your case fits into that admittedly rather narrow, but necessary, definition. We simply do not have the resources to expand into other areas for now." I knew that Hurst's reasoning was faulty and to prove it to myself I reviewed my back issues of THE QUILL, which reported contributions from the legal fund to various entities. From December of 1976 through January of 1979 financial contributions had been made to at least 15 cases that were not designated as "open meetings and open records laws" matters. I could find only five contributions noted for "open meetings and open records laws" cases. In spite of the conflict between Hurst's logic and the published record, there was nothing I could foresee doing to change his mind. The society just did not have much money to give away.

I had only asked the society for financial assistance. I had not asked for a legal opinion about the merits of my case. Not knowing that Hurst had already responded to my correspondence, Scott Aiken, chairman of the society's Freedom of Information Committee, wrote to me on April 20, 1979, from his place of employment, THE CINCINNATI ENQUIRER. His letter, in full, read as follows:

"The executive officer of the Society of Professional Journalists, Russell E. Hurst, has asked me to look into your request for assistance in dealing with your dismissal by the Laguna Beach newspaper.

"I am doubtful that we can do much to help you. The Society of Professional Journalists does not involve itself in employer-employee relations generally.

"The one area in which we do believe we have a right to speak up is that of freedom of the press. That is, if an employer seeks to dictate the contents of a news story so as to breach the professional ethic of fairness and of factual reporting we would seek to help the reporters and editors.

"But embodied in the principle of a free press--and in the principles of a free society--is the right of the employer to dismiss an employee whose job is not protected by the National Labor Relations Act. It is also the right of the employee to 'dismiss' an employer. That there can be wrongs done, especially to the employee, I have no doubt at all.

"I know this is small comfort to you. I shall let you know what the result is of our examination of your particular case."

I never did hear from Aiken again. I am sure that he did not bother to research the law about the First Amendment and conspiracies. Nor do I believe that he ever researched cases similar to mine. If he had done either he might have discovered that the First Amendment is not just for a church, a news establishment or any group to freely worship, write or assemble. The First Amendment was meant to give every individual the right to free expression. Shortly before

165

receiving Aiken's letter I had received a form letter from the society seeking financial contributions to the Legal Defense Fund. The letter proclaimed that the society "has been the acknowledged leader for decades in assuring that the public's business is conducted in public--and that First Amendment rights are asserted and protected." Since my request to the society was for financial assistance to assert my First Amendment rights, there was no logical reason for me to receive a legal opinion from Aiken, who was concerned with freedom of information, not freedom to report without governmental interference.

The NEWS-POST had aligned itself with the Laguna Beach city government to suppress my rights to report without illegal intrusion. My opinion that the NEWS-POST was trying to please the government was enforced when I saw an article in the NEWS-POST announcing that Jill Solomon, the wife of City Manager Fred Solomon, was the new lifestyles editor. Also, if I had truly been "laid off" from employment, I should have been contacted about such a job opening. None of my relatives, however, were employed by the City of Laguna Beach.

At least Rohde seemed to understand the First Amendment right that I was claiming. In his letter to Landau of the reporters committee, he wrote, "We believe that the case presents a sinister example of the management of a newspaper becoming dependent upon government largess to the detriment of the independence of its reporters." I had read of Landau and seen him on television concerning court decisions he considered to be setbacks for the First Amendment. It was possible that the American public was not aware of the need of the society and others for financial assistance to preserve the rights guaranteed by the First Amendment. It was also possible that many Americans resented the idea that many reporters talked of the First Amendment as if it was just meant to protect the news establishments and not citizens as individuals. Even indirectly, the First Amendment benefits the public because when the press and reporters are allowed to freely report the news, the public is then better informed about its government.

Several months had passed and Rohde had not received any response from Landau or anyone else at the reporters committee. I had been in contact with Rohde for 10 months and the three-year statute of limitations for filing a lawsuit would expire in approximately six months. He was not interested in writing on my behalf to another group, the Clarence Darrow Foundation, to seek financial support for my lawsuit. I had read about the group, which was established in 1977 to finance litigation involving the First Amendment and to recognize individuals exemplifying the goals and ideals for which Clarence Darrow, an attorney, had fought. It was an ad hoc group based in Los Angeles and Ramona Ripston of the ACLU was the executive director. I apparently had just wasted my time with Rohde. I telephoned Fred Okrand of the ACLU regarding the alleged agreement he made with Rohde that the ACLU would pay certain court costs for my case. Okrand said he never heard of Rohde and that the ACLU could not provide court costs or refer me to an attorney. Okrand denied that the ACLU had a roster of volunteer attorneys even though I saw mention of one in a LOS ANGELES TIMES article.

To follow through on Rohde's request to the reporters committee, I visited its offices in Washington, D.C., in June of 1979 after a business trip to New Jersey for the law firm of Haight, Dickson, Brown and Bonesteel. Larry

Marscheck, a friend and fellow journalism graduate from Pepperdine University, lived in Washington, D.C., and worked as manager of publications and editor of George Washington University's alumni magazine. On a Saturday morning he accompanied me to the reporters committee offices where representatives had no knowledge of me or my First Amendment case even though Rohde had written to them. They provided me with the names, addresses and telephone numbers of three attorneys in Southern California who were listed on the committee's roster. Back in California I was unable to locate any of the attorneys.

Two months later I was very surprised to receive a telephone call at work from Ann Christman of the reporters committee in Washington, D.C. It was her second to the last day working as an intern and she had come across Rohde's letter and the summary of my case. Explaining that she got my telephone number from Rohde's office, Christman apologized profusely for the delay in responding to his letters, the last of which was dated April 9, 1979. It was now August. Christman agreed that I had a First Amendment case and would try to have Jack Landau call me concerning my request for financial aid. She admitted that the committee probably could not provide such assistance but could at least refer me to an attorney who would handle my case without charge. She suggested I call the committee in a few weeks since Landau was out of town just then. On August 22 I called to speak to Landau but instead spoke with Peter Lovenheim, a 26-year-old attorney hired two months earlier to do freedom of information research for both the Reporters Committee for Freedom of the Press and the Society of Professional Journalists. He suggested I call after Labor Day when Landau was expected to return.   On September 5 I again reached Lovenheim instead of Landau.   Although I did not ask him for his opinion concerning my case, Lovenheim proceeded to tell me that I did not have a First Amendment case because an employer has a right to "fire" an employee.   It took my time, expense and effort to conclude that neither the committee nor the society could be counted on to help a journalist in need. Those two groups were supposed to be the pillars of the journalism profession, yet they displayed so much ignorance about the First Amendment, which was the reason for their existence and the right for which they devoted much of their own energy.   They limited the First Amendment's protection to such cases as closed meetings, closed records, gag orders and subpoenas.

Besides doing legal research regarding my case and other illegalities concerning the Laguna Beach city government, Dallas Anderson had also been trying to find an attorney to represent me. It had been almost three years since my dismissal from the NEWS-POST.   Dallas could have gone to law school himself in that time period and then represented me in my case.   A year earlier Dallas had done legal research and found out that the City of Laguna Beach's plan to purchase Sycamore Hills for $6.75 million from Rancho Palos Verdes Corp. violated Article 16, Section 18, of the state Constitution because the amount exceeded the City's annual revenue.   Ronald Steinberg, a Laguna Beach resident, had gone to court to seek an injunction to block the sale. City Attorney George Logan had told the city council that the sale would be legal.   Dallas asked Steinberg if his attorney, Roger Golden of Los Angeles, knew that the proposed sale was unconstitutional.   More than once Dallas had told the city council at public meetings that the sale would violate the state Constitution.   Steinberg asked Golden, who decided that the law had been repealed. By the time of the court hearing in July of 1978, Golden had found out that Dallas was right but it was too late to include it in his written brief. Judge James Judge, who had presided over the jury trial of LAGUNA PUBLISHING COMPANY vs. CAPISTRANO VALLEY PUBLISHING CORP., told Golden that an oral citation of the state Constitution was not sufficient. The judge let the May 30, 1978, purchase agreement stand and Steinberg chose not to appeal the case even though Dallas told him that an unconstitutional act does not have to be cited in writing, that judicial notice is sufficient. Months later City Attorney Logan requested a legal opinion from the law firm of Stradling, Yocca, Carlson and Rauth concerning the sale. Thomas Clark of the firm wrote on January 23, 1979, in a confidential letter to Logan, that Article 16, Section 18, of the state Constitution made the sale illegal. On June 26, 1979, Councilwoman Sally Bellerue was quoted in the DAILY PILOT as saying that the purchase was unconstitutional, according to another letter prepared by the new city attorney from the law firm of Rutan & Tucker. The press did not mention then or a year earlier that the city council had been told several times by Dallas that the sale would be unconstitutional. It was just another example of the press not doing its job in investigating and reporting on illegalities in city government. On June 28, 1979, the DAILY PILOT quoted Councilmen Jack McDowell and Kelly Boyd in criticizing Bellerue for taking council problems to the public. Neither one of them was quoted, however, concerning the fact that the council had violated a section of the state Constitution, which along with the United States Constitution, they had sworn to uphold when they took their oaths of office.

170

McDowell, as I already knew, objected to an open government. In an editorial, the DAILY PILOT criticized McDowell for breaking his promise to keep the public informed concerning the $6.75-million purchase of Sycamore Hills. The editorial quoted McDowell as saying, "I think it would be all wrong for (citizens) to get out in front on things...and by so doing have the excitement that tends to want to destroy a good plan (Sycamore Hills) by criticizing it and constantly taking advantage of the opportunity to come to the floor at council meetings and criticize." The DAILY PILOT had made a 180-degree turn in its treatment of McDowell, who still was able to command favorable press treatment from the NEWS-POST at least. The editorial concluded by telling McDowell that allowing input from the citizens is the "purpose of city council meetings...It's called open government." McDowell's dictatorial manner reminded me of Nikolai Lenin's similar viewpoint of wanting to govern without any negative comments from the citizenry.

The Laguna Beach city government very well knew that ideas were dangerous. The city council expressed displeasure whenever Dallas pointed out the illegalities it was committing. Howard Miller, the Rancho Palos Verdes Corp. consultant who attended all of the city council meetings, told Dallas that if he had not stressed the unconstitutionality of the Sycamore Hills purchase, that it would have gone through as planned. It was just one week after the City had failed to make a payment on the purchase that Bellerue announced publicly that the sale was illegal. Now Miller was warning Dallas that "they" were going to put a contract out on him if he did not stop trying to make the city government handle the matter according to law.

Roger Golden, the attorney who had ignored

171

Dallas' information about the Sycamore Hills purchase violating the state Constitution and as a result his client lost the case but still had to pay Golden his fees, was suggested by Dallas as an attorney who might be able to represent me in my fight against the city government and the NEWS-POST newspaper. Dallas thought that since Golden had been proven wrong in that instance that he would be more likely to accept advice and information in the future regarding my case. Dallas accompanied me to my meeting with Golden at his office in a luxury high-rise building in Century Park East in Los Angeles. Thirty-one years old and a graduate of UCLA's law school, Golden discussed my case with us and said he understood the legal theories and facts. He was willing to take the case if that was my desire, which it was. At that time I had not yet read consumer activist David Horowitz's book FIGHT BACK! which warns about young attorneys claiming to be knowledgeable and competent to handle almost any type of case.

I subsequently sent a four-page summary of cases related to mine which Dallas and I had researched at the law library. I also cited some of the applicable laws for bringing the First Amendment case to the federal courthouse in Los Angeles. They included Title 42, Section 1983 of the UNITED STATES CODE, which prohibits conspiracies done "under the color of law" (meaning a government official or employee was involved). Federal laws are cited by title and section in the UNITED STATES CODE, the codification of federal laws, arranged by chapters. When cited in a brief filed with a court the law would be written as 42 U.S.C. 1983. On October 9, 1979, I received the fruits of my $1,500 retainer fee to Golden. He had prepared a 14-page memorandum based on his legal research and cited 42 U.S.C. 1983, which Dallas and I had read many times in

172

relevant cases at the law library. Entitled Section 1983 of Title 42 of the UNITED STATES CODE, "Civil Action for Deprivation of Rights," it reads as follows:

"Every person who, under color of any statute, ordinance, regulation, custom, or usage, or any state or territory, subjects, or causes to be subjected, any citizen of the United States or other person within the jurisdiction thereof to the deprivation of any rights, privileges, or immunities secured by the Constitution and laws, shall be liable to the party injured in an action at law, suit in equity, or other proper proceeding for redress."

As agreed, I would be paying Golden $75 an hour, which I would pay at the rate of $500 a month, in addition to all costs. On November 27, 1979, the complaint was finally filed in United States District Court in Los Angeles, four days before the three-year statute of limitations expired. The 12 named defendants were the City of Laguna Beach; council members John McDowell, Carl Johnson Jr., Jon Brand, Sally Bellerue and Phyllis Sweeney; Municipal Services Director Stanley Scholl, City Manager Alfred Theal; Laguna Publishing Company, Vernon and Marjorie Spitaleri and Thomas Michael Eggers. Golden had not made some of the corrections which I had sent in writing to him with my signed verification. He also dated the complaint so as to make it appear that I had read and approved the final version before I had signed and dated my verification. He left in his false assumption that Eggers was an officer of the corporation, Laguna Publishing Company. Golden had become confused by the facts that Eggers had falsely testified in court that he was vice president and that the NEWS-POST had printed a story announcing his "promotion." The Secretary of State, however, had no record of him being an

173

officer of the corporation. Just two months earlier, in September of 1979, Eggers had left the NEWS-POST to form his own public relations company with his wife Candace.

Because my lawsuit was now filed I had something concrete to send to the ACLU to try once again to seek funding or support since it supposedly stood ready, willing and able to assist reporters around the country. On January 10, 1980, Susan McGreivy, a staff attorney, wrote me the following two-sentence letter:

"Thank you for your inquiry. Unfortunately, there is not enough information available to us in your complaint to determine if there are any constitutional violations." The First Amendment to the United States Constitution apparently did not count with McGreivy.

The following month, on February 29, 1980, I read in the DAILY PILOT that Eggers had apparently left his public relations business and was the new marketing director of J.R. Phillips, a mobile home park planning firm in El Toro.

My second small claims court case went to trial on March 1 and the judgment in my favor helped boost my morale. I was awarded damages of $137.50 plus costs for hair damage that a beauty salon had caused and had refused to give me a refund before I decided to file the suit.

A more stunning victory for Dallas and me occurred on March 20, 1980, at a Laguna Beach City Council candidates' forum sponsored by the local Business and Professional Women organization. Dallas attended the forum and during the question-and-answer portion asked a question of McDowell, who was seeking reelection to the city council. Dallas asked McDowell why he had not listed Eggers on his campaign expenditures statement in 1976, the first time he ran for city council. During the 1980 campaign Eggers, who was no longer employed by the

174

NEWS-POST, was publicly listed as the campaign manager for both McDowell and Steven Riggs, another candidate for the two seats available on the council. Dallas read aloud part of Eggers' trial testimony wherein he admitted to working on McDowell's campaign brochure but that he had been paid only a small amount--$200 or $300. Dallas had tape-recorded the question-and-answer part of the forum and played it back for me to hear McDowell twice proclaim, "I didn't pay him (Eggers) anything," and also state, "Mr. Anderson, you ask the darndest questions." The following day Sally Bellerue, who was at the forum and was also seeking reelection, told Dallas that she had never seen McDowell so surprised and set back as the night before when Dallas posed his question about McDowell's failure to report his payment to Eggers for the 1976 campaign work. The state's Fair Political Practices Act required candidates to file statements listing all expenditures in a campaign. Trevor Cushman told Dallas that during the 1976 campaign Virginia Cankar had made a habit of making crank calls in the middle of the night to Arnold Hano, an unsuccessful candidate. As McDowell's campaign manager in 1976, Cushman also confirmed that McDowell had met with Spitaleri and Eggers many times during the 1976 campaign at Spitaleri's home and at the NEWS-POST offices to develop strategy and also to uncover any useful information to discredit Hano. I was a witness to the same events, except for the meetings at Spitaleri's home.

Even though a reporter from THE REGISTER newspaper was at the candidates' forum when Dallas asked McDowell about the 1976 campaign, there was no mention of it in the next edition. Dallas consequently took the trial transcript, the 1976 campaign expenditure statements filed by McDowell, and the tape recording

175

of the exchange with McDowell to reporter Steve Mitchell at the DAILY PILOT office in Laguna Beach. Mitchell laughed excitedly and said, "Unbelievable," while reading Eggers' testimony about his education and his involvement in McDowell's 1976 campaign. The headline bannered across the top of the front page of the DAILY PILOT on April 2, 1980, just six days before the election, read, "Probe of McDowell Expenses Sought," and reported that Dallas had requested an investigation. McDowell and Eggers had been given time to prepare their lies, yet they still contradicted each other in their separate versions about the 1976 campaign. When Dallas had presented the discrepancy in Eggers' testimony and the lack of Eggers' name on McDowell's 1976 campaign expenditure statement, the city clerk had written to the District Attorney's Office requesting an investigation. She had also sent McDowell a copy of her letter. The DAILY PILOT pointed out in the story that while Eggers said he was paid for consultation after the 1976 election, McDowell said he had paid Eggers before the election to fly up to San Francisco with him to meet his son-in-law concerning a newspaper venture that might have involved Eggers. Mitchell told Dallas that he had heard that when Spitaleri saw the DAILY PILOT story he was absolutely "livid."

The NEWS-POST had previously reduced its editions from twice a week to once a week, on Wednesdays. The DAILY PILOT story appeared in a Wednesday edition and the election was scheduled for the following Tuesday, April 8, 1980, so Spitaleri would not be able to print anything in an attempt to salvage not only the reputation of McDowell but that of himself, since he was the employer of Eggers during the 1976 campaign. On April 7, the day before the election, McDowell told Mitchell that he had heard a rumor that people were going to be boycotting the DAILY PILOT and that if Mitchell heard anything about it he was to let McDowell know and he would take care of it. Just such an attempt to control the press was one of the reasons McDowell and the other council members had been named as defendants in my lawsuit. On the evening of April 8, McDowell was having what was supposed to be a celebration party at a local restaurant. Television monitors were set up in the party room for McDowell and Riggs, and their supporters to watch the results being tallied at city hall. When it became obvious that Bellerue and Neil Fitzpatrick were easily defeating all the other candidates for the two vacancies, McDowell walked over to Dallas and told him the party was by "invitation only." Very irate, McDowell told Cushman, his campaign manager in 1976, that he, too, should leave. After Cushman responded that Riggs had invited him, McDowell verified it and conceded, "You were invited; but I wish you hadn't come." The post-election edition of the LOS ANGELES TIMES quoted McDowell as saying he had not thought much about his defeat. The next I heard he was on vacation in Carmel. Another sign of Dallas' effect was the fact that the city council had finally switched to the appropriate term of mayor pro tempore instead of vice mayor. Dallas had lectured the city council and pointed out the ignorance of the city attorney, who at that time was Logan, for not knowing the titles designated in the California GOVERNMENT CODE.

Four months later the District Attorney's Office finally completed its investigation of the McDowell matter. Before becoming a judge, Jean Rheinheimer, as deputy district attorney and head of the special assignment section, wrote the following to the city clerk on August 26, 1980:

"On August 21, 1980, our investigators concluded their final interviews in the matter and I have reviewed the entire file. Based on the information available it is my opinion there is insufficient evidence to justify any criminal proceedings against Mr. McDowell or Mr. Eggers. Mr. Eggers advised us that his testimony at the 1978 court proceedings was in error. Mr. McDowell states he did not pay Mr. Eggers to work on his campaign. We have no evidence to the contrary, especially in view of Mr. Eggers' statement that he had erred in so testifying in 1978. We are, therefore, concluding our investigation in this matter and closing the file."

A copy of the letter was sent to the Fair Political Practices Commission by Rheinheimer since McDowell had been required to file copies of his 1976 campaign expenditure statements, signed under the penalty of perjury, with the commission as well as with the City Clerk's Office. Having investigated the District Attorney's Office's past performances, it did not surprise Dallas or me that McDowell would not be prosecuted for concealing a damaging fact about his 1976 campaign. The District Attorney's Office did not want to do any investigation which would produce sufficient evidence. No one had interviewed Trevor Cushman, McDowell's campaign manager for the 1976 election. It was apparent that no other witnesses besides McDowell and Eggers had been interviewed by the District Attorney's Office. There was also no indication that financial records, such as cancelled checks and bank withdrawals and deposits had been examined. The court of public opinion, however, the electorate, had rendered its own judgment when it chose to not reelect McDowell.

Chapter 6

On about April 17, 1980, I read in the LOS ANGELES TIMES that U.S. District Judge Mariana Pfaelzer's home had been robbed. Among the items she reported missing were her driver's license and a badge which she carried in the same case. If stopped by a law enforcement officer for any reason and asked to produce her driver's license, an officer would see the badge next to it and perhaps be unjustly influenced.

Several days later, on April 21, Judge Pfaelzer ruled on the defendants' motion to dismiss my suit. The second cause of action, Title 42 UNITED STATES CODE Section 1985(3), which alleged I had been a member of a class, that of newspaper reporters, was dismissed. The other cause of action, 42 U.S.C. 1983, was allowed to stand. At the courthouse after the hearing, Golden agreed to let the defense attorneys take my deposition before I would be allowed to take the depositions of any of the defendants. When Dallas and I told Glenn Watson about the arrangement, he said it was an "ass backward" way to prosecute a civil rights lawsuit. We already knew that. Golden did not. My deposition was scheduled for May 13, 1980, but was postponed because the defense attorneys decided they wanted me to first produce copies of all the city government stories I had written and which were published in the NEWS-POST. They wanted to review them for a month before deposing me on June 4, 1980. Again the deposition was rescheduled, this time for July 3, 1980. Golden later informed me that the deposition would be taken sometime in mid-August instead. I was shocked and irate when Golden telephoned me at my home on August 19 at 6:05 p.m. and asked if I was going to appear the following day. Unbeknownst to me, my deposition had been scheduled for 10:00 a.m. the next day. I asked Golden the date he had written or called to inform me of the new date. He was unable to say because he had done neither. Although that was not his first mistake in my case, Golden had the gall to say that he normally did not fail to inform a client of a deposition date.

Just three weeks earlier, on July 28, 1980, I had joined the law firm of Beam, DiCaro, D'Antony & Stafford in Santa Ana as a paralegal. I had not wanted to move to Santa Monica, where the pharmaceutical division of Haight, Dickson, Brown & Bonesteel had moved from its Newport Beach location. The next morning I telephoned my immediate superior to say I would not be at work that day because I was being deposed. Defendant Alfred Theal attended the deposition, which was held at the Santa Ana offices of Rutan & Tucker, which was representing the municipal defendants. Arthur Tuverson of Santa Monica represented the newspaper defendants at the expense of their insurance company, The Atlantic Companies. Even though the California GOVERNMENT CODE stated that an individual, not a law firm, was to be designated as a city attorney for a general law city, the City of Laguna Beach and various other cities in Orange County had retained the law firm of Rutan & Tucker as its city attorney. The LOS ANGELES TIMES, in an article about Orange County law firms, characterized Rutan & Tucker as the "monolith" law firm and quoted one of the senior partners as saying it was trying to preserve the status quo.

Marc Winthrop, who was then assuming the title of assistant city attorney of Laguna Beach, took my deposition, during which he asked many harassing questions such as my political affiliation and my parents' address. I could see that Golden, who rarely made an objection to a question, buckled under to Winthrop. They had attended UCLA law school at the same time, with Golden graduating in 1974. Both Winthrop and Tuverson had much more experience than Golden in litigation and they used psychology, a major tool of an attorney, in gaining the upper hand over Golden.

Winthrop ascertained through questioning that I had obtained my B.A. degree in journalism in three years and that I received "A" grades in all of my journalism classes. During a break in the deposition, Golden, who had never bothered to ask me those questions during any of our conversations, was obviously favorably impressed having just found out that I was a well-qualified journalist. He had been my attorney for more than a year and I had paid him several thousand dollars yet it took questioning by the defense attorneys for him to find out what he should have known long before. Golden had been concerned that even though I had lost income by not being employed for more than a year after the NEWS-POST dismissed me, my salary as a paralegal at a law firm was more than I had received as a reporter/photographer/paste-up artist/proofreader. I had to point out to him that my chosen profession was that of a journalist and that the defendants could be required to pay punitive damages, not only special and general damages which cover actual monetary losses, and mental and emotional injuries.

In early September, Dallas and I heard that the state's 4th District Court of Appeal had overturned Judge Charamza's decision about the First Amendment issue raised by Spitaleri concerning entrance into the private community of Leisure World. Only two of the three appellate court justices had heard and ruled on the appeal. Glenn Watson and Mitchell Abbott would be seeking a rehearing, according to a September 9, 1980, report in the LOS ANGELES TIMES. The new decision seemed to mean that anyone could enter a private community, including Emerald Bay where Spitaleri lived.

The second session of my deposition was held September 17, 1980. Tuverson liked to give the impression that he felt my testimony elicited by Winthrop was boring. Tuverson would yawn and act like he was asleep but would sure perk up when something detrimental to his clients was said. With two years of experience in working in law offices, I knew that once in a while a person was deposed twice, such as I had just been. It was extremely unusual, however, to be deposed more than twice. My attorney was allowing the defense attorneys to harass me with irrelevant questions, such as the balance in my bank account, my apartment rent and the kind of car I drove. Golden was more concerned about impressing the defense attorneys than he was with properly representing me. Instead of voicing ob-

182

jections to Winthrop's harassing and irrelevant questions, Golden would tell me during breaks that I gave the impression of having been hurt by the defendants. Why else was I suing if it were not for the fact that I had been damaged? Golden also criticized me because I had not been friendly when I had passed Winthrop on a sidewalk in Santa Ana. Winthrop had obviously told Golden that when I had passed him on a sidewalk several days earlier I had not greeted him. It was not enough that Winthrop was purposely increasing the amount of money I had to pay to Golden for the hours he just sat listening to Winthrop depose me, but Winthrop also was trying to hinder my civil rights lawsuit by trying to get Golden to join his side. I would not be surprised if Winthrop, who had done better both professionally and financially than Golden since they left law school, had privately intimated to Golden that he might be able to join Rutan & Tucker at some later time.

Without yet taking the depositions of any of the defendants or witnesses, Golden allowed a third session of my deposition to be scheduled for October 22, 1980. During his questioning of me, Winthrop found out that I had prepared a declaration outlining the conspiracy by the defendants and that I had obtained portions of Spitaleri's and Eggers' testimony transcripts from the LAGUNA PUBLISHING COMPANY vs. GOLDEN WEST PUBLISHING CORPORATION trial. Without my permission, Golden told the defense attorneys that he would produce copies of both for them. Both had been prepared in anticipation of my litigation against those responsible for having me removed from my employment with the NEWS-POST. They were my work product, which was privileged, and not subject to discovery by the defense. During a break I told Golden that he had no authority to release the documents to the defense because he had not obtained my permission and case law allowed me to refrain from producing them. Yet just like with the errors he had made in preparing the complaint for filing with the court, Golden would not correct his mistake. He chose to ignore my instructions as a paying client but chose also to delay in producing the items for the defense.

Golden allowed my deposition to be taken at a fourth session on November 4, 1980. Several of the questions Winthrop asked concerned the City's legal advertisements being published in the NEWS-POST instead of in the TIDES AND TIMES. Winthrop, who by then was assuming the position of city attorney, must have already known that the NEWS-POST's Affidavits of Publication were perjured because they stated the NEWS-POST was published and printed in the city of Laguna Beach when it was not. Two years later I found out that on the same day, November 4, 1980, City Manager Kenneth Frank had written to the NEWS-POST and the TIDES AND TIMES informing them that the City's legal notices would be placed in the TIDES AND TIMES if it was adjudicated as a newspaper of general circulation for the City of Laguna Beach. Spitaleri wrote to Frank on November 7, 1980, claiming that the NEWS-POST met a grandfather clause requirement that it be adjudicated before 1923 in order to move out of the city limits and still receive the City's ads. He falsely stated that the NEWS-POST had been adjudicated to receive the City's ads in 1919, which contradicted his 1976 opposition to the TIDES AND TIMES court petition when he falsely claimed the NEWS-POST was adjudicated in 1922. Both statements were lies because the City was not even incorporated until 1927 and the County Clerk's Office had no record of any adjudications in 1919 or 1922. On November 14, 1980, TIDES AND TIMES publisher Earl Shelley, who had bought the newspaper from Larry Campbell some time earlier, filed a petition with the Superior Court to have his newspaper adjudicated for publishing the City's legal advertisements. Campbell had only obtained adjudication for the County of Orange in 1976. Shelley's application was approved on December 3, 1980, but it was not until February 5, 1981, that Frank finally informed Spitaleri that the TIDES AND TIMES was the only newspaper, in the city attorney's opinion, that was "legally entitled" to print the ads.

Disgusted with Golden's representation of me, I was actively seeking a qualified attorney to take an aggressive approach in prosecuting my case. By his actions and inactions at my depositions, Golden gave the impression that he had very little experience in litigation. Before retaining him, I had known that he had never before worked on a civil rights case. His failure with Steinberg's case had not taught him a lesson about accepting free information from Dallas and me which he could have verified. The FEDERAL RULES OF CIVIL PROCEDURE and case laws protected me from having to produce work prepared in anticipation of litigation. His agreement on the record in the transcript of my deposition had not been retracted by him because he was too proud to correct himself in front of Winthrop. From September 17, 1979, through November 8, 1980, I had paid Golden $7,474.70 in fees and costs. At four sessions of my day-long depositions he had done little more than just sit there. His preparation of the complaint and the briefs in opposition to the defendants' motions to dismiss the complaint was the only work he had done. Many of the citations had been provided to him earlier by Dallas and me. Golden had not done any discovery on my behalf, such as deposing the defendants or contacting witnesses.

185

On October 30, 1980, Golden and the defense attorneys had signed and filed with the court a joint discovery schedule listing the order and the dates on which the defendants would be deposed. On my own I had telephoned Gary Frolenko, a former employee in the City's Municipal Services Department, who had moved to Santa Barbara. Frolenko signed and sent to me a declaration in which he stated that Scholl had been unhappy with my news stories and that something had been going on, but he did not know about Scholl actually pressuring the NEWS-POST to get rid of me.

On November 24, 1980, I retained another inexperienced, but receptive, attorney to represent me. Dallas had been in contact with James Bishop, an attorney who lived and worked in Laguna Beach. Bishop admitted that he did not have much experience but was willing to receive and implement advice from Dallas and me. He had just graduated the year before, in 1979, from Western State University law school in Fullerton. Thirty-five years old, Bishop was married to a law student. Bishop was open to suggestions and was knowledgeable about local community and government activities. Like Golden, he would be paid handsomely for doing hardly any work. The fact that he charged $60 an hour, $15 less than Golden, did not really help me since he had to spend a lot of time to review the file to acquaint himself with what Golden supposedly already knew.

On January 13, 1981, I happened to look at the current EDITOR & PUBLISHER magazine at the Santa Ana Public Library and noticed an article which listed all sales of newspapers in the country during the previous year. I checked to see if the NEWS-POST had been sold. Instead, I saw that Golden West Publishing Corporation had been sold to Media General Inc. for $8 million.

After I told Dallas he telephoned Richard Birchall, who was impressed that we kept so well-informed because the sale, he said, had just been recorded on January 13. Birchall added that he had received $4 million and that Smith was still president of Golden West.

Within three days Birchall met with Dallas at the courthouse to discuss hiring him to investigate the appellate judges because he felt that McCray or Spitaleri was using illegal influence on at least one of the three. Dallas turned down the offer, citing that there was not enough time before the February 3 rehearing and that to obtain such evidence was next to impossible. Birchall offered to help with my case in any way possible, even testify. All I really needed was a lot of money to hire a good attorney, but I was not there to tell Birchall that.

A few days before the fifth scheduled session of my deposition, Winthrop had admitted to Bishop that he really did not know what questions he would ask me. Bishop had written to Winthrop and Tuverson noting that my testimony already consisted of more than 400 pages and indicated that not all of the questions asked had been relevant to the case. Winthrop had been using me to find out about his nemesis, Dallas Anderson, who continued to apprise the city council at public meetings about various illegalities, including the firm of Rutan & Tucker, instead of an individual, being named as the city attorney in their contract. William Keiser, an attorney at Rutan & Tucker, had been designated by the firm, instead of by the city council as required, to be the individual with the title of city attorney at public meetings. Since the firm's contract with the City, Dallas had publicly referred to Keiser as the "illegal city attorney" many times before he left the law firm in September of 1980. Winthrop subsequently assumed the position and became the recipient of Dallas' expositions.

The "Deposition of Janice Brownfield--Part V," as Golden had referred to it earlier a la the television movie "Shogun," was held February 12, 1981. In place of Tuverson was Gary Moorhead of a Santa Ana law firm. On the record Bishop asked him what authority he had to attend the deposition in Tuverson's place. Moorhead was not of the law firm which employed the attorney of record for the newspaper defendants and consequently was not duly authorized to be there. Winthrop smirked when Bishop also stated that any off the record remarks would need to be prefaced with the words "off the record" if they were not to appear in the transcript. Bishop made that statement because I had told him about Tuverson's sarcastic comments being edited out of the previous transcripts by the court reporter transcribing the depositions.

One of the reporters, Beth Strayer, had been at a deposition which was attended by John West, one of the attorneys at the law firm where I worked. That deposition was in another case and was not related to my case in any way. Strayer had asked West if he knew me. She had then proceeded to tell him about my lawsuit against the City of Laguna Beach and the other defendants. When she found out he did not know anything about it, she apparently decided not to say anything more. Back at the office, West told me of the conversation. A more interesting revelation after my deposition occurred when I was reading the TIDES AND TIMES. I noticed that the City's legal advertisements were being published there instead of in the NEWS-POST.

After reading it for more than a year, I finally finished David Halberstam's 736-page book, THE POWERS THAT BE, on March 1, 1981. The book documents the rise of CBS, TIME, the WASHINGTON POST and the LOS ANGELES

TIMES and examines how some of them gained enough power to unseat a president of the United States and became highly profitable corporate entities at the same time. I paid particular attention to the instances in which the federal government had pressured the press institutions to get rid of or relocate reporters who did not provide favorable coverage to those in public office. Those officials on the federal level were comparable to a local official like Scholl who would give allegedly newsworthy handouts in exchange for his choice of a reporter covering his official duties.

I do not recall Halberstam mentioning where he got the title for his book, nor mentioning the name anywhere in the book. The term, "the powers that be," probably was first used in the King James translation of the Bible commissioned in the 16th century in England. "Let every soul be subject unto the higher powers. For there is no power but of God: the powers that be are ordained of God." That is the King James version of a portion of the apostle Paul's letter written in the year 55 to the Christians in Rome. The verse is more popularly referred to as Romans chapter 13, verse one. The Living Bible translates Paul's letter as follows: "Obey the government, for God is the one who has put it there. There is no government anywhere that God has not placed in power." I do not believe that God or the apostle Paul intended for us to obey an evil government, or to place our faith in the media giants. As documented by Halberstam, some of the media have acquired so much power that they are able to manipulate some high level government leaders.

The defense attorneys in my case continued in their efforts to obtain the declaration and the trial excerpts I had prepared and obtained, respectively, for the purpose of prosecuting my

189

lawsuit. Bishop told them that he could not be held to an agreement that Golden had made. Consequently, Winthrop assigned Donna Snow Wolf, an attorney at Rutan & Tucker, to begin preparing a motion to seek a court order for the production of the documents. Rutan & Tucker employed at least 30 attorneys at that time and it seemed that this was another incident that was more than just coincidental. Bishop had just begun to share his office space with Alan Wolf, an attorney who was also the husband of Donna Snow Wolf. When Bishop found out that Mrs. Wolf had been assigned to the case he could no longer leave the file cabinets unlocked or my case papers on his desk when he left the office for fear that Alan Wolf would pass information on to his wife.

In trying to follow the joint discovery schedule of October 30, 1980, Bishop had witnesses Frank and Virginia Cankar and Trevor Cushman served with subpoenas to give deposition testimony at his office. The Cankars were deposed April 2, 1981, and claimed that they did not have any conversations with Thomas Michael Eggers or Cushman regarding the city government pressuring the NEWS-POST to remove me from the editorial department. I had not spoken with the Cankars for several years and did not know whether they would tell the truth under oath. I certainly did not contact them after their depositions had been scheduled because I did not want to be accused of trying to influence witnesses. I had also not been in contact with Cushman, but he chose to tell the truth about the conspiracy. Unlike the Cankars, who were friends with Eggers and showed an unusual interest in Sycamore Hills, Cushman did not try to protect anyone with his testimony. The defense attorneys failed to discover that Cushman had signed a declaration on October 2, 1978, outlining his knowledge of the

190

conspiracy. It would be more than a year before they would know of the existence of such a declaration by him and also one by Dallas signed the same day.

The joint discovery schedule was not being faithfully adhered to by the defense attorneys in that they failed to produce their clients for depositions, claiming they were away on vacations or business trips. Plaintiffs and defendants in cases are termed "parties" and do not need to be subpoenaed for depositions as witnesses are. Notices are sent to their attorneys requesting their attendance at depositions. While my attorneys had notified me of such requests, albeit just the night before on one occasion, and I had voluntarily appeared for not just one or two sessions, but five sessions of a deposition, the defense attorneys were trying to prevent their clients from appearing as requested by my attorneys. Consequently, I had Bishop have Eggers and Marjorie Spitaleri served with subpoenas to enforce their compliance with the discovery schedule. Their attorneys, however, went to court and had the service of the subpoenas quashed. Bishop had been notified of the court hearing but had not gone to argue my position. My disappointment in him was to be expected since he was extremely inexperienced. Even though I was not an attorney I knew from my work in law firms that corrections, deletions or additions to a deposition transcript are to be listed in letter form and sent to all attorneys so that they are aware of any changes in the testimony. Although I did not make any changes in the substance of my testimony, I sometimes made additions and duly gave them to Golden and Bishop. Neither one had sent the changes to the defense attorneys. Bishop, in fact, had said that he would just put the list of changes in front of the transcript and then produce it at the time of trial. I could not be with Bishop every moment to educate him on such elementary procedures. From November 28, 1980, to April 1, 1981, I had paid him $2,500 and had received little in return. On April 19, 1981, I sent a Mailgram to the court, with copies to the defense attorneys and to Bishop, requesting a delay in all proceedings until I had obtained new counsel.

If I were wealthy I would have had no problem in hiring a competent attorney. Being female and relatively young also had its disadvantages. If I had been a middle-aged male, I am sure that it would have been easier and that I would not have been removed from my job in the first place. The Orange County Bar Association's Attorney Referral Service listed attorneys who specialized in various fields of law even if the attorneys did not have any experience with the types of cases they wanted to be listed as being able to handle. I told the service that I was looking for an attorney to prosecute a civil rights lawsuit and was given the names of George Comroe and others seeking such cases. Comroe had already proven that he was not an expert in the field. The State Bar of California, the agency responsible for admitting attorneys to the practice of law in California, had established certain requirements for attorneys to be certified as specialists in various fields of law. Civil rights was not one of them. William Dougherty was certified in criminal law, which would not necessarily have made him proficient to prosecute a civil case since he usually defended individuals charged with federal crimes. Many attorneys are interested in getting personal injury cases, which are taken on a contingency basis with the hope of obtaining a large recovery. Very few attorneys have experience in civil rights litigation.

One of the names I received from the service was that of Marc Block, who had taken

192

Comroe's cases when he retired from the law practice after only a few years in the profession. Comroe, not remembering I had spoken with him in 1978, told me by telephone that Block had not been doing justice to the cases he received from Comroe. Having previously experienced Comroe's lack of ability and knowledge, I got the feeling that their animosity was a case of the pot calling the kettle "black." Like Golden, Block was one of those young attorneys whom David Horowitz in his book FIGHT BACK! cautioned readers against hiring. After my talking to Block on the telephone for only a couple of minutes, he said, "I'll take your case." He had not looked at the file but the prospect of receiving $500 a month was the only enticement he needed. Told that he had been a law clerk at the U.S. District Court in Los Angeles where my lawsuit was on file, I was under the false impression that Block would be knowledgeable about cases such as mine and would be able to successfully prosecute it. Thirty-three years old, he had been graduated from the University of West Los Angeles law school three years earlier, in 1978.

On July 16, 1981, I agreed to retain him for $100 an hour and a $1,500 retainer. On August 12, 1981, Block took the depositions of Carl Johnson, a former city council member, and Marjorie Spitaleri, the vice president of Laguna Publishing Company. Like the other four council members who were in office during the conspiracy against me, Johnson had been named as a defendant because he was responsible for protecting my civil rights from being violated by municipal employees and officials. The council members, who had taken oaths of office to uphold those rights, and the City were negligent for not having a policy regarding city employees' relations with members of the press. Johnson claimed that he did not know of any pressure by the city government to have me terminated by the NEWS-POST. The transcript of Mrs. Spitaleri's deposition indicated that the proceedings began at 9:45 a.m. and ended at 11:05 a.m., and consisted of 52 pages. Compared to the 400+ pages of testimony by me, she was not subjected to the type of examination that a defendant in her position should have received. Mrs. Spitaleri testified that the reason she let me go from the NEWS-POST production department on January 20, 1977, was because Laguna Publishing Company did not have enough money to keep me employed. Since my December 1, 1976, removal from the editorial department I had continued my part-time work as a proofreader and paste-up artist in the production department. Her testimony did not include any reason why my independent contractor position of delivering the NEWS-POST to racks was also taken away from me on the same day. My payment for that position had been one-third of the profits from the racks. Therefore, she could not claim that Laguna Publishing Company could not afford to pay me. After reading her transcript I subsequently looked at old issues of the NEWS-POST which Dallas had kept. I found NEWS-POST advertisements in their classified section seeking a paste-up artist and proofreader in several different editions published February 9, 16 and 19, 1977, just several weeks after dismissing me for what she now claimed was a lack of finances.

Defendants Sally Bellerue and Jon Brand, council members during the time I reported on the city government, were deposed and claimed to know nothing of a conspiracy against me. Brand was a traveling partner of Scholl, and Eggers had featured them in a NEWS-POST article following a trip to Russia. Douglas Schmitz, the City's planning director, had gone with them and was a confidante of Scholl. Schmitz was the one who had been overheard by Councilman Jack McDowell in identifying Scholl as the one who was trying to pressure the NEWS-POST to terminate me. Since that time Schmitz had moved to the state of Washington and he failed to return two telephone calls I placed to his office at the city hall in Bellevue. The municipal defendants were adamant in seeking my work products and had scheduled a court hearing for November 16, 1981, concerning them.

On November 12, 1981, the NEWS-POST announced that it had been purchased by Media General Inc., the Virginia firm which had also acquired Golden West in January of the same year. The story stated that purchase details were not disclosed and that Spitaleri was retained as a consultant. Dallas telephoned Richard Birchall, who explained that the purchase was part of the settlement of Spitaleri's lawsuit against Golden West. In addition to receiving approximately $500,000, according to Birchall, Spitaleri would be paid $75,000 a year for five years to work as a consultant to Carlton Smith, his archenemy, who was now publisher of the NEWS-POST as well as the SADDLEBACK VALLEY NEWS, LEISURE WORLD NEWS and CAPISTRANO VALLEY NEWS. Smith eventually removed himself from the scene by moving to the Bahamas.

For two months I had been living in Coronado in San Diego County because the law firm for which I worked had a case in trial there and I was needed to provide paralegal services. Because Block failed to keep me informed of the status of my own lawsuit, I telephoned the clerk's office of the U.S. District Court in Los Angeles and found out about the scheduled hearing of November 16, 1981, just a few days before it was to be held. I then telephoned Block, who had promised me several times in the past that he would send the two pages of legal opposition

195

he had sent to the defense attorneys. Dallas and I had earlier researched many cases in support of my position that I was not required to produce my declaration and the trial transcript excerpts. Block had not gone to the law library and found the numerous cases that we had. Instead, he just used a federal law book in his office and used the few cases it cited. Block had assured me that in addition to the two pages he would then list many other cases in opposition to the defendants' motion. Having heard him brag about lying to judges and others in other cases, I should have known that he would lie to me, too. The court ruled in the defendants' favor and ordered me to pay $800 in attorneys' fees to them for their preparation of the motion to acquire the declaration and the trial transcript excerpts.

Having been psychologically influenced by the defense attorneys, Block sent me a substitution of attorney form the next day, November 17, 1981, naming me as my own legal representative. I did not receive his correspondence until after he attended the first session of Dallas' deposition on November 19, 1981. If he had telephoned me and advised me of his intention to remove himself as my counsel, I would have requested a postponement of the deposition until I had retained an attorney who was on my side. I wrote back to Block, informing him that he would be dismissed as my attorney only after I had retained new counsel. Daniel Sullivan, one of the associate attorneys at the firm where I worked, was also in San Diego assigned to the trial that caused me to be there. I told him for the first time about my lawsuit and my inability to obtain competent representation. He said he would represent me if he were not so busy and then suggested that Garrett Gregor, another associate at the Santa Ana office, might be able to assist me. Sullivan knew firsthand about Block's incompetence because our firm had defended the County of Orange in a federal lawsuit in which Block had represented the plaintiff. The court had ruled in the County's favor because Block failed to prove that his client, a County employee, had been discriminated against when he was passed over for a promotion. It was Block's handling of the case that caused Sullivan to form his negative opinion of him.

On December 15, 1981, I returned to the Santa Ana office after three months in Coronado. I retrieved my files from Block, who had not bothered to have any papers received or generated by him placed in the files. There was nothing in the file to indicate when he had sent the declaration and the trial transcript excerpts to the defense attorneys. The court had instructed that they were to pay half the cost that I had paid to have a court reporter transcribe the portions of the trial transcript which I had ordered. Block chose instead to give the copies away for free, charging me for them. Included in my files were papers belonging to other case files at his office. I spent hours organizing the files, which had grown to a total of approximately two feet thick.

In an attempt to recoup the $800 Block had caused me to have to pay to the defense attorneys, I filed a small claims court case against him. The judge chose to rule in his favor. At the hearing Block had his secretary serve me with a summons and complaint he had filed against me in municipal court for $1,800 he claimed that I still owed him. From July 16, 1981, to November 17, 1981, I had paid him $2,400, which at his hourly rate of $100 amounted to 24 hours of billed time. The transcripts of the four depositions he had taken showed the starting and ending times, which amounted to less than four hours total. For just sitting at Dallas' deposition, which only lasted a few hours for that first session, and not making any objections to the defense attorneys' irrelevant questions such as the names of Dallas' children, I was charged $100 an hour when he knew, and I did not, that he had sent me a substitution of attorney form executed by him. The two pages of legal argument he had prepared in opposition to the defendants' motion to compel production of the documents indicated that he could not have spent more than one hour in that endeavor. Even allowing 10 hours for the maximum amount of time he could have spent working on my case, that meant that the remaining 14 of the 24 would have been spent just in reviewing the files for background information. Yet it was evident that he had spent precious little time in reviewing the files.

While Garrett Gregor and I had signed a substitution of attorney form on December 14, 1981, and had Block sign it two days later, Block subsequently sent me an investigator's report dated January 8, 1982, and wanted me to pay the invoice of $109. During the first three months that he was my attorney, Block had lied in telling me that the investigator, Gary Derks, was busy interviewing witnesses for my case. In reality, Derks had not done anything in that direction until the first week of January, two weeks after Block was no longer my attorney of record. Derks' report, prepared on the letterhead of Dillahunty Investigative/Security Services, Inc., epitomized the incompetence of Block. The following five paragraphs constitute the full investigative efforts employed by Derks and for which he sought $109:

"As you requested, an investigation was conducted into the firing of Ms. Janice Brownfield from the editorial staff of the Newpost (sic) Newspaper. It was learned from Mr. Larry

Campbell, 645 Anita, Laguna Beach, California, home telephone (714) 494-0651, that Ms. Brownfield was at no time employed by the New-post (sic) Newspaper.

"Her position with the paper was in the capacity of a contributor only. Ms. Brownfield would write an article and submit it for publication in the paper, however, was not expecting reimbursement for these articles.

"Ms. Brownfield was socially involved with Mr. Vern Spitaleri, who was the owner of the Newpost (sic) Newspaper, and was doing all work on a voluntary basis, knowing there was to be no compensation.

"With this information in mind, it is felt that further investigation would not prove to be in the best interest of Ms. Brownfield.

"Thank you for allowing us to be of service to you at this time, and if in the future we may be of further assistance, please feel free to call."

Derks obviously was unaware that Campbell had been the publisher of the TIDES AND TIMES newspaper to which I had submitted stories without any expectation of compensation. It was preposterous that Block expected me to pay for such a report. The defendants had already admitted in their answer to my complaint on file in court that I had been an employee of the NEWS-POST. Marjorie Spitaleri, the vice president of Laguna Publishing Company, the publisher of the NEWS-POST, had been deposed more than four months earlier regarding my employment there. It was very time consuming for me to have to compile all of the documentary evidence to defend myself against Block's complaint for breach of contract. Dallas assisted me by doing legal research in supporting my position that an attorney cannot recover on a contract where his services had no value. At the hearing in municipal court I also pointed out that Block had

199

consistently overcharged for his alleged services. On November 11, 1981, Block had charged me $200 for two hours of "Anderson deposition," according to his billing sheets. In reality, there had been no deposition that day because Block had failed to inform Dallas of a deposition to be held that day and so Block, the defense attorneys and a court reporter had shown up at Block's office with no one to depose. Since Dallas was a witness, not a party to the lawsuit, the defense attorneys were to have subpoenaed him, which they did not do. Although I argued to the court that I believed the $2,400 I had already paid Block was far more than he was worth, the judged ruled in his favor. I did enjoy a partial victory, however, in that the judge reduced the $1,800 he was seeking down to $1,000 since I had shown the worthlessness of Derks' report and its reflection on Block's work quality, and the fact that Block had over-charged me, not to mention charged me for a two-hour deposition that had never occurred. It was still disturbing that another attorney, the judge, would rule in an attorney's favor, seemingly thinking that he had to award at least a respectable amount of money to Block, whether or not he had earned it.

Back at the Santa Ana office, Timothy Stafford, one of the partners of Beam, DiCaro, D'Antony & Stafford, told me about the case in which Sullivan had experienced Block's incompetence. In fact, Stafford was the one defending the County of Orange in that case and Sullivan was assisting him. Referring to Block as "Blockhead," Stafford said that at the trial in federal court Block had produced a character witness to testify on behalf of his client. The witness testified about the plaintiff's excellent workmanship and other admirable traits. The testimony was completely irrelevant, however, because the County had promoted a more capable person than the plaintiff. The County had never argued the fact that the plaintiff was a good worker and fine person.

It was just not to be my fate to have a competent or truthful attorney represent me. Gregor was 35 years old and had been graduated from the Western State University law school four years earlier, in 1978. He had said that my case sounded interesting and he was willing to represent me. Having been represented by Golden, Bishop and Block, I had decided that I would like to have an attorney where I worked represent me so I could do most of the work and provide needed information. I also wanted to have more firsthand observations of the psychological tactics employed by the defense attorneys in manipulating my legal counsel. Since Beam, DiCaro, D'Antony & Stafford was primarily an insurance defense firm, receiving business from insurance companies which insured individuals and businesses subsequently named as defendants in civil lawsuits, Gregor had more experience in representing defendants than plaintiffs. After being my attorney for only a few days he said that he had reviewed my case file and decided that even though I believed there had been a conspiracy against me at the NEWS-POST he just did not believe that the defendants had done me any harm. Gregor suggested that I look for another attorney; but when I asked him if he could name a single civil rights attorney in Orange or Los Angeles counties he said he did not know any. A short while later he suggested Timothy Flynn, an attorney with the Center for Law in the Public Interest which was based in Los Angeles. I contacted Flynn, but as expected, the center would only represent litigants in cases which directly affected many people, not just me.

My boss, Byron Beam, the senior partner at Beam, DiCaro, D'Antony & Stafford, for some unknown reason apparently thought that I would be better off with a female attorney representing me. He suggested Eleanor Weaver or Corrine Adams as a possible substitute for Gregor. Weaver worked for the law firm of Kinkle, Rodiger & Spriggs, another insurance defense firm in Santa Ana. After discussing my case with her by telephone, she informed me that she would not be able to represent me because of a conflict of interest in that her law firm had represented the City of Laguna Beach, a defendant in my lawsuit, in other matters. Like Weaver, Adams was in her early forties. She had turned to the legal profession as a second career. Adams was working as a law clerk at the Orange County Superior Court because she did not have enough clients to provide her with sufficient financial security. Beam had failed to mention to me that Adams was seeking employment with his law firm. I did not discover that Adams was using me for her own interests until after she insisted on meeting with me at my place of employment. She told me she had been interviewed by John DiCaro, one of the partners. When I confronted Beam with the information, he stated that Adams was seeking a larger salary than the firm was willing to pay her.

John West, the associate attorney who had been informed of my lawsuit by certified shorthand reporter Beth Strayer, suggested I contact attorney Fred Anderson, a former deputy district attorney, who had gone into private practice years earlier. At my meeting with Anderson I was disappointed to learn that I would have to give him an entire education about federal civil rights case laws and exceptions to the federal hearsay rules if he became my counsel. Michael McKay, an attorney who had worked at Haight, Dickson, Brown & Bonesteel while I was there, suggested Gary Moorhead, who, unbeknownst to

McKay, had been at the fifth session of my deposition on behalf of the newspaper defendants even though he was not their attorney of record. Remembering that Fulton Haight was a member of the State Bar Board of Governors, I decided to telephone him even though I had only met him a couple of times at the Los Angeles office of Haight, Dickson, Brown & Bonesteel. Having been an attorney in the Los Angeles area for more than 30 years and being involved with the State Bar which oversees all attorneys in the State of California, Haight was in a position to know the name of at least one civil rights attorney whom he could recommend. I was wrong. Haight had his secretary call me the next day to inform me that he did not know of one. I again turned to the Orange County Bar Association's Attorney Referral Service for the name of a civil rights attorney. Steven Delbridge, 49 years old and a 1974 graduate of the Pepperdine University law school, was very generous with his time, I thought, in reviewing the facts of my case and discussing possible strategy with me and one of his associates. After being charged $75 for his time and being told that he would be glad to represent me at his usual rate of $150 an hour, I went back to the office and told Gregor that I did not have the financial resources to hire an attorney at that rate.

Gregor had resigned himself to representing me through the final outcome of my litigation. Without saying so, he had no plans to do anything more than the absolute minimum required. He would just follow the October 30, 1980, joint discovery schedule and take the depositions of the remaining defendants on the list, ask them a few questions and then let them leave. Never having been involved in a case such as mine and not having researched the federal case law on civil rights conspiracies, Gregor was oblivious to the

203

fact that the federal courts had established that circumstantial evidence and hearsay testimony were admissible in proving conspiracies because the conspirators go to great efforts to hide the direct evidence. Conspirators do not sign an agreement to violate a citizen's civil rights. There is no police report identifying the violator of the California VEHICLE CODE so that all an attorney in a civil suit has got to do is go through the motions to get one-third the recovery of a plaintiff injured in a motor vehicle accident. Gregor had been instructed by Beam to provide me with copies of all correspondence and pleadings which he sent out or received in my case. Gregor was also told to allow me to actively participate in the prosecution of my case. Beam gave those instructions only after he and David Brobeck, another partner in the law firm, had failed to persuade me to drop my lawsuit to affirm their belief that Christians are not supposed to file lawsuits.

Perhaps they were thinking of the apostle Paul's first letter to the Corinthians, chapter six, verse one, which states, "How is it that when you have something against another Christian, you 'go to law' and ask a heathen court to decide the matter instead of taking it to other Christians to decide which of you is right?" Later, in verse seven, Paul asked, "Why not just accept mistreatment and leave it at that?" Those verses were the only ones listed in my concordance concerning lawsuits and they certainly did not seem to apply to my lawsuit in that they regarded complaints which should be settled in church among other members. Another argument of Beam's which I did not accept was his advice that if I could not beat the city politicians that I should then run for city council and join them. Beam obviously did not understand that I chose to be a journalist, not a politician, and that his idea was inappropriate for redress of my grievance.

Beam, who was 43 years old and a 1965 graduate of the University of California at Berkeley law school, known as Boalt Hall, had just become a Christian in November, two months earlier while we were in San Diego together for work on a trial there. In the few weeks before he became a Christian he had asked me questions about Christianity on several occasions and if I did not have the answers I looked them up for him and provided him with written material that had additional information. I had been a Christian for 19 years and had never heard of Beam and Brobeck's theory that Christianity precluded the pursuit of justice through the court system established by society. I wondered if they planned to return to former and present clients all the moneys they had received for participating in such a "sinful" profession of defending and prosecuting lawsuits. While the law firm primarily represented defendants in civil cases, it also had quite a few plaintiffs' cases. Those were mainly personal injury cases in which the plaintiffs were physically injured in accidents caused by the defendants. Beam and Brobeck apparently believed that it was Christian to file lawsuits for physical injuries against people who accidentally caused them. From their point of view, it seemed that it was not Christian, however, to sue people who intentionally injured someone in her profession and damaged her mentally and emotionally. A broken arm was seemingly a more serious injury than a ruined career.

It was especially hypocritical for Brobeck to be siding with Beam against me in my desire to proceed with my civil rights lawsuit against the defendants because he was suing the City of Laguna Beach for injuries his younger daughter had sustained when she was struck by an automobile while riding a bicycle. The accident

205

occurred on September 12, 1977, at an intersection near Brobeck's home. The City of Laguna Beach was being charged with negligence because the intersection apparently had a blind spot which prevented those approaching from seeing others entering the intersection. Five years later, in September of 1982, while the case was in trial, the Brobecks received a settlement of $3.9 million to pay for their daughter's medical expenses, which included round-the-clock nursing care because she was still unable to talk, walk or care for herself. Brobeck and his wife expressed the belief that others had become Christians through their testimony about their daughter, who was seven years old when the accident occurred.

Both Beam and Brobeck seemed to criticize me for my interest in the city government. If Brobeck or other citizens had gone to the Laguna Beach city government and complained about the dangerous intersection, perhaps his daughter would not have been accidentally injured. Beam, who lived in Lagunita, an unincorporated part of Orange County immediately south of the Laguna Beach city border, at one time said he did not know if he resided within the city limits. He did not seem to have enough interest in government to know that he did not even have the opportunity to vote in the municipal elections. If I had too much civic interest, it made up for those who had too little. It is every citizen's responsibility to be a watchdog on their governments at every level--federal, state, county and city.

I have heard it said and I believe that it is true, if you do not exercise your rights, such as the First Amendment, you will lose them. I am sure that Beam and Brobeck would think it perfectly all right to prosecute a First Amendment lawsuit if it was for freedom of religion. But because my First Amendment lawsuit was for freedom of speech and press they somehow did not think it was worthwhile. I think that one of Beam's true reasons for not wanting me to prosecute my lawsuit was revealed when he told me of his acquaintanceship with Victor Bellerue, husband of defendant city council member Sally Bellerue. Mr. Bellerue is an attorney who is a deputy in the Orange County Counsel's Office, with which Beam's law firm had contact concerning various lawsuits in which the firm represented the County.

At 38 years old, Brobeck was five years younger than Beam and had been graduated in 1970 from the law school of the U.S. International University. It appeared that Brobeck was taking sides with Beam only because Beam was the senior partner of the firm and I was only a paralegal. Within a few years the name of the firm was changed to Beam, DiCaro, D'Antony, Stafford & Brobeck.

Because the municipal defense attorneys were pressuring Gregor to dismiss the city council member defendants, including Sally Bellerue, Beam was trying to convince me that I should agree to such a dismissal. Just because Beam was an attorney did not mean that he knew anything about federal civil rights conspiracies, the appropriate case laws, statutes and evidence requirements. He had limited his law practice to the state courts, and usually represented the defendants in medical malpractice, land subsidence and bad faith insurance cases. Beam wrongly thought and stated that the city council members had been named as defendants on a "respondeat superior" basis, meaning they were responsible for the actions of municipal employees, defendants Stanley Scholl and Alfred Theal. Beam apparently thought he could apply the same principles of the cases in which he worked to my lawsuit, which was governed by an entirely different set of laws, cases and codes.

207

Beam's law firm was not offering any charity in allowing Gregor to represent me. I was being billed at the usual rate of $65 an hour, for which I had paid $1,000 at the start as a retainer. Gregor did not heed Beam's orders to keep me informed of the status of my case and to provide me with copies of all letters and court documents which he prepared or received. I had suspected that Gregor lied at the beginning when he told me and Beam that he had thoroughly reviewed my case files and did not see a basis for any lawsuit against the defendants. Like Beam, Gregor did not have any experience in a federal civil rights conspiracy case and he did not know how to prosecute such a case. That was also true of Golden and Bishop. Block had experience but he lacked ability. Gregor allowed the defense attorneys to take my deposition for a sixth time on January 27, 1982. As evidence that he did not know even the basic facts concerning my employment at the NEWS-POST, Gregor had to interrupt the deposition to ask me questions on the record because he did not understand the fact that I had worked in both the editorial and production departments until December 1, 1976, when I continued to work in just the production department at the newspaper's offices.

According to the transcript, Gregor stated, "If I may just interject. Before December 1st, 1976, you were working in two departments of the newspaper?" I answered, "Yes." He then asked, "And afterwards you were working in one?" I again answered, "Yes." It was very embarrassing for me to again have an attorney who was so ignorant he had to display his lack of knowledge in front of the defense attorneys, making him even more vulnerable to their manipulations. It is very rare for an attorney to ask his own client questions at a deposition taken by the opposition. It is an unwritten rule that an attorney never should ask his client questions there, but if he does, he should already know the answers beforehand.

The same day, January 27, 1982, Dallas had been deposed for the third time, the second session being just the day before. Like all attorneys, the defense attorneys are officers of the court, and yet they abused their positions by asking irrelevant questions of Dallas because they were concerned with his criticisms of the city government and of the city attorney, who now was Winthrop. A fourth session was held on January 28, 1982.

It was not until February 24, 1982, that one of the main defendants, Vernon Spitaleri, was deposed. The transcript consisted of only 58 pages and showed, through the questions asked by Gregor, that Spitaleri was not being subjected to proper interrogation. I had drafted questions for Gregor to ask all of the defendants because he had acted like the whole case was just too much for him to handle. He asked just some of the questions and did not pin Spitaleri down on specifics. At the second session of his deposition, Spitaleri testified that the main reason I was removed from the editorial department was because of the NEWS-POST's financial problems. A secondary reason was because various co-workers of mine were complaining about me to him, describing me as a "pain in the neck." Scholl's deposition was taken between the first and second sessions of Spitaleri's depositions. Apparently because Scholl had testified about the October of 1976 meeting, Spitaleri had to concede that he had, indeed, met then with Scholl. The City's municipal services director at the time, Scholl had complained to him about a story allegedly written by me, Spitaleri testified. It apparently was a short technical story with many factual errors.   To offset his role as a conspirator, Spitaleri also testified that I had a "good grasp of the English language."   It was several weeks before the court reporter had transcribed the deposition transcripts so that I could read them to find out exactly what Spitaleri had said.   Two of Gregor's main mistakes at those depositions and throughout the rest of the litigation were accepting as fact Spitaleri's testimony that co-workers had complained about me and that I had written a short technical story with many errors.

On March 3, 1982, Gregor took the deposition of defendant John McDowell, a former city council member, who mainly offered criticisms of Dallas Anderson.   Since McDowell had lost his reelection bid two years earlier, very possibly because of the DAILY PILOT article about McDowell not disclosing that he had paid Eggers to work on his 1976 campaign, it was not surprising that McDowell would still be bitter toward Dallas, who had supplied the DAILY PILOT with the information.   McDowell should have directed the blame at himself, however, for not lawfully disclosing the payment to Eggers on his campaign expenditure statements that were required by state law.

Following the October 30, 1980, joint discovery schedule, Gregor had taken the deposition of Stanley Scholl on March 9, 1982, about one year after it was originally scheduled.   I was disgusted by the fact that Gregor let Scholl leave after just 40 pages of questions and answers which did not even come close to eliciting the truth from him.   Scholl had acknowledged that in October of 1976 he, Spitaleri and defendant Alfred Theal, who was then the city manager, met for lunch at the Top of the Mark restaurant in El Toro, near the NEWS-POST offices, to discuss the inaccurate article allegedly written by

210

me. I remembered that Spitaleri only went to the Top of the Mark when he was trying to favorably impress others. Scholl testified, "That was an occasion when there was a news article which I had determined that there were plus or minus 20 errors in it, and I circled all the errors and explained why each one was an error and gave that to him (Spitaleri) at lunch." Scholl claimed that it was written by me. Gregor again made the mistake of not having the alleged article identified. On June 23, 1980, I had produced for the defense attorneys copies of all the articles I had written for the NEWS-POST. Since the luncheon was in October of 1976, the defendants should have been able to locate the alleged article in the copies I produced or in the NEWS-POST volumes of newspapers for the months of September and October of 1976. Under oath, Scholl denied that he had pressured the NEWS-POST to terminate me. He also denied ever contacting the NEWS-POST, Eggers, Dorothy Korber, me or anyone else to come to Laguna Beach to take photographs of his municipal services department projects. Korber had written two columns, which were published in the NEWS-POST, about Scholl's excessive demands for press coverage, but Gregor did not bother to show copies of them to Scholl or ask him about them. Even the defense attorneys were somewhat surprised when Gregor let him off the hook after less than an hour of questioning. When Gregor said, "I don't have anything further," attorney Paul Bickenbach of Arthur Tuverson's law firm asked, "Why didn't you tell me this 20 minutes ago?" When Gregor hesitated, Bickenbach exclaimed, "Jesus."

The fifth and final session of Dallas' deposition was on March 11, 1982. By the end of the five sessions there were 402 pages of testimony of him answering mostly irrelevant, harassing, intimidating and oppressing questions that were not objected to by Gregor. Dallas told them that he was going to court to get a protective order if they tried to take his deposition another time. Gregor allowed the defense attorneys to take my deposition for a seventh time, on March 15, 1982. In all of the cases I have seen in more than six years as a paralegal, I have never heard of anyone being subjected to the experience to which Dallas and I were exposed. The total number of pages for my depositions amounted to 609. It was part of the defense attorneys' apparent strategy to increase my attorney's fees so that they could perhaps discourage me through financial pressure to drop my lawsuit.

On March 17, 1982, Gregor took the deposition of Phyllis Sweeney, a defendant city council member who testified that my physical appearance deteriorated during the time I worked for the NEWS-POST. It was ironic that Sweeney, who was not known for her good appearance, would falsely make such a remark about me. The last deposition in the case, that of defendant Thomas Michael Eggers, was taken on March 31, 1982. It exemplified the "ass backward" order that attorney Glenn Watson had described earlier. In a conspiracy case, the alleged conspirators, not the victim plaintiff, are to be deposed first because it is well established by the courts that conspirators go to great lengths to hide the evidence. Just as Vernon Spitaleri had testified, Eggers claimed that the main reason I had been removed from the editorial department was because of the NEWS-POST's financial problems. Gregor showed him the advertisements which had been published in the California Newspaper Publishers Association's CONFIDENTIAL BULLETIN on October 11 and 18, 1976. The only reason Gregor had them was because I had prepared the

212

subpoena duces tecum for Gregor to sign so that the information that had been supplied by my former journalism professor, James Fields, by telephone on November 27, 1976, would be corroborated. Eggers had advertised for a reporter, he testified, because he had been informed that Dorothy Korber would be leaving the NEWS-POST staff. Gregor failed to ask Eggers the proper questions because he did not know the facts himself.

Korber did not leave the NEWS-POST until February of 1977, at which time Marshall Krantz was hired to replace her. On December 1, 1976, Marilyn Angell became a full-time employee in the editorial department. If the NEWS-POST did not have enough money to keep me, a part-time editorial department employee, it certainly did not have the resources to hire a full-time editorial department employee. Gregor, however, did not go into that, choosing instead apparently, to believe Eggers' testimony that Angell had been hired to replace Korber. I could have done a better job than Gregor in interrogating Eggers. Also like Vernon Spitaleri, Eggers testified that the second reason I was removed from the editorial department was because my co-workers had complained to him about me. When shown the glowing letter of recommendation he had written to Pepperdine University, stating I had done "A" work in my internship at the NEWS-POST, Eggers tried to claim I had practically forced him to write what an "excellent" journalist I was. Several years earlier, after deciding to commence litigation, I had written to JoAnn Carlson at Pepperdine University to ask for a copy of the letter Eggers had written to her at the end of July, 1975. Instead of sending me a copy, she sent me the original, for which I was grateful.

While the defense attorneys had listed

Dorothy Korber on the joint discovery schedule because they had planned to take her deposition, they chose not to do so. It was probably because they had found out she would not be a cooperative witness. Dallas Anderson had telephoned her several years earlier and she had told him that when she left the NEWS-POST to work for the Long Beach INDEPENDENT, PRESS-TELEGRAM, Eggers had accused her of stealing a 12-inch ruler from the NEWS-POST. Now married to David Levinson, an editor at the Long Beach paper and her former boss, she was expecting their first child and told Dallas she did not want to have anything to do with the NEWS-POST. She had often complained at the NEWS-POST that she, and not I, should have the Laguna Beach beat. If any of my co-workers had complained to Spitaleri and Eggers about me, it would have been Korber. Her complaints would not have been well-founded, however, because her motive was to have the Laguna Beach beat for herself. It was very well for her that she had gotten what she had wanted and that I no longer had a career in my chosen profession. She wanted to close the book on that chapter of her life and not look at the consequences.

At that time I did not yet know that it was Korber who had contacted Angell to work at the NEWS-POST. The two women had attended California State University at Long Beach together and knew each other in the journalism department there. While manipulating Spitaleri and Eggers to get the Laguna Beach beat for herself, which fit in nicely with the defendants' plan to remove me from the editorial department because of the city government's pressure, Korber contacted Angell to replace her on the San Juan Capistrano/South Shores beat. Because Gregor was not interested in successfully prosecuting my case, I decided to contact my former co-workers, with the exception of Korber, to ask them to sign declarations under the penalty of perjury that they had never complained about me to Spitaleri or Eggers, that they had not heard any complaints about me, and that they had not noticed any decline in my physical appearance while I was employed at the NEWS-POST. One of my former co-workers was Peggye Swenson, who was living in Texas and commented that Angell, who had left the NEWS-POST to move to Arizona, was back in Orange County and living in Huntington Beach, about a half-hour drive from my home. I was sure that Eggers had no idea when he gave his false testimony that Angell could be easily contacted to dispute his statements.

Part of the declaration which Swenson signed on May 24, 1982, stated the following:

"At no time did I consider Janice to be a pain in the neck or a disruptive influence. She did not cause me any problems and in no way did she interfere with my work. There were activities in the editorial department which disrupted my work but Janice was not involved in those. I did not hear anyone in the editorial or production departments complain about her."

To counter the nasty and false remarks made by Phyllis Sweeney at her deposition, I used some of the exact words she said in another part of the declaration, which read as follows:

"During the entire time that Janice worked at the NEWS-POST I never observed her to be zombie-like with a blank stare or to have a deteriorating physical appearance."

I had already gotten the same or similar declarations signed by William Doherty, on March 28, 1982; David Cunningham, on April 13, 1982; and Richard Manly, on April 18, 1982. In addition, because Vernon Spitaleri had testified that production department workers had also complained about me, I also got Adena Gay to sign a

215

similar declaration on May 20, 1982. I was unable to locate Kathy Jordan, who had moved out of the state. Marcie Eden, whose daughter Cathy had married the Spitaleris' son Eric earlier in 1982, decided to show the declaration to the Spitaleris instead of signing it and returning it to me as the others had. The Spitaleris in turn sent it to their attorney, who sent it to Gregor. Eden seemed to be more concerned about her family and financial relationships with the Spitaleris than she was with telling the truth. I had spoken with her on the telephone previously and she was aware that I had been unemployed for more than a year after the NEWS-POST terminated me. Again, because Gregor and my previous attorneys had not done any adequate investigation for my case, I decided to telephone Korber to ask her if she knew why the NEWS-POST had terminated me. She feigned ignorance. When I asked about Angell, she did not volunteer that she was the one who had contacted Angell to work at the NEWS-POST.

While he had not previously supplied me with any copies of correspondence or court documents, Gregor slammed a copy of the defendants' motion for summary judgment on my desk on May 24, 1982. Obviously intimidated by the 31-page motion accompanied by affidavits of all the defendants stating they did not conspire to have me terminated, Gregor did not like the idea of having to do any work on my case. He would do as he had at the depositions and just go through the motions of representing me, but not adequately. As further evidence that he had lied when he had said he had thoroughly reviewed my case files in December of 1981, Gregor indicated that he was not aware the case laws and arguments used by the defense attorneys were the same ones they had used two years earlier in their motion to dismiss the complaint. I got out from the files the copy of the motion they had made at that time and pointed out the often verbatim arguments they were now making. Scheduled for a hearing on June 14, 1982, in the U.S. District Court in Los Angeles, Gregor had just seven days to prepare an opposition brief so that the defense attorneys would then be able to prepare a reply.

Meanwhile, in the same month the state's 4th District Court of Appeal, Division Two, reversed the jury verdict entered four years earlier in Orange County Superior Court in Laguna Publishing Company's case against Golden Rain Foundation of Laguna Hills. After a five-month trial the jury had entered judgment against Laguna Publishing. The appellate court held that Golden Rain had discriminated against the NEWS-POST by denying it distribution rights which for many years had been afforded to a rival newspaper, the LEISURE WORLD NEWS, in violation of the free speech and press rights provided by the California Constitution. The trial court was directed to determine whether such exclusion had caused any damages to Laguna Publishing.

In the meantime, on June 2, 1982, without my permission, Gregor filed with the federal court a dismissal from the case for defendants Sally Bellerue, John McDowell, Jon Brand, Phyllis Sweeney and Carl Johnson Jr., who had been city council members when the NEWS-POST removed me from the editorial department. It was a move that the defense attorneys, as well as my boss Byron Beam, had been pressuring Gregor to do for a long time. Gregor's plan for his opposition brief to the defendants' summary judgment motion was to present a "very simple" outline pointing out the genuine issues of material fact and focusing on the October, 1976, meeting of Scholl, Theal and Spitaleri. Not allowed to see a copy of the opposition brief until after he had

217

already sent the original to be filed with the court, I knew when I read it that the judge would rule in the defendants' favor. Gregor made no mention of the fact that I had been told in October of 1976 on several occasions that the city government was pressuring the NEWS-POST to terminate me. All of the facts were laid out in the deposition testimonies of me, Dallas and Trevor Cushman, as well as in our signed declarations.

One part of the defendants' motion for summary judgment read as follows:

"Assuming for the sake of argument only that defendants did indeed act to remove her as a reporter from the NEWS-POST staff, plaintiff has not presented any evidence or even alleged that defendants thus prevented her or the NEWS-POST from entering City Council Chambers and attending Council meetings or appearing at press conferences." As in the motion to dismiss the complaint, the defendants' attorneys contended that the only First Amendment rights to which I was entitled were freedom of access and freedom from prior restraint. They were attempting to ignore the facts of the case and thereby confuse the court with diversionary arguments as to what I was claiming. Gregor correctly responded with the following in the opposition brief:

"Plaintiff hastens to point out that prior restraint and denial of access to news are not the only ways protected rights can be infringed upon. Retribution for exercising First Amendment rights can also form the basis of a Section 1983 action."

He then cited a case which I had found years earlier and supplied to Golden to show that if a lifeguard has a First Amendment right to have letters printed in a newspaper without being terminated from his employment, then I also had the same right as a newspaper reporter. The case was DONOVAN vs. REINBOLD, 291 F. Supp. 930 (C.D. Cal. 1968 affirmed 433 F. 2d 738 [1970]). The notations after the case name mean that the case originated in the central district of California, the same court in which my case was filed, in 1968 and was summarized in a case law book known as the FEDERAL SUPPLEMENT, in volume 291 on page 930. The case was affirmed on appeal in the plaintiff's favor and was summarized in the FEDERAL REPORTER, second series, in 1970.

Not knowing that I had contacted former co-workers, who signed declarations under the penalty of perjury claiming, among other things, that I had never been a disruptive influence at the NEWS-POST, the defendants' attorneys placed heavy reliance upon a case known as GRASECK vs. MAUCERI, 582 F. 2d 203 (2d Cir. 1978), cert. denied, 439 U.S. 1129, which meant that the case had been on appeal from a district court to the Second Circuit Court of Appeals, whose decision was left to stand by the U.S. Supreme Court after a writ of certiorari was denied. The defense attorneys tried to compare me to the plaintiff in the GRASECK case who was an attorney who had been discharged from his employment with a legal aid society because, according to the defendants in that case, he had been a disruptive influence. The plaintiff had contended that judges had pressured the society to terminate him because his actions in court were not pleasing to them.

Like DONOVAN, another case that was more similar to mine and which was first used by Golden in his opposition brief to the defendants' motion to dismiss the complaint, Gregor cited PHABY vs. KSD-KSD-TV, INC., 476 F. Supp. 1051 (1979). The plaintiff had been a reporter for the defendant television station and his duties had included reporting on local political and governmen-

219

tal activities. Sheriff Percich of the local government complained about Phaby's endorsement of a competing candidate for sheriff. Phaby's employment was then terminated. The court hearing that case concluded that if the sheriff "used the power and prestige vested in him due to his office, even though acting outside the scope of his authority granted by law, his actions would sufficiently constitute state action," meaning the plaintiff was entitled to sue under 42 U.S.C. 1983, conspiracies to violate civil rights under the color of law. Stanley Scholl was Sheriff Percich in my case.

Although I had acquired declarations from former NEWS-POST co-workers contradicting the testimony of Spitaleri and Eggers, Gregor chose not to use them in his opposition brief. It was my contention that if the defendants were proved to be lying about one of the reasons they claimed motivated them to terminate me, then their credibility was at question and needed to be tested at a trial before a jury, the trier of fact. That was the reasoning given in numerous case laws. Gregor also did not point out that Scholl had testified that he only saw Spitaleri about once a year, which would make their October, 1976, luncheon a rare occasion and provide more circumstantial evidence that Scholl was strongly motivated to speak with Spitaleri about me and have me terminated. While he was trying to gain employment for himself with the City of Santa Monica, Scholl certainly did not want any negative press in the NEWS-POST. In his opposition, Gregor assumed the false position that there actually was in existence an article that I had written that contained about 20 errors which Scholl had taken to Spitaleri at the October, 1976, luncheon. Gregor wrote, "Mr. Spitaleri and Mr. Scholl have both admitted attending such meeting and discussing the article and Ms.

Brownfield, although each has denied mentioning termination, or other punitive action toward Ms. Brownfield."

As I expected, the court ruled in favor of the defendants' motion for summary judgment on June 14, 1982, thus precluding me from having a trial, which would have been the real day in court to which I was entitled. Just like Block after the court had ruled in the defendants' favor seven months earlier when they sought my declaration and the partial trial transcript, Gregor had a substitution of attorney form prepared and signed, naming me as my own legal representative. Beam himself gave it to me on June 23, 1982, which was three years later than I should have begun representing myself in my litigation. At a law firm where the number of hours billed to clients each month is the bottom line, Gregor had charged me more than $10,000 for just sitting at depositions of me and Dallas which should not have been taken, for taking only hour-long depositions of the defendants, and for preparing an opposition to the defendants' motion for summary judgment with the aid of work Golden and I had already done two years earlier.

On June 28, 1982, I filed with the district court a motion for reconsideration pursuant to Rule 59 of the FEDERAL RULES OF CIVIL PROCEDURE. One of the exhibits which I attached to the motion was a declaration that Marilyn Angell had signed just that morning. I had telephoned her before travelling to her home in Huntington Beach to obtain it. Signed under the penalty of perjury, her declaration stated that she had begun working for the NEWS-POST on December 1, 1976, for more than $680 a month after the NEWS-POST had contacted her. The amount of Angell's salary was $130 more than mine, which showed that I was not removed from the editorial department because of financial

221

problems.   Also, I only worked in the editorial
department   18   hours   a   week,   which   further
evidenced   the   falsity   of   Spitaleri's   and   Eggers'
testimonies   since   my   work   in   that   department
would   have   been   compensated   at   the   rate   of
about   only $200   a   month.   I   also   attached   the
February   9,   16   and   19,   1977,   NEWS-POST   advertisements   seeking   a   proofreader/paste-up   artist   to
impeach   Marjorie   Spitaleri's   testimony   that   financial   troubles   had   also   prompted   my   termination
from   the   production   department   on   January   20,
1977.   The   declarations   of   my   former   co-workers,
Gay,   Doherty,   Manly,   Cunningham   and   Swenson,
were   attached   to   contradict   the   testimonies   of
Vernon   Spitaleri   and   Eggers   that   they   had   said   I
was   a   disruptive   influence,   a   secondary   reason
they   had   given   for   my   termination   from   the
editorial   department.

In   addition,   I   pointed   out   that   at   his
deposition,   Scholl   denied   yelling   at   me,   "You   don't
write   stories   the   right   way!"   That   contradiction
in   our   testimonies   constituted   a   genuine   issue   of
material   fact,   which   is   required   to   be   shown   at
hearings   for   summary   judgments   in   order   to   allow
a   case   to   proceed   to   trial.   The   circumstances   of
October   14,   25,   26   and   31,   1976,   when   I   was   told
of   the   defendants'   conspiracy   against   me,   and   the
event   of   November   26,   1976,   when   I   was
terminated,   represented   a   more-than-coincidental
sequence   of   events.   They   represented   the
defendants'   conspiracy   to   have   me   terminated   effective   December   1,   1976.   The   information   which
Dallas   gave   to   me   on   October   14   and   31,   1976,
was   hearsay   testimony   because   he   had   received   it
from   Cushman,   who   had   received   it   from   Virginia
Cankar,   who   in   turn   had   been   told   about   the   city
government's   pressure   on   Eggers   by   her   husband
Frank   Cankar,   who   was   Eggers'   father   figure.
Rule   803   of   the   FEDERAL   RULES   OF   EVIDENCE
allowed   hearsay   testimony   as   admissible   evidence

as long as the defendants were unable to prove that the testimony was false. The defense attorneys had not even attempted to challenge the testimonies of me, Dallas Anderson or Trevor Cushman. They merely ridiculed the conspiracy information that I received in October of 1976 as being fifthhand. Rule 805, however, allowed hearsay within hearsay.

Years earlier I had heard the saying among attorneys that if the facts are not on your side of a case, then argue the law. If the law is also not on your side, then argue emotion. In their opposition to my motion for reconsideration, the defendants' attorneys chose to argue emotion by claiming that my allegation of a conspiracy was based on a "wild imagination," "paranoia" and "insecurity." Having been told of the conspiracy on October 14 and 31, 1976, and then being told on October 25, 1976, of a meeting to be held the next day between Spitaleri, Theal and Scholl to discuss me, seeing Spitaleri leave the offices on October 26, 1976, and then return to tell Eggers, "You've got it!" and then be told on November 26, 1976, that I was being terminated effective December 1, 1976, proved that I was not suffering, as the defendants' attorneys falsely and maliciously charged, from the above-mentioned mental and emotional aberrations. Regarding the declarations and testimonies of me, Dallas and Trevor about the October, 1976, conspiracy information, the defendants' attorneys claimed that in order to be admitted as evidence, such hearsay statements needed to be accompanied by the witnesses' addresses. In my reply to their opposition, I attached copies of pages from our deposition transcripts in which we provided them with our addresses, and copies of the declarations they received, in November of 1981 by court order, in which I listed our addresses. With documentary evidence and declarations by non-defendants, I told the court in my briefs that every single reason the defendants gave for my termination had been proven false, thus necessitating a trial of the issues.

On July 26, 1982, Judge A. Wallace Tashima denied my motion, claiming all of the evidence I had produced was irrelevant, that it had been available to Gregor at the time of the summary judgment hearing, and that hearsay was not acceptable. The judge chose to ignore the hearsay rules, that the evidence was relevant because all of it pertained to the reasons for my termination, which my lawsuit concerned, and that I had just obtained Angell's declaration on June 28, 1982, the same day I filed the motion.

It was at this exact point in writing this book on April 14, 1984, that I watched the movie THE VERDICT for the first time when it was shown on HBO cable on television. It was a little more than a year earlier that the movie had been released at the theatres and my boss had been one of many people interviewed for a newspaper story concerning local attorneys' opinions about the accuracy of the film's portrayal of the legal profession. Being an attorney, and one who received most of his business from insurance companies, oftentimes to defend doctors accused of committing malpractice, Beam was almost typecast, at least as far as his specialty at that time. He condemned the film, which exposed the unethical practices of defense law firms in trying to obstruct justice. From my own experience I agreed with the movie's depiction of defense attorneys trying to use every strategy at their disposal in trying to pervert the legal system. As in my case, the evidence was on my side, but the defense attorneys tried to latch on to insignificant technicalities to prevent the evidence from being admitted and considered by the trier of fact. I do not believe the movie would have been made if the verdict had not been in the plaintiff's favor. The events in the film very conceivably could have happened, and if in fact they had, I think it is also an injustice by the publishing and film-making industries to not use the real names of the people involved. The film reminded me of an incident in the LAGUNA PUBLISHING COMPANY vs. GOLDEN WEST PUBLISHING CORPORATION trial. Glenn Watson, one of the defense attorneys, had his girlfriend Grace pose as a student observing the trial. She went to the front row and sat next to Spitaleri. Pretending she was doing research for a term paper, she asked him questions about the case, and appeared to attempt flirting with him also. More interested in his lawsuit, however, Spitaleri ignored her and she gave up after a few hours.

Within a few months after Judge Tashima's denial of my motion on July 26, 1982, attorney Paul Bickenbach, representing the newspaper defendants, telephoned me to ask if I was planning to appeal the decision and if so, he was willing to offer $6,000 to have his clients dismissed from the case. Retained by The Atlantic Companies, the insurer paying his legal fees for the newspaper defendants, Bickenbach probably made the offer in that amount because that was the going rate for defense attorneys to charge an insurance company for the preparation of a reply brief to an appeal. I told Bickenbach that $6,000 did not even come close to covering the amount of money I had already spent on attorneys' fees and that he would know soon enough if I was planning an appeal to the U.S. Court of Appeals for the Ninth Circuit. I did not tell him that I was already in the midst of preparing my appeal brief, which was served on him and the other defense attorney on November 5, 1982. Beginning in February of 1983 the defense attorneys began to garnishee my salary for their $7,000+ costs, which they had accumulated by deposing me seven times and Dallas five times.

Shortly before a three-member panel of the appeals court was to hear any oral arguments on March 11, 1983, I received correspondence from the court clerk's office stating that the three appellate judges would thoroughly read the briefs submitted so that they would be fully knowledgeable about the case. One of my previous attorneys, Garrett Gregor, had made the same sort of claim but I thought I could trust the appellate judges to be true to their word. At the hearing, the municipal defendants' attorney brought another case citation to be added to their reply brief. There was no mention of the name of the case. The fact that the defense wanted to add another citation at the last minute, at the time of the hearing, told me that I had presented an impressive appeal brief to the court.

One of the three judges was Bruce R. Thompson, senior U.S. district judge for the district of Nevada, sitting by designation. Judge Thompson stated the following:

"There is a matter that isn't covered by the briefs that interests me, and that's that after reviewing the whole record, I can't find any action under color of state law under 1983 and under 1985. I don't believe that newspaper reporters are a class that can be designated as being discriminated against. So I don't see how these states (sic) are praying for release, but that's not argued very extensively in any brief that I read."

If Judge Thompson had read the briefs he would have known that the 42 U.S.C. 1985(3) cause of action, regarding discrimination against a class, was dismissed on April 21, 1980. The attorney for the municipal defendants responded as

226

follows:

"Your Honor, the City's brief does go into that question quite extensively, and we have argued consistently that there was no action under color of law and that therefore, she cannot maintain action under 42 USC 1983." To edify the judge, she then had to add, "Well, the allegation under 42 USC 1985 was dismissed."

One of the three appellate judges was Harry Pregerson, who was in the midst of conducting a months-long trial concerning the Oakland Raiders football team moving to Los Angeles. There were stories in the newspapers every day concerning his activities in that trial, which apparently had begun while he was still a district judge, not yet appointed to the appellate court. On March 31, 1983, the appellate court issued its ruling, declaring that Judge Tashima had properly granted summary judgment to all defendants. In its two-page memorandum decision, the appellate court proved that it had not even read the defendants' reply briefs thoroughly. In at least three places the appellate court referred to the "city council members" as if they were still defendants in the case. They had been dismissed more than nine months earlier. The appellate court failed to address the allegations against former City Manager Alfred Theal and former Municipal Services Director Stanley Scholl, the remaining municipal defendants, along with the City of Laguna Beach. The court wrote, "Even if all of the facts plaintiff alleged are true, she still failed to establish any conduct by city council members, in conjunction with her employer, which impinged on her free expression rights in violation of 42 U.S.C. 1983." The court misconstrued the case laws submitted by both the defendants and myself.

In a petition for a rehearing I pointed out the appellate court's faulty references to "city

227

council members." On May 19, 1983, the court issued an order amending its March 31, 1983, decision, changing "city council members" to "city officials" but rejecting my petition for a rehearing "en banc," meaning a hearing before all members of the appellate court and not just three members. For those who have not had such direct and firsthand experience with the legal system they may not understand what a miscarriage of justice had just occurred.

Chapter 7

On August 15, 1983, I filed with the United States Supreme Court a petition for writ of certiorari seeking a review of the district and appellate courts' rulings because they contradicted the rulings by the Supreme Court in similar cases. While the appellate court was required to review every case submitted on appeal, the Supreme Court is not required to do so. In fact, it is rare for the Supreme Court to grant a petition, meaning it would then listen to both sides before reaching a decision. Very few of the many cases submitted to the Supreme Court each year are selected for such a review. I used the maximum limit of 65 pages in booklet form to summarize the history of my case at the district and appellate court levels, and to argue why those lower court decisions were unjust.

The Supreme Court convened for the October Term 1983 on the first Monday in October.

Eight days later, on October 11, 1983, the court clerk wrote me a letter stating that my petition had been denied.

Meanwhile, Vernon Spitaleri, who was no longer publisher of the NEWS-POST, agreed to accept a $1.85 million settlement from the Golden Rain Foundation to end his 10-year legal battle regarding distribution of the newspaper to non-subscribers in the private community of Leisure World. A story in the October 20, 1983, edition of the NEWS-POST stated that Golden Rain, the last remaining defendant in the case, chose to settle instead of incurring more legal expenses in a trial which was scheduled to start on January 3, 1984.

I assumed it was Spitaleri who told the LOS ANGELES TIMES about the Supreme Court denying my petition. It was not until about January of 1984 that a woman whom I have never met in person told me that she had read a newspaper account of my lawsuit several months earlier. Thinking that she may have read such a story in the NEWS-POST, I subsequently contacted Annette McCluskey, who had been the editor since Media General Inc. bought the newspaper as part of the settlement concerning Spitaleri's lawsuit regarding entrance into Leisure World. McCluskey told me that the story was probably in the TIMES because one of its reporters had asked her for a comment about my litigation. She had told the reporter that she did not have any comment because my lawsuit concerned the previous owner, Laguna Publishing Company. Not until I read the story in June of 1984 did I know that I had been libeled by the TIMES.

Headlined "High Court Rejects Ex-Reporter's Suit Against Laguna," the story published on October 26, 1983, read as follows:

"The U.S. Supreme Court has refused to hear a $350,000 lawsuit filed by a former

230

newspaper reporter against Laguna Beach and a newspaper, thereby upholding two lower court decisions against the reporter.

"Janice Brownfield, who had been fired as a reporter for the Laguna News-Post, contended that city officials conspired with the newspaper on her firing because of articles she wrote about the city.

"In November, 1979, charging that her civil rights had been violated, Brownfield sought general damages of $100,000 and punitive damages of $250,000 in U.S. District Court against the City Council and the Laguna Publishing Co., which owned the News-Post.

"Attorneys for the publishing company said in court that Brownfield was fired because of poor work.

"The court ruled against Brownfield, saying there was no basis for the suit. The 9th Circuit Court of Appeals in San Francisco also found in favor of the city and newspaper.

"Since the lawsuit was originally filed, the News-Post, along with several other papers in the south county area, has been sold to Golden West Publishing Inc., a subsidiary of Media General Inc., based in Richmond, Va."

I read and copied the story in the microfilm department of the library at the University of California at Irvine, which was the only location in the county where back issues of the TIMES were available for public viewing. Besides erring in stating that I was "fired" and in naming the city council instead of Scholl and Theal, the TIMES falsely libeled me in stating that I had been terminated because of "poor work." Neither the defense attorneys nor their clients had ever given that reason to the courts. The story, although about a judicial proceeding, was not obtained directly from the court records, and was not fair or accurate. The defendants had testified at their depositions that Laguna Publishing Company's financial problems was the main reason and that co-workers complaining about me being a disruptive influence was a secondary reason. I had proven both of those reasons false with declarations by five former NEWS-POST co-workers and one by Marilyn Angell.

My legal research concerning libel confirmed what I had learned in a communications law class at Pepperdine University. There are three defenses for publishing a libelous story-- truth, fair comment or privilege. Not one of those defenses was applicable to the story published by the Times Mirror Company in the LOS ANGELES TIMES. Only if in fact the attorneys for the publishing company had said in court that I had been fired because of poor work would the Times Mirror Company be able to claim the privilege defense. The real reason for my termination of employment would not have mattered.

After Eggers' column in October of 1978 which mentioned the City's reputation for eating "green reporters," Eggers had stayed on the beat until February of 1979 when Kathryn Ayres' bylines began appearing over Laguna Beach city government stories. They were replaced in May of 1979 by the name of Don Chapman, who stayed 11 months, until April of 1980. The next three months Ken Barnes, the former Marine who had covered the Leisure World and Laguna Beach beats, resumed the latter beat. His replacement, Marc Wutchke, took over the beat in July of 1980 and lasted 12 months, until July of 1981, when Len Hall assumed the job. After the NEWS-POST was sold in November of 1981, Hall continued on the beat for the new owner.

Until the story in the TIMES I had not seen or heard of any other newspaper stories concerning my lawsuit. In fact, an October 6, 1983, NEWS-POST story summarizing lawsuits against the City of Laguna Beach, headlined "Laguna's Legal Tangles," made no mention of my suit. Because of the TIMES' false and libelous story about me, I wrote a letter requesting a retraction. Jeffrey Klein, the TIMES' legal counsel, wrote back denying my request and stating that my lawsuit was a "public controversy." There had been no stories about my lawsuit, filed in 1979, until the TIMES story in 1983. In addition, I was a private individual, not a public figure or official.

The fact that there was no published story until after the U.S. Supreme Court declined to hear my case indicated that whoever supplied the information believed that was the final step in my litigation. My last recourse, however, was to file a petition for rehearing, which I did on November 3, 1983. The first part of the nine-page petition began as follows:

"This petitioner is the victim of a serious miscarriage of justice.

"It is apparent that more supervision in the justice system is needed. When manifest injustice is perpetuated from one court to the next with clear indication that papers are not properly read, that they are not read in enough detail to clearly understand the litigation at bar, then the United States Supreme Court should exercise its function of supervision."

On the same day, November 3, 1983, the NEWS-POST published another article about Spitaleri's legal victories. He had been awarded a $69.5 million default judgment in Orange County Superior Court in his claim of infringement of freedom of press rights and restraint of trade after he was prevented from distributing his paper free on a door-to-door basis in Leisure World. To collect the $69.5 million, which included triple damages because of anti-trust findings, Spitaleri would then have to sue six or

233

seven insurance companies. Spitaleri's attorney, W. Mike McCray, would receive $3.75 million in attorney fees, according to the article.

My final legal defeat in my pursuit of justice and vindication of my civil rights ended on November 28, 1983, when the Supreme Court denied my petition for rehearing. The rulings and settlements in Spitaleri's favor, both in his own litigation and in mine, proved to me once more that there is no equal justice on this earth so long as evil is allowed to flourish. While Spitaleri was being awarded absurd amounts of money, I was having my paychecks garnisheed to pay the defendants' costs of more than $7,000. I had already paid more than $25,000 for my own costs and attorneys' fees and was still making payments on more than $5,000 owed in attorneys' fees.

Rather than ever offering me a monetary settlement, the law firm of Rutan & Tucker, which represented the municipal defendants, had chosen to line its own pockets with legal fees. In response to a written inquiry, the firm refused to divulge the amount it had billed to the City of Laguna Beach for the defense of my lawsuit. Recalling the sanctions ordered three years earlier concerning the firm's efforts to obtain my declaration and the partial trial transcript, it was reasonable to assume that Rutan & Tucker had charged the City an incredibly large amount. A city hall watchdog who checked the City's public records got the impression that the City had paid Rutan & Tucker $150,000 in 1983 alone for the defense of my case.

My journalism studies, both formally and independently, had not prepared me for the experiences I encountered since my graduation eight years earlier from Pepperdine University. I had known before that as a reporter I could expect to find corruption in government. My studies

before graduation had not disclosed such an aber-
ration in newspaper management as well. I had
been more interested in working in Laguna Beach,
which only had one newspaper in early 1975, than
I was in investigating the background of that
newspaper and its management.

The flaws in this country's judicial system
became much more apparent after I had become
a victim of a conspiracy by the city government
and newspaper officials. The system does not
provide equal justice for all. Taxpayers are
required to financially support their governments,
which then have an almost limitless source of
funds with which to defend themselves against
lawsuits filed by citizens. A citizen who does
not have adequate financial resources may not be
able to retain a competent attorney. Chief Justice Warren Burger has also recognized the
system's ineffectiveness. In 1984 he stated that
"for some disputes, of course, trials will be the
only means, but for many, trials by the adver-
sarial contest must in time go the way of the
ancient trials by battle and blood. Our system is
too costly, too painful, too destructive, too inef-
ficient for a truly civilized people." Appointed
to the Supreme Court by Richard Nixon while he
was president of the United States, Burger is a
critic of the journalism profession as well as of
the legal profession.

Besides being disenchanted with the judicial
system, I had also lost faith in the journalism
profession. Because I considered the Society of
Professional Journalists to be an ignorant and un-
helpful organization, I allowed my membership to
expire at the end of 1982. A year later I received a form letter dated December 16, 1983,
asking me to rejoin by sending a check for $40,
with no penalty added for not paying 1983 dues.
Citing its 75 years of "service," the society
claimed a membership of "24,000 people who are

dedicated to high professional ideals." I disagreed with the letter's statement that I could not afford losing my membership in the society.

While the press has been known as the "Fourth Estate," after the three estates of the executive, legislative and judicial branches of government, it is the judicial branch, namely the United States Supreme Court, that has more official power. It is that court which has the final word on litigation, including those lawsuits concerning the First Amendment. But the press has the unofficial last word in being able to submit stories to the people, the court of public opinion. Burger seems to levy more criticism toward attorneys than he does toward the court system. In a 1984 "20/20" television program on the ABC network, Burger was cited as the biggest critic of the "tidal wave of litigation" in this country. It was predicted that 15 million civil lawsuits would be filed in 1984 in courts across the nation. Only half of those cases would be decided in the plaintiffs' favor if they went to trial. One of the deterrents, the program noted, is that the attorney usually acts as judge and jury when first receiving a complaint from a prospective litigant. Seeking out-of-court settlements which frequently benefit the attorneys more than the victims, they were described by Burger as "hordes of lawyers, hungry as locusts" in a 1984 LOS ANGELES TIMES series.

Focusing on just the lawsuits that are filed in the federal courts in the United States, the TIMES article stated that more than 240,000 civil lawsuits were filed in 1983. That was twice the number filed in 1975. It was predicted that by the year 2010 the annual federal docket will reach one million new cases, requiring 5,000 judges, compared to the 684 on the federal bench in 1984. Rather than the citizens making this country a litigious society, the TIMES story indicated that there just are not enough judges. There are 67.7 judges for every million residents, placing the United States far behind the ratio in other civilized countries. The ratio of attorneys to judges is also far greater in this country. There are more than 620,000 attorneys with 35,000 graduates coming out of this nation's law schools each year. That means there is one lawyer for every 375 Americans, compared to one for every 632 citizens, in 1976, according to the TIMES.

The courthouse built for Orange County in 1900 became too small, after more than 60 years, to handle the growing caseload generated by the increased population and number of attorneys. A much larger courthouse was built nearby and the old one, designated a state historical landmark, was used in the filming of "Gideon's Trumpet," a television movie starring Henry Fonda which was first aired several years ago. The featured character, Clarence Earl Gideon, was portrayed by Fonda. The movie was made shortly after I began working as a paralegal at Beam, DiCaro, D'Antony & Stafford, which had offices in downtown Santa Ana a couple of blocks from the old courthouse. Before the law firm relocated its offices, I walked by the landmark every day on my way to work and remembered when I read the book, also entitled GIDEON'S TRUMPET. James Fields, one of my journalism instructors, had required that we read the book, which was written in 1964 by Anthony Lewis. The title for the book came from a verse in the Bible. As it was written in Judges, the sixth chapter, verse 34, "But the Spirit of the Lord came upon Gideon, and he blew a trumpet." Through faith in God, the Biblical Gideon was able to kill 250,000 Midianites with just 300 Israelite soldiers.

In 1963, Clarence Gideon faced a similar obstacle--the U.S. Supreme Court. Gideon had

237

been tried and convicted of a misdemeanor theft without the right to counsel. From his prison cell he handwrote a petition for a writ of certiorari to the United States Supreme Court. Like myself, he was representing himself, "in propria persona," one of the many Latin phrases used in the judicial system. One of the law clerks at the Supreme Court read Gideon's petition and took a personal interest in his case. From there his petition made its way to the justices, who eventually ruled that his due process rights guaranteed by the Fourteenth Amendment had been denied when he was not provided with an attorney. At the second trial in the Florida state court, Gideon was represented by an attorney and was found innocent of the crime. GIDEON vs. WAINWRIGHT became a landmark decision, leading to the establishment of legal aid programs for indigents, and forming the foundation for the ESCOBEDO and MIRANDA decisions.

The stories of the Gideon in the Bible and the Gideon in "Gideon's Trumpet" indicate that faith is obtained when people take action. The author of the eleventh chapter of the book of Hebrews in the Bible cited Gideon as an example of the good results that can be achieved by those who have faith that God is in control. Almost 10 years after reading of Clarence Gideon's plight I had taken action when I had found myself in a similar predicament. I had sent a petition to the United States Supreme Court, trusting that justice would result. Unlike myself, Clarence Gideon was fortunate to have found justice in an imperfect justice system in an imperfect world.

A. Wallace Tashima, the U.S. District Court judge who granted the defendants' motion for summary judgment and denied my petition for a rehearing, was quoted in the DAILY JOURNAL shortly after he was appointed to the federal bench. Tashima stated that even though the U.S.

Supreme Court had upheld the decision to relocate Japanese-Americans during World War II, he remained convinced that the internment was unconstitutional. Tashima said he thought the relocation was a "result of political and economic forces in which racism played an overriding part."

Racism did play a part in the killing of six million Jews in Europe during World War II. "The Holocaust," the term given to German dictator Adolf Hitler's extermination of the Jews, remains very much alive in the memories of those who survived the death camps and in those who are outraged by injustice. Simon Wiesenthal, a well-known Nazi hunter who for 40 years has kept the memory alive, still tracks down for persecution those responsible for the killings and other war crime atrocities. In response to my petition to the U.S. District Court for a rehearing of the summary judgment motion, the defendants' attorneys--rejecting the facts and the law but not emotion--criticized me in their opposition brief by stating that it had been six years since my termination of employment and, therefore, I should not continue to use the court system to question the actions of the defendants. In my reply brief I wrote, "The mere passage of time does not right a wrong, restore a property right or uphold a constitutional right. The passage of more than forty (40) years has not dampened the fervor of those attempting to locate and prosecute Nazi war criminals. Although plaintiff's life was not taken away by the defendants, her chosen means of livelihood was."

One of the famous quotations which I have long believed, was spoken in 1770 by Edmund Burke, an Irish political figure and government reformer. His original statement in "Thoughts on the Cause of the Present Discontents" was, "When bad men combine, the good must associate; else they will fall one by one, an unpitied sacrifice in a contemptible struggle." The modern version of the quotation attributed to him is, "The only thing necessary for the triumph of evil is for good men to do nothing." The defendants were able to conspire against me because people who were in a position to prevent it chose to allow evil to prevail.

Burke's quote was paraphrased by actor Edward Asner when he narrated "Auschwitz and the Allies," a television documentary which aired in 1984. In the introduction of the program, Asner stated, "Evil flourishes when good men do nothing." He then presented the facts of his case in attempt to prove, for the court of public opinion, that Hitler was able to exterminate six million Jews only because the Allies, the so-called good countries which included the United States, failed to allow immigration of the Jews to their countries. Hitler established the first internment camp for Jews in 1933. Up until December 9, 1941, Asner stated, Hitler would have allowed the Jews to leave Europe in order to fulfill his eradication attempts. The Western press corps conspired with the Allied governments by failing to run film in 1943 of the extermination of three million Jews. Anti-Semitism in the U.S. State Department was revealed in a January 13, 1944, report to the secretary of state. Entitled "Acquiescence of this Government in the Murder of the Jews," the report disclosed a conspiracy to silence news of the extermination and to cover the Allies' guilt by means of concealment, misrepresentation and false statements.

Because the Holocaust involved so many people, many of whom still live, and represented one of the most extreme examples of evil, it is cited by many authors when they write about other injustices in life. Some of the authors and their books include M. Scott Peck, PEOPLE OF THE LIE; Harold Kushner, WHEN BAD THINGS

240

HAPPEN TO GOOD PEOPLE; and C.S. Lewis, MERE CHRISTIANITY.

"Of the Holocaust as well as of lesser evils it is often asked," Peck wrote, "'How could a loving God allow such a thing to happen?'" If an evil person were given a nation, Peck believes that he would likely become a Hitler. It was a rare instance, however, that an evil person such as Hitler was given such an extraordinary degree of political power. Evil people, according to Peck, are usually perceived to be "solid citizens--Sunday school teachers, PTA members, bankers or policemen." The "crimes" of evil people are usually subtle and covert, Peck added. It seems that a conspiracy to terminate a newspaper reporter could be an example. Peck defined evil as the use of political power to destroy others for the purpose of defending or preserving the integrity of one's sick self.

Many people besides myself have been victims of evil on a smaller scale than Hitler's Holocaust. Harold Kushner, a rabbi, wrote WHEN BAD THINGS HAPPEN TO GOOD PEOPLE after his son Aaron died of progeria in 1977. In writing of his own grief and that of others who have suffered misfortunes, Kushner wrote that Hitler's extermination of Jews was allowed to occur because certain human beings chose to be cruel to their fellow man. "The Holocaust happened because thousands of others could be persuaded to join him in his madness, and millions of others permitted themselves to be frightened or shamed into cooperating," Kushner stated. That opinion was also offered by Edmund Burke and Edward Asner in talking about group evil. Television evangelist Paul Crouch of the Trinity Broadcasting Network has said that Christians were responsible for failing to convert Hitler to Christianity. Kushner and Peck, however, express the belief that every person chooses to be evil or good.

"To say of Hitler, to say of any criminal, that he did not choose to be bad but was a victim of his upbringing, is to make all morality, all discussion of right and wrong, impossible," Kushner claimed. From my own view of the legal system, I would agree with Kushner's statement that another reason the Holocaust happened was "because Hitler was able to persuade lawyers to forget their commitment to justice."

During the Holocaust on continental Europe, C.S. Lewis, a Christian theologian, was living in England and wrote his classic book, MERE CHRISTIANITY. Based on his radio talks, the book was directed toward millions of people who, viewing the Nazis' persecution of the Jews, questioned the existence of God. Lewis commented that if there were no real sense of right and a real morality, the Nazis could not be in the wrong because there would be no civilized or Christian morality with which to compare them. Lewis compared Christ's instruction, to "Take up your cross," to going to be beaten to death in a concentration camp. Jesus Christ must be accepted as either the Son of God or as a fool, according to Lewis. "A man who was merely a man and said the sort of things Jesus said would not be a great moral teacher. He would either be a lunatic--on a level with the man who says he is a poached egg--or else he would be the devil of hell."

Corrie ten Boom and her sister Betsie experienced Hitler's concentration camps firsthand. The Ten Boom family had participated in the Dutch underground in Holland by hiding Jews in their watch shop and home. When captured by the Nazis, the sisters were able to hide a Bible inside the death camp and read of the sufferings Jesus endured before and during his death on the cross. Corrie ten Boom told of their experiences in THE HIDING PLACE. Betsie ten Boom died in Ravensbruck, a women's extermination camp in Germany where 96,000 died. Before she died, Betsie told Corrie, "The most important part of our task will be to tell everyone who will listen that Jesus is the only answer to the problems that are disturbing the hearts of men and nations. We shall have the right to speak because we can tell from our experience that His light is more powerful than the deepest darkness."

After 15-year-old Anne Frank died in one of Hitler's extermination camps, a diary she had kept was found and published as THE DIARY OF A YOUNG GIRL. The last entry in the diary had been made a few days before she, her family and friends were found by the Nazis hiding in an Amsterdam warehouse. Her writings contained humor and insight, and revealed the power of the indomitable human spirit. In one of her diary entries she wrote, "I know there will always be comfort for every sorrow, whatever the circumstances may be." As a Jew, Anne Frank apparently found comfort in knowing that God did not cause her misfortune but was able to provide strength in overcoming her adversity. In his book, Rabbi Kushner assures readers that God does not cause our misfortunes and that they are not part of any grand design on God's part. While God cannot prevent evil people from hurting us, He can provide help in overcoming our problems. I agree with Kushner's statement that it is wrong for people to believe "in a world to come where the innocent are compensated for their suffering" if they use it as "an excuse for not being troubled or outraged by injustice around us, and not using our God-given intelligence to try to do something about it."

Those who died in Hitler's concentration camps suffered death at the hands of human evil, just as Jesus Christ did. "It was evil that raised Christ to the cross, thereby enabling us to see

243

him from afar," M. Scott Peck wrote in both of his books, THE ROAD LESS TRAVELED and PEOPLE OF THE LIE. The chief priests and scribes viewed Jesus as a public enemy because he was usurping their power and they were afraid that more people might start following Him instead of them. Consequently, they conspired together in order to arrest Jesus by stealth and have Him put to death. At the fourth trial of Jesus, the crowd told Pilate, the governor, that Jesus had told the people to not pay taxes to the Roman government and that Jesus was causing riots against the government. Even though Jesus was found innocent of leading a revolt against the Roman government, He was given to the crowd, which had demanded that He be crucified and that Barabbas, who was in prison for murder and insurrection against the government, be freed.

Even though I believe that Christ was the Messiah and that He is coming again soon, probably in my lifetime according to Bible prophecies, I do not understand some of the verses in the Bible which seem to try to explain why all of us experience misfortunes and injustices of various types. In the apostle Paul's letter to the Romans, chapter 8, verse 28, he wrote, "And we know that all that happens to us is working for our good if we love God and are fitting into His plans." In Mark 11:24 it is written that Jesus said, "You can pray for anything, and if you believe, you have it; it's yours!" From the time the defendants began conspiring against me in 1976 I prayed that I would not lose my job; and when I did lose my job, I prayed that I would find justice through a lawsuit. The courts ruled against me. All that was necessary for me to have a trial in the district court was for me to lie and say that defendant Thomas Michael Eggers had told me directly that I was being removed from the editorial department because the city government was pressuring him to get rid of me. That would have made the conspiracy information which I had acquired firsthand instead of fifthhand, which the district court ruled was inadmissible evidence because it was hearsay. Claiming that my co-workers had complained about me was inadmissible hearsay that the defendants had offered at their depositions. The courts indicated that they wanted me to use firsthand knowledge to prove the conspiracy rather than proving false all of the defendants' reasons for my termination. That was in spite of the fact that the courts had not required such evidence from plaintiffs in cases similar to mine.

In reading Robert Schuller's TOUGH TIMES NEVER LAST BUT TOUGH PEOPLE DO! I was glad when he assured coach Bear Bryant that Christians do not have to understand everything written in the Bible. Also, after reading that an associate minister had conspired to replace him as the senior minister of his church, now known as the Crystal Cathedral, I empathized with the corruption Schuller had experienced among evil people calling themselves Christians.

MOURNING SONG was written by Joyce Landorf as her "grief work" following the deaths of several members of her family. In the loss of my job as a newspaper reporter and the larger loss of my chosen profession of journalism, I experienced the same stages of grief of which Landorf wrote. I have chosen to write this book not only as a grief work for myself but also as a means of warning others planning to become journalists that corruption exists throughout the world, not just in governments. If they know that even the hallowed field of journalism is imperfect, then perhaps they will not be so disillusioned when they find out for themselves in a firsthand experience. As Rabbi Kushner wrote, "We can give bad things meaning by asking, 'Now that this has happened to me, what am I going to do about it?'" Through this book I want to continue to help rid our lives of the influence of evil people, indwelled by Satan as was Judas when he helped in the conspiracy against Jesus.

In the story of Joseph in the Bible, Moses wrote in Genesis that Joseph's brothers had sold and abandoned him. Because Joseph was able to make the most of his predicament he was able to later tell his brothers, "You meant it for evil but God meant it for good." That is how I want to turn my experiences into benefit for others in the journalism field.

Julie Wallace, an idealistic young woman like myself who wanted to be a journalist, is the heroine in JULIE, the last novel written by Catherine Marshall before her death in 1983. The daughter of a Christian minister who resigned from a church and moved his family to a steel mill town where he bought the last surviving newspaper, Julie yearned to be a journalist who could change the world, including Adolf Hitler, not just the corrupt town in which she lived. I wish the book had been written at least 10 years earlier so that I could have read it before my idealism and illusions were dimmed by my experiences at the NEWS-POST.

Suzanne Rista, a 1983 graduate of Laguna Beach High School, became so disillusioned by her journalism experience on that school's newspaper that she abandoned her pursuit of a journalism career. In April of 1985 the Southern California Investigative Journalism Award was created as a result of the furor caused by the first article she wrote, which was critical of the school's drama department. Teachers harassed her and told her friends that she was a "lousy journalist."

Bruce Hopping, a Laguna Beach resident and city hall watcher, conceived and endowed the

$1,000 annual award to encourage students to write investigative stories which may have unpopular political or social reactions. As president of the Kalos Kagathos Foundation, Hopping solicited and received support for the award from the American Civil Liberties Union (ACLU), the Society of Professional Journalists, the Scholastic Press Association and the Journalism Educators' Association. Ramona Ripston, executive director of the ACLU, was quoted as saying that nothing could be more vital than reinforcing the importance of the First Amendment with those who will be entrusted with its future. From my experience with the ACLU and the Society of Professional Journalists, I wonder if student journalists will receive such support from those organizations when they become professional journalists in need of help.

Twelve years after commencing his litigation in 1973, Spitaleri is still embroiled in seeking compensation for deprivation of his First Amendment rights in Leisure World. On May 5, 1984, the LOS ANGELES TIMES reported that the Orange County Superior Court had nullified the $69.3 (not $69.5) million default judgment previously awarded to Spitaleri. It appeared that attorney McCray had not informed the insurance companies of the October 24, 1983, court hearing at which $69,301,853 was awarded to his client. The reporter wrote, "McCray admitted that a major problem with rescinding the settlement would be returning the money (the $1.85 million settlement) to Golden Rain." McCray also stated that Spitaleri would file an appeal.

Effective April 8, 1985, McCray was suspended, for disciplinary reasons, from the practice of law for one year by the State Bar of California. I obtained that information from the State Bar after Dallas Anderson told of a conversation he had with an individual who had wit-

247

nessed the LAGUNA PUBLISHING COMPANY vs. GOLDEN WEST PUBLISHING CORPORATION trial. The records I received from the State Bar revealed that McCray had been disciplined by the Bar five times before, with the first time being in 1964.

On October 23, 1984, I filed a lawsuit for libel per se against the Times Mirror Company for the false and libelous LOS ANGELES TIMES story printed almost a year earlier. On February 1, 1985, the Times Mirror Company served its answer to my complaint, denying that it had falsely libeled me. The answer was signed by attorney Susan Erburu Reardon of the Los Angeles law firm of Gibson, Dunn & Crutcher. According to the MARTINDALE-HUBBELL directory, Reardon had been graduated summa cum laude a few years earlier from Harvard Law School.

After taking my deposition on July 9, 1985, she wrote me a letter asking about the possibility of settling my lawsuit. In a telephone call to me the following week, Reardon asked if I would dismiss my lawsuit in exchange for a retraction printed in the LOS ANGELES TIMES. Nothing was said about my reputation, interrupted career, or expended time and money. There also was no mention as to the reason for the offer to print a retraction. I felt as if I had actually been slapped in the face over the telephone. Reardon subsequently submitted a written declaration by Daniel Nakaso, the reporter who wrote the article when he was 22 years old. He confirmed that he had never checked any court records before writing the story. After I requested a retraction of the story, Nakaso continued, he telephoned attorney Paul Bickenbach, who told him "that he had probably said in court that Ms. Brownfield was fired because of poor work, as well as because of an editorial reorganization at the Laguna News-Post." The latter reason, and Nakaso's al-

248

leged attempts to reach me, were not mentioned in the story.

On July 22, 1985, Carla Block, the former secretary and wife of attorney Marc Block, began work as a secretary assigned to one of the associate attorneys at Beam, DiCaro, D'Antony, Stafford & Brobeck, which employs 19 of the more than 8,000 attorneys in Orange County. Her expression, upon seeing me, indicated that she had forgotten I worked there. According to records at the County Clerk's Office, she and I have one thing in common. Both of us have been sued by Marc Block. Their divorce became final the week before she started the job. The court records do not support her earlier claim that she is an attorney specializing in real estate law. The condition of my files on receipt from Marc Block's office indicated that she was not a secretary either.

On August 25, 1985, THE REGISTER newspaper featured on the front page an exposition of Eggers, described as a political opportunist concerning his work as a congressional aide in the southern Orange County area. Among numerous charges about conflicts of interest, it was reported that Eggers had aligned himself with two political action committees that had direct ties to a fireworks magnate who was awaiting sentencing on political corruption and bank bribery charges. Some constituents accused Eggers of serving his own personal financial interests instead of the public. It seemed that his mode of operation had not changed since leaving the NEWS-POST.

On October 2, 1985, the Times Mirror Company agreed to pay me a specified amount in exchange for dismissal of my lawsuit for libel per se. The Times required that the terms of the settlement agreement be kept confidential.

249

Index

C

D

E

F

251

N

Nader, Ralph, 27
NEW YORK TIMES, 235
Nixon Administration, 21, 155, 235

O

Orwell, George, 71

P

Peck, M. Scott, 240, 241, 244
Pepperdine University, 21, 22, 25, 27, 28, 35, 61,
    168, 203, 234
PHABY vs. KSD-KSD-TV, INC., 219
Political campaigns, 36, 38, 39, 124-126, 129,
    174-178, 210
POWERS THAT BE, THE, 188, 189

Q

QUILL, THE, 153, 163, 164

R

Reagan, Ronald, 36, 37
REGISTER, THE, 9, 15, 33, 68, 96, 97, 104, 121,
    143, 149, 157, 175, 176
Reorganization, 61, 70
Reporters Committee for Freedom of the Press,
    162-164, 166-169
Rockwell, Norman, 19

S

SANTA MONICA EVENING OUTLOOK, 65
Scholastic Press Assocation, 247
Schuller, Robert, 245
Scripps-Howard, 132
Sigma Delta Chi, 22, 35, 134, 153
"60 MINUTES," 161, 162
Society of Professional Journalists, 22, 35, 36,
        134, 153, 163-166, 168, 169, 235, 236, 247
Southern California Investigative Journalism Award,
        246, 247
Sta-Hi Corp. 3, 6, 11, 91, 92, 133, 153

T

Tarkington, Booth, 19
Ten Boom, Corrie, 242
Terminated, 56, 59, 63, 65, 127, 130, 163, 194,
        195, 211, 216, 218, 220-224, 231, 245
THINKING BIG, 158
TIME, 21, 188
Times Mirror Company, 248
"20/20," 236

U

UNITED STATES CODE, 172, 173, 179, 220, 226,
        227
United States Congress, 118
United States Constitution, 14, 20, 21, 163, 170,
        174
United States Marine Corps, 112, 114, 117, 119,
        136, 141, 145
United States Postal Service, 13, 119, 120
United States Supreme Court, 20, 229-239, 248